Whelks
to
Whales

Whelks
to
Whales

Coastal Marine Life
of the
Pacific Northwest

Rick M. Harbo

HARBOUR PUBLISHING

Published by

HARBOUR PUBLISHING
P.O. Box 219
Madeira Park, BC Canada
V0N 2H0

Cover photos: R. Harbo: dire whelk (p. 110), snakelock anemone
(p. 45), bat star (p. 133), quillback rockfish (p. 164), bull kelp
(p. 205). Alexandra Morton: killer whale (p. 183).

Cover design, page design and composition by
Martin Nichols, Lionheart Graphics

Printed and bound in Canada

Harbour Publishing acknowledges the financial support of the
Government of Canada through the Book Publishing Industry
Development Program (BPIDP), the Canada Council for the Arts,
and the Province of British Columbia through the British Columbia
Arts Council, for its publishing activities.

Canadian Cataloguing in Publication Data

Harbo, Rick M., 1949–
    Whelks to whales

Includes bibliographical references and index.
ISBN 1-55017-183-6

1. Marine animals—Northwest, Pacific—Identification.
2. Coastal animals—Northwest, Pacific—Identification. I. Title.
QH95.3.H38 1998   591.77'09795'09146   C98-910223-8

THE CANADA COUNCIL | LE CONSEIL DES ARTS
FOR THE ARTS | DU CANADA
SINCE 1957 | DEPUIS 1957

Contents

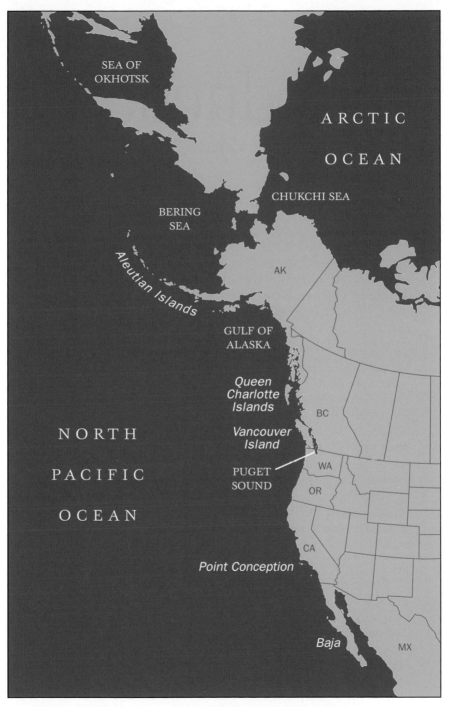

Northeast Pacific Ocean and the Pacific Northwest coast.

Introduction

The shorelines of Alaska, British Columbia, Washington, Oregon and northern California—the Pacific Northwest area of North America—is so generously populated with marine animals and plants that divers, beachcombers, whale watchers, naturalists and biologists from all over the world come here to enjoy the natural wonders of the coastline. At any time of year, for experts and first-time beach walkers alike, every trip to the ocean can be a great pleasure and a learning experience.

The gentle climate and warm ocean currents of this region support thousands of plants and animals, from the microscopic planktonic algae that bloom and colour the water, to the smallest snails on the seashore, to the blue whale, one of the largest animals that has ever lived on earth. The Pacific Northwest is home to the world's tallest anemone (plumose anemone, p. 41) and many of the world's largest species, including the giant Pacific octopus (p. 121), the two largest scallops, the weathervane scallop and the rock scallop (p. 91), the largest sea slug (orange peel nudibranch, p. 117), chiton (giant Pacific chiton, p. 125), barnacle (giant barnacle, p. 84) intertidal clam (geoduck, p. 98) and sea urchin (red sea urchin, p. 145).

More than 400 fascinating marine plants and animals of the Pacific Northwest are included in *Whelks to Whales*. Most are commonly found along the seashore, in habitats ranging from tidepools to rocky reefs, while some of the whales, porpoises and dolphins may be found seasonally in coastal waters and range even farther, out to the continental shelf and beyond. Many of the species illustrated are conspicuous in size, shape and colour, and have some unique and interesting features to help in their identification.

OUR RICH MARINE LIFE

The abundance and diversity of marine life of this region is due to temperate water conditions, the age of the Pacific basin and the geographic diversity of the coast, among other factors. Upwelling at the edge of the continental shelf during the summer months brings nutrient-rich waters to the surface. The many inlets, coastal reefs and thousands of islands create a diversity of water currents and wave exposures and a multitude of habitats.

Short plumose anemones and soft coral.

Extensive scientific information is available on some groups of organisms, and almost none on others. Taxonomic specialists tend to study one group of species at a time, and much of the coast of northern British Columbia and Alaska is too remote and wild for the establishment of long-term studies. Based on what we do know, experts estimate that the invertebrate species, numbering to 8,000, comprise approximately 90 percent of the species of the region. Invertebrates are animals without backbones, including the sponges, crabs, shrimp, sea stars and many others. The vertebrate species of this region include some 400 fishes, close to 200 marine birds and 30 marine mammals. Approximately 640 species of seaweeds and seagrasses also grow along our shores.

DISTRIBUTION OF SPECIES

The Pacific Northwest (a land-based reference) is also commonly referred to as cold temperate Northeast Pacific waters (an ocean-based reference). It is one of seven zones or biogeographic regions accepted by most authorities to describe the distribution of marine life of the world. These zones are the Arctic in the north, the cold temperate northern hemisphere (our region), the warm temperate northern hemisphere, the tropics, warm and cold temperate regions of the southern hemisphere and the Antarctic in the south.

Most animal and seaweed species have a broad distribution. The northern boundary of our region (see map, p. 7) is generally the Pacific rim of the Aleutian Islands, and northeast Siberia. The southern boundary is often at Point Conception, California, a large headland where distribution of life changes dramatically. Many species range outside of this zone, and a few species, including the sail jellyfish (see p. 47),calcareous tube worm (p. 53), pelagic goose barnacle (p. 85), spiny dogfish (p. 159) and killer whale (p. 183–84), are cosmopolitan, being found in all oceans of the world.

A number of the bivalves, gastropods, worms, bryozoans, algae and other organisms included in this guide are exotic species, introduced when Japanese and Atlantic oysters were shipped to our waters for commercial production. The discharge of ballast water from ships can also introduce species. Although many are regarded as pests, some have been beneficial. The introduction of the Manila clam (see p. 97) has led to the development of a valuable fishery.

Basket star.

HABITATS

Many animals and plants have very specific requirements that limit their survival to particular kinds of habitats, defined by physical conditions such as wave shock, tidal exposure, type of bottom (sand, mud, rock, etc.), chemical factors such as salinity (saltiness of the water) and the amount of dissolved oxygen from wind, waves and currents. Biological factors such as predation, competition between species and the ability to tolerate exposure at low tides are also key elements.

Tidal exposure: The water at the seashore rises and recedes, drawn by the gravitational forces of the moon and, to a lesser extent, the sun. A daily tidal cycle in our region typically has two unequal high tides and two unequal low tides. Tidal changes can be extreme, with changes of 20' (6 m) in water height or depth at some locations, and can cause swift currents at passes and narrows where the water flow is restricted by land masses.

Some species are found only in the intertidal zone and shallows, limited by predators or environmental conditions. These species have a great tolerance to exposure to air, higher temperatures and fresh water from rain and runoff. They often seek refuge at low tide in cracks and crevices, in shadows or under rocks. Some, like barnacles, are specially adapted to "close up tight" to minimize water loss. Many other species are found anywhere from the intertidal zone to great depths below the tides.

Official tide tables are published by government agencies and are available at marinas and sporting good stores. The tables also appear daily in many newspapers. The best times to view marine life are during the hours before and after the lowest tides, which are generally less than 2' (.6 m) in the USA or less than 3' (1 m) height in Canada (the two countries measure tidal heights from different reference points).

Wave exposure: Some animals and plants (e.g. California mussel, p. 89, and sea palm, p. 207) are well adapted only to outer or exposed coast areas, where water is saltier (not diluted by coastal rivers and freshwater runoff) and wave action is stronger. Wave action provides a highly oxygenated environment and an abundance of food washed up on the shore. Other species (e.g. bay mussel, p. 89, and eelgrass, p. 212) prefer protected bays and sheltered habitats.

SCIENTIFIC AND COMMON NAMES

Carolus Linnaeus (1707–1778), a Swedish scientist, developed a system of giving each species a unique name composed of two words. These scientific names are used throughout the world and provide a standard, precise way of communicating about an organism, regardless of the language of the scholar. Type specimens are designated against which additional specimens can be compared. Today the International Commission of Zoological Nomenclature sets the rules for scientific naming of animals, and names of marine algae (including seaweeds) and seagrasses are governed by the International Code of Botanical Nomenclature.

Species also have common names, given by people who live in the area or by specialists who study them. These names seldom change, unlike scientific names that are constantly under revision. But because common names are not unique names, they have limited use in international study and published reports. Some species have several common names, and sometimes two or more species are known by the same common name in different regions.

Species differ from one another in at least one characteristic and generally do not interbreed with one another where their ranges overlap in nature. An organism's scientific and common names often reflect its unique features—structural attributes, colours or colour patterns, ecological characteristics, geographic distribution—or honour a person associated with it. Scientists generally discourage names that are not descriptive, but these names persist.

Scientific naming and classification of animal and plant species is constantly under review and is frequently changed, as species demographics change, and as biological study all over the world continues and new information is found and exchanged.

MARINE SPECIES AND THEIR ENVIRONMENT

This guidebook has been written and illustrated to help you observe and identify animals and plants in their natural surroundings without disturbing them, as this is the best way to understand the relationships between organisms and their environment. Whenever possible, please capture the seashore with your camera, sketchbook or notebook and leave the beach undisturbed for others to see. Avoid stepping on plants and animals, and return any overturned rocks to their original positions. If you dig holes, fill them in.

If you do take specimens, please keep these guidelines in mind to cause minimal disturbance to habitats and the organisms that live there:

- Whenever possible, collect specimens from man-made structures such as docks and pilings. If you turn any rock to inspect the underside, replace it carefully and immediately.

- Take the minimum number of specimens necessary. Do not collect individuals that are laying or guarding eggs, or engaged in any other reproductive behaviour. Familiarize yourself with local park or seasonal closures, bag limits, requirements for licences and other regulations for conservation.

- Before harvesting for food, consult with local fisheries or health authorities for closures due to pollution or to harmful algal blooms such as "red tides."

Scientific Classification of Species

The system of classifying and naming species developed by Carolus Linnaeus in the eighteenth century is still used by scientists all over the world today. The following outline shows where the species in this guide belong in the overall scientific classification of living things. The number of species described worldwide in each category is shown in parentheses. As more information becomes available and species change in distribution and behaviour, details of this outline shift in response.

KINGDOM ANIMALIA

INVERTEBRATES - Animals without backbones

PHYLUM PORIFERA (Approx. 5,000 species)
    Class Calacarea - Calcareous sponges
    Class Hexactinellida - Glass sponges
    Class Demospongiae - Common sponges

PHYLUM CNIDARIA (Approx. 9,000 species)
    Class Hydrozoa
        Order Hydroida - Hydroids, hydromedusae (see below)
        Order Stylasterina - Hydrocorals
        Order Siphonophora - Small jellyfish (see below)
    Class Anthozoa
    Subclass Octocorallia - Octocorals
        Order Pennatulacea - Sea pens
        Order Alcyonacea - Soft corals
        Order Gorgonacea - Sea fans
    Subclass Zoantharia
        Order Scleractinia - Cup corals
        Order Corallimorpharia - Club anemones
        Order Zoanthidea - Zoanthids
        Order Actiniaria - Anemones
    Class Scyphozoa
        Order Semaeostomeae - Large, bell-shaped jellyfish
        Order Stauromedusae - Stalked jellyfish

PHYLUM CTENOPHORA - Comb jellies (Approx. 1,000 species)

PHYLUM ANNELIDA - Segmented worms (Approx. 9,000 species)
    Class Polychaeta
    Subclass Sedentaria - Tube worms
    Subclass Errantia - Free-swimming worms

PHYLUM NEMERTEA - Ribbon worms or nemerteans (Approx. 800 species)

PHYLUM PLATYHELMINTHES
    Class Turbellaria - Free-living flatworms (Approx. 3,000 species)

PHYLUM BRYOZOA (ECTOPROCTA) - Moss animals (Approx. 6,000 species)
    Class Stenolaemata - Bryozoans
    Class Gymnolaemata - Bryozoans

PHYLUM ARTHROPODA (Approx. 900,000 species)

SUBPHYLUM CRUSTACEA
    Class Malacostraca
        Order Decapoda
            Suborder Pleocyemata

Infraorder Thassinidea - Mud shrimp, ghost shrimp
Infraorder Anomura - Hermit crabs, king crabs, lithodid crabs, galatheid crabs, porcelain crabs
Infraorder Brachyura - "True crabs"
Infraorder Caridea - Most shrimp
Order Isopoda - Isopods
Order Amphipoda - Amphipods
Class Cirripedia - Barnacles

PHYLUM MOLLUSCA (Approx. 50,000 species)
Class Bivalvia - Clams, mussels, oysters, scallops
Subclass Pteriomorphia - Mussels, oysters, scallops
Subclass Heterodonta - Cockles, clams
Class Gastropoda
Subclass Prosobranchia - Abalone, limpets, snails
Subclass Opisthobranchia - Bubble shells, nudibranchs
Order Nudibranchia - Nudibranchs
Class Cephalopoda - Octopus, squid
Class Polyplacophora - Chitons

PHYLUM BRACHIOPODA - Lampshells (Approx. 300 species)

PHYLUM ECHINODERMATA (Approx. 6,000 species)
Class Asteroidea - Sea stars
Class Ophiuroidea - Brittle stars, basket stars
Class Holothuroidea - Sea cucumbers
Class Echinoidea - Sea urchins, sand dollars
Order Echinoida - Sea urchins
Order Clypeasteroida - Sand dollars
Class Crinoidea - Feather stars

PHYLUM UROCHORDATA (Approx. 3,000 species)
Class Ascidiacea - Solitary, social and colonial-compound ascidians
Class Thaliacea - Pelagic tunicates (salps)

VERTEBRATES - Animals with backbones
PHYLUM CHORDATA
(Approx. 21,000 species of fishes)
Class Elasmobranchii - Sharks, rays
Class Holocephali - Ratfish
Class Actinopterygii - Bony fishes
Class Mammalia (Approx. 4,500 species)
Order Cetacea - Whales, dolphins, porpoises (Approx. 80 species)
Suborder Odontoceti - Dolphins, porpoises, orcas, toothed whales
Suborder Mysticeti - Baleen whales
Order Carnivora - Seals, sea lions (approx. 35 species) river otters, sea otters

KINGDOM PLANTAE (Approx. 7,000 seaweeds and 50 seagrasses)
PHYLUM (DIVISION) CHLOROPHYTA - Green algae
PHYLUM (DIVISION) PHAEOPHYTA - Brown, golden, yellow-green algae
Class Phaeophyceae - Brown algae, kelps
PHYLUM (DIVISION) RHODOPHYTA
Class Rhodophyceae - Red algae
PHYLUM (DIVISION) ANTHOPHYTA - Flowering plants
Class Monocotyledoneae - Seagrasses
Class Dicotyledoneae - Sea asparagus

Sponges

PHYLUM PORIFERA

The phylum Porifera ("hole or pore bearers") comprises the sponges, fixed or sedentary animals that are common in most marine habitats from the intertidal zone to waters deeper than 2,300' (700 m). A few species inhabit fresh waters. Sponges may be thin encrusting mats or erect tube-like, vase-like or branching growths reaching heights of 7' (2 m). There are more than 275 species in our waters. The well-known bath sponges are harvested in the Mediterranean, Red Sea and West Indies.

LOCOMOTION

A sponge does not have a developed musculature or a nervous system, although some species can contract and seem to move very slowly. Many live in association with other animals, such as scallops and

---

17

hermit crabs, which helps both sponge and host escape predators and enjoy other benefits.

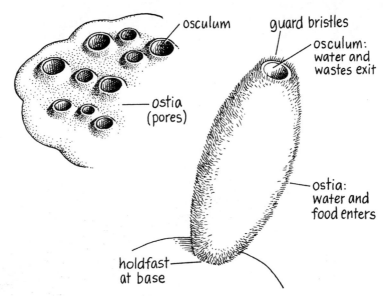

Physical features of sponges.

PREY–PREDATORS

Most sponges feed by drawing water through canals and chambers in their bodies, ingesting nutrients and filtering out bacteria. Water enters the sponge through small pores (ostia) and exits through large, often volcano-like pores (oscula).

Sponges are often eaten by sea stars such as the blood star (see p. 134) and leather star (p. 133), snails such as the blue topsnail (p. 103), chitons such as the black katy chiton (p. 125) and nudibranchs such as sea lemons (p. 112) and leopard dorid nudibranch (p. 113). The sponge's skeletal rod-like structures (spicules) serve as a defence, and some have a strong repellent odour as well.

REPRODUCTION

Sponges reproduce by broadcasting gametes and also by asexual budding. Some sponges alternate genders, being male one season and a female the next.

CAUTION: Be careful when handling sponges. Many of them, particularly the glass sponges, contain a meshwork of hard, sharp spicules which cannot always be seen but which can puncture your skin and cause severe irritation. In other parts of the world, in subtropical waters, some sponges are highly toxic and cause severe skin blisters if handled.

Calcareous Sponges Class Calcarea

The calcareous sponge species are marine and few in number. They are common in shallow (sometimes intertidal) to moderate depths of 100' (30 m) and more. The spicules are made of calcium carbonate.

VASE SPONGE
Scypha compacta (Lambe, 1894).
Etymology: *Scypha* = cup.
Size: to 4" (10 cm) high, 1" (2.5 cm) diameter.
Range: Aleutian Islands to BC.
Habitat: Subtidal on rocks, 50–100' (15–30 m).
Description: Vase-shaped sponge attached at the base, fringe of bristles around the narrow osculum. Whitish body bristles collect sediments.
Comments: Species is also found in Japan.

STALKED SPONGE
Leucilla nuttingi (Urban, 1902).
Alternate names: Urn sponge; Nutting's sponge.
Etymology: After C.C. Nutting.
Size: To 2" (5 cm) high, 3/8" (9 mm) diameter.
Range: Aleutian Islands to Baja California.
Habitat: Low intertidal to 510' (155 m). Protected in shallows in crevices or undersides of rocks, on floats and in the open, at depths. In current-swept passages.
Description: Stalked, slender vase usually in clusters of 5–10 or more individuals.

BRISTLY VASE SPONGE
Leucandra heathi Urban, 1905.
Alternate names: Spiny vase sponge (*Scypha ciliata*); Heath's sponge.
Etymology: Named after Dr. Harold Heath.
Size: To 4 3/8" (11 cm) high, 3 1/2" (9 cm) wide.
Range: Aleutian Islands to Baja California.
Habitat: Intertidal to 600' (183 m) on rocks and floats.
Description: Small, bristly, pear-shaped body with fringe of long guard bristles at top opening. White to grey. Crushes easily when handled.

TUBE BALL SPONGE
Leucosolenia eleanor Urban, 1905.
Etymology: *Leuco* = white; *solen* = pipe.
Size: Individual tubes less than 1/8" (3 mm) diameter; balls to 2–6" (5–15 cm).
Range: Aleutian Islands to southern California.
Habitat: Intertidal and shallow subtidal, on rocks, often on open coast to 90' (27 m).
Description: Small branching tubes, forming compact growths resembling balls attached by a thin stalk. Species often moves in the surge.
Comments: Species is also found in Japan.

TUBE SPONGE

Leucosolenia nautilia de Laubenfels, 1930.
Size: Individual tubes to 1/8" (3 mm) diameter, loose growths to 2-6" (5-15 cm) diameter.
Range: BC to southern California.
Habitat: In harbours, on floats and on rocks, intertidal and shallow subtidal.
Description: Small branching tubes, forming "loose" growths, white to off-white.
Comments: More than 100 species of *Leucosolenia* have been described worldwide.

Glass Sponges Class Hexactinellida

The glass sponges are typically deep-water sponges but some large species are found at moderate depths (40–100'/12–30 m) in our waters. These sponges form massive living growths often to 6 1/2' (2 m) wide or high. Be careful when handling these sponges: the sharp glass-like spicules that support the structure of the sponge are made of silica, and can penetrate the skin and be very irritating. In one species, the spicules are more than 3' (1 m) long! The silica spicules typically have a six-point arrangement, inspiring the class name Hexactinellida.

GOBLET SPONGE

Chonelasma calyx Schulze, 1887.
Alternate name: Vase sponge.
Etymology: *calyx* = cup.
Size: To 3' (1 m) diameter, 24" (60 cm) high.
Range: Bering Sea to southern California.
Habitat: On rocks, usually in flat locations rather than on walls. As shallow as 16' (5 m) in current-swept areas but usually at depths of 80' (25 m) and deeper.
Description: Bowl-shaped, often with drooping formations. White-cream to yellow.
Comments: Shelters rockfish and others. Species is also found in Japan.

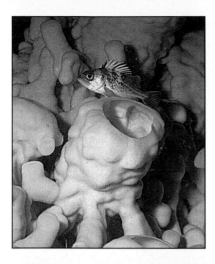

CLOUD SPONGE

Aphrocallistes vastus Schulze, 1887.
Etymology: *Aphro/callistes* = foam/cup.
Size: To 10' (3 m) diameter.
Range: Bering Sea to Mexico.
Habitat: Typically in inlets, 80' (25 m) and deeper.
Description: Massive erect branching tubular, convoluted or cloud-like growths on rock walls. White to orange.
Comments: Cavities host a variety of other animals: juvenile rockfishes and other small fishes, crabs and various shrimp. Has a fast growth rate but may be very old—some suggest hundreds of years old.

CHIMNEY SPONGE

Rhabdocalyptus dawsoni (Lambe, 1893).
Alternate name: Boot sponge.
Size: To 5' (1.5 m) high, 3' (1 m) diameter.
Range: Alaska to southern California.
Habitat: Hanging on rock walls or standing on rocks.
Description: Large, long tube. Lip of osculum is thin and sharp-edged. Body bristles trap sediments.
Comments: Shelters rockfish, shrimp and a variety of other organisms. Generally shallower than *Staurocalyptus dowlingi* (below).

CHIMNEY SPONGE

Staurocalyptus dowlingi (Lambe, 1894).
Alternate name: Boot sponge.
Size: To 5' (1.5 m) high, 3' (1 m) diameter.
Range: Alaska to southern California.
Habitat: Hanging on rock walls or standing on rocks.
Description: Large, long tube. Lip of osculum is rounded.
Comments: Shelters a variety of organisms. Generally deeper than *Rhabdocalyptus dawsoni* (above).

Encrusting Sponges, Scallop Sponges, the Hermit Crab Sponge Class Demospongiae

Approximately 95 percent of living sponges are in the class Demospongiae. They exhibit a variety of forms.

Several sponges are typically but not exclusively associated with scallops. The shell of the rock scallop (*Crassadoma gigantea*), is often infested with the boring sponge (*Cliona*), and the swimming scallops (*Chlamys* spp.) are typically encrusted with sponges. The sponge helps protect the scallop by providing camouflage and helping prevent sea star predators from grasping the scallop with their tube feet. In turn, the swimming scallop often carries the sponge away from nudibranch predators.

YELLOW BORING SPONGE

Cliona celata Grant, 1826; var. *californiana* de Laubenfels, 1932.
Alternate name: Sulphur sponge
Size: Yellow patches protrude from holes to 1/16–1/8" (1-3 mm) diameter.
Range: Pacific coast.
Habitat: Typically in shells, sometimes encrusting patches on rocks or in limestone rock.
Description: Clear yellow to sulphur yellow patches on shells of rock scallops and in calcareous shells of barnacles, moonsnails and others.
Comments: There are likely a number of *Cliona* species in west coast waters, and species is found in many other regions. This sponge breaks down shell litter and is sometimes considered a pest to oyster fisheries.

ROUGH SCALLOP SPONGE

Myxilla incrustans (Esper, 1805–14).
Size: To 3/8" (9 mm) thick.
Range: Arctic Ocean to southern California.
Habitat: On shells of scallop (*Chlamys* spp.).
Description: Thick crust on scallop shells, gold to light brown. Does not have thick fibre structure. "Lumpy" oscula (pores) to 1/4" (6 mm) diameter.
Comments: Species is also found in Japan. It is often eaten by nudibranchs, including the leopard dorid (see p. 113) and yellow margin dorid (p. 114).

SMOOTH SCALLOP SPONGE

Mycale adhaerens (Lambe, 1894).
Size: To 3/8" (9 mm) thick.
Range: Bering Sea to Washington.
Habitat: On shells of scallop (*Chlamys* spp.).
Description: Yellow-brown to violet crust on scallop shells. When torn, thick, prominent fibres are visible. Thinner crust and smaller oscula (pores) than the rough scallop sponge (above).

HERMIT CRAB SPONGE

Suberites suberea forma *latus* Lambe, 1893.
Alternate name: Often listed as the Atlantic *Suberites fiscus,* similar but not the same.
Size: Lumps to 3" (7.5 cm) high and wide.
Range: Gulf of Alaska to San Diego, California.
Habitat: Settles on and dissolves shells inhabited by hermit crabs. Low intertidal to 120' (36 m).
Description: Firm and dense. Grey or brown to dark orange.
Comments: Associated with a variety of hermit crabs, which grow within sponge and do not have to fight for larger shells as they grow. Sponge is mobile and less vulnerable than other sponges to nudibranch predators.

PURPLE ENCRUSTING SPONGE

Haliclona? permollis (Bowerbank, 1866).
Size: To 15/8" (4 cm) high, 3' (1 m) wide.
Range: BC to central California.
Habitat: Intertidal, on rocks to 20' (6 m).
Description: Thin, smooth crust with volcano pores. Pink to lavender to purple.
Comments: Widespread on both Pacific and Atlantic coasts. May be separate species or subspecies. Often eaten by leopard dorid (see p. 113).

BREAD CRUMB SPONGES

Halichondria spp.

Etymology: *Hali/chondria* = sea/lump.
Size: To 2" (5 cm) high; greater than 12" (30 cm) wide.
Range: Alaska to southern California.
Habitat: Shallow subtidal, on rocks in current areas.
Description: Looks like bread crumbs. Prominent, low, volcano-like oscula (pores). Spicules are similar to *Halichondria bowerbankia*.

Comments: Has a strong odour. This yellow subtidal sponge appears to be different from the green to yellow intertidal crumb of bread sponge *Halichondria panicea* (Pallas, 1766), found on exposed shores (left). *H. panicea*, when broken, smells like exploded gunpowder.

VELVETY RED SPONGE

Ophlitaspongia pennata (Lambe, 1895).
Size: Crust to 1/4" (6 mm) thick, to 3' (1 m) wide,.
Range: Alaska to Gulf of California.
Habitat: High intertidal to 295' (90 m), on rocks,.
Description: Thin, smooth patches. Coral red, red-brown to mustard colour.
Comments: The red sponge nudibranch (see p. 112) is usually found feeding on this sponge and laying a red ribbon of eggs.

YELLOW ENCRUSTING SPONGE

Myxilla lacunosa Lambe, 1893.
Etymology: *Myxilla* = slime.
Size: Crust to 5" (12.5 cm) high; to 12" (30 cm) or more wide.
Range: Aleutian Islands to BC.
Habitat: On rocks in current-swept areas, 30' (9 m) and deeper.
Description: Slimy, thickly encrusting sponge, sometimes in lumps. Orange-yellow.
Comments: Often eaten by various sea lemon nudibranchs (see p. 112).

RED VOLCANO SPONGE

Acarnus erithacus de Laubenfels, 1927.
Size: Crust to 6" (15 cm) thick, to 4" (10 cm) diameter.
Range: Southern Alaska to Baja California; in Gulf of California.
Habitat: On open coast, low intertidal to 2,300' (700 m).
Description: Firm, massive clumps. Bright red-orange.
Comments: Sometimes eaten by red sponge nudibranch (see p. 112).

ORANGE BALL SPONGE

Tethya californiana (de Laubenfels, 1932).
Alternate names: Orange puffball sponge; *Tethya aurantia*.
Etymology: *Tethya* = a sea goddess.
Size: To 6" (15 cm) diameter.
Range: Southeast Alaska to central Baja California.
Habitat: Intertidal and subtidal. Can tolerate sedimentation. At 20' (6 m) and deeper.
Description: Firm ball, firmly attached. Orange or yellow to green.
Comments: Species is also found in Europe, New Zealand and other regions. It is often eaten by the vermilion star (see p. 130).

TENNIS BALL SPONGE

Craniella villosa Lambe, 1894.
Alternate names: *Tetilla villosa*; gray puffball sponge. *Tetilla arb* may be an alternate name or a southern species.
Size: To 6" (15 cm) diameter.
Range: Southeast Alaska to Washington.
Habitat: Intertidal and subtidal to 65' (20 m) and deeper, on rocks.
Description: Round grey exterior with ridge and holes at top. White to yellow interior with large radiating spicules. Firmly attached.
Comments: Widely distributed, commonly encountered. Sometimes eaten by nudibranchs and sea stars.

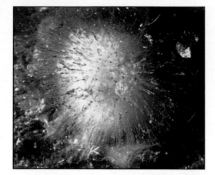

SPINY TENNIS BALL SPONGE

Craniella spinosa Lambe, 1894.
Alternate name: *Tetilla spinosa.*
Size: To 1¹/₂" (4 cm) diameter.
Range: Aleutian Islands to BC.
Habitat: Shallow subtidal, on rocks.
Description: Small bristly balls attached to rocks.
Comments: Easily distinguished from the smooth tennis ball sponge (see p. 25).

GLOVE SPONGE

Neoesperiopsis digitata (Miklucho-Maclay, 1870).
Alternate name: *Isodictya digitata;*
Esperiopsis quatsinoensis.
Size: To 12" (30 cm) high.
Range: Bering Sea to BC.
Habitat: On rocks in current-swept areas.
Description: Clump of finger-like branches, flexible in strong currents. Off-white to yellow-orange.
Comments: The glove sponge is also found in Japan. There are different forms and colours in the field, and there may be several species involved here!

ORANGE FINGER SPONGE

Neoesperiopsis rigida (Lambe, 1893).
Alternate name: *Isodyctia rigida.*
Size: To 8" (20 cm) high.
Range: Southeast Alaska to BC.
Habitat: Intertidal and shallow subtidal, on rocks.
Description: Flexible, erect finger-like branches. Orange to yellow.
Comments: Often eaten by the leopard dorid (see p. 113). Usually in a smaller mass and found in more protected waters than the glove sponge (above).

TRUMPET SPONGE

Stylissa stipitata de Laubenfels, 1961.
Etymology: *Stylus* = column; *stipi* = stalked.
Size: To 10" (25 cm) high.
Range: Southeast Alaska to Washington.
Habitat: Subtidal in current-swept areas.
Description: Strong, flexible stalk, trumpet-shaped growths. Cream-yellow.
Comments: Often eaten by the Monterey sea lemon.

AGGREGATED VASE SPONGE

Polymastia pacifica Lambe, 1894.
Alternate name: Western nipple sponge.
Etymology:*Poly/mastia* = many breasts.
Size: Mat to 1/4" (6 mm) thick and 12" (30 cm) wide. Oscula (pores) to 3/8" (9 mm) high.
Range: Amchitka Island, Alaska to California.
Habitat: Intertidal to 600' (180 m).
Description: Nipple-like pores in a cushion-shaped mat. Cream-yellow.
Comments: Species is eaten by sea lemon (see p. 112). It is similar in appearance to *Polymastia pachymastia*.

SALT AND PEPPER SPONGE

Penares cortius de Laubenfels, 1930.
Size: To 2" (5 cm) high, 12" (30 cm) wide.
Range: Southeast Alaska to southern California.
Habitat: Intertidal and subtidal.
Description: Firm ridges or patches. Bright conspicuous oscula (pores) along the ridges. White or grey to brown.

PEACH BALL SPONGE

Suberites montiniger Carter, 1880.
Size: To 8" (20 cm) wide.
Range: BC to Baja California.
Habitat: In current-swept passages, 15–100' (5–30 m).
Description: Irregular balls of sponge. Pink to apricot colour.

IOPHON SPONGE

Iophon chelifer Ridley & Dendy, 1886; var. *californiana* (de Laubenfels, 1932).
Size: To 12" (30 cm) high, 3' (1 m) wide.
Range: Alaska to Gulf of California.
Habitat: On rocks, in currents. At 65' (20 m) and deeper.
Description: Encrusting to large, erect, branching growths. Cream to yellow.
Comments: Species is eaten by the wrinkled star (see p. 131). It turns black in alcohol. Several *Iophon* species live in Northwest Coast waters; others are found in Europe and on the east coast of North America.

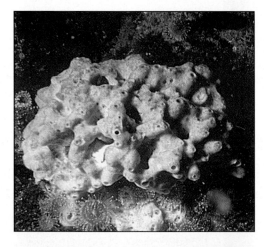

WHITE SPONGE

Adocia sp.
Size: To 4" (10 cm) high, 8" (20 cm) wide.
Range: BC.
Habitat: Subtidal, 30' (9 m) and deeper. On rocks in current-swept areas.
Description: Convoluted mounds with oscula (pores) raised on chimneys. Crispy outer layer. White.
Comments: Species is similar to *Reniera mollis* Lambe, 1893, not shown here.

CHOCOLATE PUFFBALL SPONGE

Latrunculia sp.
Size: To 4" (10 cm) high, 6" (15 cm) across.
Range: BC.
Habitat: Subtidal to 65' (20 m) or deeper, on rocks in protected waters.
Description: Thin, fragile appearance. Dark chocolate brown.
Comments: Species is abundant at some locations in the Strait of Georgia, BC.

Hydroids, Corals, Sea Anemones, Jellyfish, Comb Jellies

Cnidarians and Ctenophores

PHYLUM CNIDARIA

The Cnidarians, or sea nettles, are invertebrates characterized by the stinging capsules in the tentacles around the mouth. (The Greek *cnidos* means "stinging nettles.") There are some 9,000 living species of cnidarians, about 340 of which inhabit the shores and shallows of the Pacific Northwest.

LOCOMOTION

Many cnidarians are sessile (permanently attached at the base and not free-swimming). Some of the anemones glide in a snail-like fashion on their pedal disks, and can move great distances. The "swimming anemones," such as *Stomphia* species (p. 46), have a dramatic escape response to predatory sea stars: they detach and flex to move away from danger. Most of the jellyfish alternately drift and swim with a pulsing action.

PREY–PREDATORS

The cnidarian feeds by stinging and paralyzing anything that gets tangled in its tentacles, where most of its intracellular stinging capsules (nematocysts) are concentrated. These stinging structures also help protect the animal from predators.

A variety of creatures feed on cnidarians, including nudibranchs, which eat hydroids and octocorals. Some nudibranchs are able to take the nematocysts from their prey and use them for their own defence. Many sea stars feed on sea pens and various anemones, and some fishes feed on drifting jellyfish.

CAUTION: Stinging capsules on the tentacles of jellyfish, particularly the sea blubber (see p. 48), can cause a painful, stinging rash. Handling the fish-eating anemone (p. 44) can also result in severe stings. Some cnidarians also contain toxins. Traditionally, Hawaiians used an extract from zoanthids to poison their speartips.

REPRODUCTION

Cnidarians have complex life cycles, with many species alternating between an attached phase and a free-swimming phase, and between a jellyfish and an umbrella-shaped medusa. The jellyfish stage reproduces sexually by producing larvae that drift, then attach to continue the cycle. Many of the attached forms, like the familiar anemone, divide by budding (asexual) or by sexual means.

EDIBILITY

The Nuu-chah-nulth (Nootka) people of the west coast of Vancouver Island traditionally gathered sea anemones in the spring, steamed them and ate them. According to stories and legends, if you were offered one, you had to eat it or become a widower.

Hydroids (Sea Firs, Sea Trees, Sea Plumes, Sea-Ferns) Class Hydrozoa

Order Hydroida

Hydroids are common, but so small they are easy to overlook. To find them, search for a solitary stalk (an unbranched stem) crowned with a ring of tentacles. Many hydroids are bushy, tree-like or feather-like colonies rising from a root-like base. The thin, stick-like branches bear numerous polyps, some on stalks and others housed in protective cups. All hydroids are eaten by nudibranchs, and nudibranch eggs can often be seen lodged in the branches of hydroid colonies.

Many hydroids alternate between an attached form and a small jellyfish (hydromedusa) stage. These miniature jellyfish are different in structure from the large medusae or "true" jellyfish (see p. 48).

The hydroids are fascinating creatures, but little study of them has been undertaken in the Pacific Northwest area.

SEA FIR
Abietinaria sp.
Size: To 6" (15 cm) high.
Range: Alaska to San Diego, California.
Habitat: On rocks, intertidal and shallow subtidal.
Description: Feather-like or fern-like stem and branches, with polyps on both sides of branches.

HYDROID
Abietinaria greenei (Murray, 1860).
Size: To 3" (7.5 cm) high, clumps to 4" (10 cm) wide.
Range: Bering Sea to San Diego, California.
Habitat: On rocks in current-swept areas, intertidal and shallow subtidal.
Description: Bushy clump of branches, bright, reflective tips.

OSTRICH PLUME HYDROID

Aglaophenia struthionides (Murray, 1860).

Size: To 5" (12.5 cm) high.
Range: Alaska to San Diego, California.
Habitat: On rocks, intertidal to 525' (160 m).
Description: Polyps on only one side of the feather-like branches.
Comments: Often seen with nudibranchs on the branches, feeding on the polyps.

RASPBERRY HYDROID

Corymorpha sp.

Size: Stem to 2" (5 cm) long.
Range: BC to Monterey, California.
Habitat: On rocks, subtidal in high current areas.
Description: Wine-red polyp on solitary, slender stalk.
Comments: Often found being eaten by a small nudi-branch, *Cuthona punicea* Millen, 1986.

PINK MOUTH HYDROID

Ectopleura crocea (L. Agassiz, 1862).

Alternate name: *Tubularia crocea*.
Size: To 5" (12.5 cm) high; colonies more than 12" (30 cm) wide.
Range: Gulf of Alaska to California; Nova Scotia to Florida.
Habitat: On rocks and hard surfaces, intertidal and shallow subtidal.
Description: Bushy, tangled clusters of straw-like stems with pink and red polyps, 2 whorls of tentacles, grape-like clusters of reproductive organs.

PINK MOUTH HYDROID

Ectopleura marina (Torrey, 1902).
Alternate name: *Tubularia marina.*
Size: Stem to 3" (8 cm) long.
Range: BC to Monterey, California.
Habitat: On rocks and floats, intertidal to 50' (15 m).
Description: Orange-pink polyp on solitary, slender stalk.

ORANGE HYDROID

Garveia annulata Nutting, 1901.
Size: Clusters to 6" (15 cm) high.
Range: Sitka, Alaska to Santa Catalina Island, California.
Habitat: On rocks and stems of kelp, sponges or coralline algae, intertidal to 400' (120 m).
Description: Easily recognized by bright orange holdfast, stem and hydranth (mouth end of polyp).

HEDGEHOG HYDROID (SNAIL FUR)

Hydractinia milleri Torrey, 1902.
Alternate name: Miller's hydractinia.
Size: To 1/8" (3 mm) high, mats to 2" (5 cm) wide.
Range: Vancouver Island to Carmel, California.
Habitat: Often on shells inhabited by hermit crabs (*Ellasochirus tenuimanus*, shown here), on shells of crabs and occasionally on rocks.
Description: Pink fuzzy masses joined at the base in a mat which unites the colony.

Comments: Several species of *Hydractinia* occur on rocks in Pacific Northwest waters.

GLASSY PLUME HYDROIDS
Plumularia spp.
Alternate name: Decorator hydroids.
Size: To 1 1/2" (4 cm) high.
Range: Alaska to California.
Habitat: On rocks or floats, intertidal and shallow subtidal.
Description: Delicate feather-like plumes.
Comments: Species is cosmopolitan. There are several species that are difficult to distinguish in the field.

Hydrocorals Class Hydrozoa

Order Stylasterina

The hydrocorals, so named because their calcareous skeletons resemble those of the true corals, are very "plastic": they may change forms from encrusting to branching according to currents and other habitat conditions. A colony may have a range of colours, from pink to red to violet.

Hydrocorals are difficult to identify positively in the field, as they vary mostly by structure of the polyps and shape of the pores. A few frequently seen species are included here.

ENCRUSTING HYDROCORALS
Stylantheca spp.
Alternate names: *Allopora petrograpta* Fisher, 1938; *Allopora porphyra* Fisher, 1931.
Size: Crust 1/8" (3 mm) thick, patches to 6" (15 cm) wide and more.
Range: BC to central California.
Habitat: On rocks in current-swept areas, intertidal and shallow subtidal.
Description: Reddish-pink to violet. Thin, hard, smooth crust without erect branches, with small holes occupied by polyps.
Comments: May be one or several species. Often confused with coralline algae.

PINK HYDROCORAL

Stylaster venustus (Verrill, 1870).
Alternate name: *Allopora venusta* Verrill, 1868.
Size: To 3" (7.5 cm) high, 3' (1 m) wide and more.
Range: BC to southern California.
Habitat: On clean, current-swept rocks, subtidal.
Description: Mass of thickly branching colonies. Rose pink to faded violet with tips of branches nearly white.

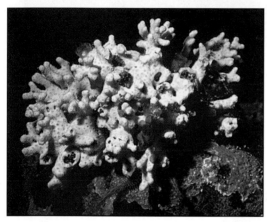

PINK HYDROCORAL

Stylaster verrilli (Dall, 1884).
Alternate names: *Allopora verrilli* Dall, 1864;
= *A. norvegica.*
Size: To 3" (7.5 cm) high, 4" (10 cm) wide or more.
Range: Aleutian Islands to Oregon.
Habitat: On rocks in current-swept areas, shallow subtidal to 30' (9 m) and more.
Description: Upright branching colonies, orange to salmon pink.

Comments: Easily confused with several similar-looking species. Microscopic examination of polyps and pores is necessary for positive identification.

Sea Pens, Soft Corals, Sea Fans (Gorgonian Corals), Anemones, Jellyfish Class Anthozoa

The sea pens, soft corals and sea fans are members of the subclass Octocorallia, named for the eight tentacles surrounding the mouth, and live in colonies.

Sea Pens Order Pennatulacea

The sea pen grows in tall, branching, feather-like colonies that project vertically from sand or sand–mud. The branches have polyps with eight tentacles. Sea pens can be seen in shallows by divers, or from boats or wharves. They can withdraw completely into the sea bottom.

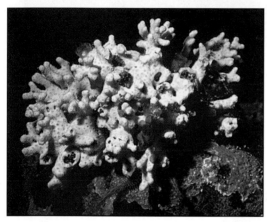

CORALS

35

ORANGE SEA PEN
Ptilosarcus gurneyi (Gray, 1860).
Alternate name: Gurney's sea pen.
Size: To 18" (46 cm) high, 4" (10 cm) wide.
Range: Prince William Sound, Alaska to central California.
Habitat: Intertidal and common in shallow subtidal, to 330' (100 m) or more.
Description: Orange fleshy stalk and branches with many polyps.
Comments: Eaten by the striped nudibranch (see p. 118), diamond back triton (p. 118) and other nudibranchs; and by several sea stars, including leather (p. 133), spiny red (p. 130), rose (p. 130), vermilion (p. 133) and other sea stars.

WHITE SEA PEN
Virgularia sp.
Alternate name: *Virgularia ? tuberculata* Marshall, 1877.
Size: To 8" (20 cm) across, 12" (30 cm) high.
Range: Alaska to California.
Habitat: Anchored in sand–mud, 50' (15 m) and deeper.
Description: Slender, delicate white branches.
Comments: Cut down and eaten by the nudibranch pink tritonia (see p. 117). There may be several species of this sea pen in the shallow subtidal.

SEA WHIP
Balticina septentrionalis (Gray, 1872).
Alternate name: = *Osteocella septentrionalis*.
Size: To 8' (2.5 m) high.
Range: Alaska to Puget Sound.
Habitat: In sand–mud, 65' (20 m) and deeper.
Description: Slender, short white branches with polyps on a thick supporting rod.
Comments: One of the largest sea pens seen by divers. Another deep water sea pen, *Acanthoptilum* sp., can reach heights to 9' (2.7 m)!

Soft Corals: Order Alcyonacea

These corals are soft, fleshy colonies, without a hard skeleton. Their tissues contain small structural rods (spicules) that are examined microscopically to identify some species.

SOFT CORAL
Gersemia rubiformis (Eherenberg, 1834).
Alternate name: Sea strawberry.
Etymology: *Gersemia* = seed bearer; *rubiformis* = berry-shaped. The genus *Rubus* includes raspberries and blackberries.
Size: Lumps to 6" (15 cm) high, 6" (15 cm) wide.
Range: Gulf of Alaska to Pt. Arena, California; Arctic to Gulf of Maine.
Habitat: On rocks in current-swept areas, rarely intertidal, subtidal to 65' (20 m) and more.
Description: Firm colonies, cream to pink to deep red. Polyps have 8 tentacles and delicate side branches, and gather in a fleshy mass. Polyps are often withdrawn, or extended to 1/4" (6 mm) beyond base.

Comments: Octocoral has spicules of calcium carbonate in body. Eaten by nudibranchs, including orange peel (see p. 117) and diamond back tritonia (p. 118). Hosts juvenile basket stars (p. 139).

PALE SOFT CORAL
Clavularia spp.
Size: Lumps to 4" (10 cm) high, 4" (10 cm) wide.
Range: BC to southern California.
Habitat: On rocks in current-swept areas, rarely intertidal, subtidal to 65' (20 m) and more.
Description: Firm colonies, cream to pink. Individual polyps rise from creeping stolons (rootlike extensions), each having 8 tentacles and delicate side branches.
Comments: Octocoral has spicules of calcium carbonate in body. Occasionally found on shells of decorator crabs (see p. 76).

Sea Fans (Gorgonian Corals) Order Gorgonacea

These corals form branched colonies, often in flat, fan-like shapes. The stiff supporting column and branches bear numerous holes from which fuzzy polyps protrude and feed. They are octocorals, having eight feathery tentacles surrounding the mouth, as in soft corals and sea pens.

SEA FAN (GORGONIAN CORAL)
Swiftia torreyi (Nutting, 1909).
Size: To 12" (30 cm) high, 24" (60 cm) wide.
Range: BC; California.
Habitat: On rocks in current-swept areas, shallow subtidal, 60' (18 m) and deeper.
Description: Fans of many short orange-red branches with many small golden polyps.
Comments: In the Pacific Northwest, found in the Strait of Georgia and in Barkley Sound in the shallow subtidal.

SEA FAN (GORGONIAN CORAL)
Calcigorgia spiculifera Broch, 1935.
Size: To 12" (30 cm) high, 24" (60 cm) wide.
Range: Southern Alaska to BC.
Habitat: On rocks in current-swept areas, shallow subtidal, 50' (15 m) and deeper.
Description: Short, wide fans of pink-peach branches and polyps.
Comments: Often has basket stars (see p. 139) attached.

Cup Corals, Club Anemones, Zoanthids, Anemones
Subclass Zoantharia

Cup Corals Order Scleractinia

These solitary limestone cups house anemone-like individuals. They are members of the same order as the reef-building "true corals," which do not inhabit Pacific Northwest waters.

ORANGE CUP CORAL
Balanophyllia elegans Verill, 1869.
Etymology: *Balano/phyllia* = acorn/leaf; *elegans* = elegant.
Size: To 1/2" (1 cm) high, 1/2" (1 cm) diameter.
Range: Alaska to central Baja California.
Habitat: On rocks, intertidal in dark places and shallow subtidal to 65' (20 m) and more.
Description: Solitary but sometimes clumped. Bright orange polyps, nearly transparent tentacles sit in a calcareous cup that partitions the digestive cavity (see photo).

TAN CUP CORAL
Caryophyllia alaskensis Vaughan, 1941.
Size: To 1/2" (1 cm) high, 1" (2.5 cm) or more.
Range: Alaska to California.
Habitat: On rocks, subtidal to 50' (15 m) or more.
Description: Beige, brown to pink polyps with many short, transparent tentacles. Solitary, but sometimes clumped.

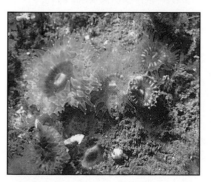

TAN CUP CORAL
Paracyathus stearnsi Verill, 1869.
Alternate name: Stern's cup.
Size: To 1 1/2" (4 cm) diameter.
Range: BC; California to Cedros Island, Baja California.
Habitat: On rocks, 30–300' (10–90 m).
Description: Dark orange-brown polyp, transparent tentacles which are fewer and longer than tan cup coral (above). Solitary.

Corallimorphs (Club Anemones) Order Corallimorpharia

These colonies of individuals resemble anemones in appearance, but are more closely related to corals in internal body structure.

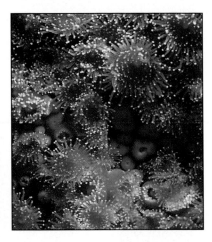

STRAWBERRY ANEMONE

Corynactis californica Calgren, 1936.
Size: To 3/4" (2 cm) high, colonies to 65' (20 m) wide.
Range: BC to San Martin Island, Baja California.
Habitat: On rocks in current-swept areas, intertidal to 70' (21 m) and more.
Description: Colony of white to pink, to red and lavender bodies with white knobs on tips of tentacles.
Comments: Colonial species closely related to corals.

Zoanthids Order Zoanthidea

The zoanthids are colonies of anemone-like individuals, joined at the base by a sheet of tissue.

ZOANTHIDS

Epizoanthus scotinus Wood, 1958.
Size: To 2" (5 cm) high, colonies to several feet (1–2 m) wide.
Range: Western Aleutian Islands to Puget Sound.
Habitat: On rocks, intertidal and subtidal.
Description: Anemone-like, orange-yellow polyps from a common base forms a mat of hundreds of individuals.
Comments: Unlike anemones, zoanthids are colonial.

Anemones Order Actiniaria

The anemone is a stalked animal, crowned by a flattened disk and rings of tentacles. It lacks a skeleton and can extend or flatten its body by changing its internal water pressure. Anemones often divide to form new individuals, but they are not joined colonies like the strawberry anemone or zoanthids (above).

SHORT PLUMOSE ANEMONES

Metridium senile (Linnaeus, 1767).
Size: To 4" (10 cm) high, usually to 2" (5 cm) wide.
Range: Circumpolar; Alaska to southern California.
Habitat: Attached to hard surfaces, on floats, intertidal to 1,000' (300 m).
Description: White, cream, brown, tan to orange. Usually with fewer than 100 slender, translucent tentacles crowning a smooth column. Oral disc not lobed.
Comments: Species spreads by pedal fragments and is often found in dense aggregations. Long threads with stinging cells from mouth and special tentacles defend territory against other colonies (clones) or anemone species. Attacked by spiny red star (see p. 130). Species is found on northern Atlantic coasts as well as Pacific Northwest.

GIANT PLUMOSE ANEMONES

Metridium giganteum Fautin, Bucklin & Hand, 1989.
Size: To 3' (1 m) high.
Range: Circumpolar; Alaska to southern California.
Habitat: Attached to hard surfaces, on floats, intertidal to 1,000' (300 m).
Description: White, brown, tan to salmon-orange. Usually with more than 200 slender, translucent tentacles, crowning a smooth column. Lobed oral disk.
Comments: Common in dense aggregations. Long threads with stinging capsules from mouth and special tentacles defend territory against other colonies (clones) or anemone species. Attacked by the shaggy mouse nudibranch (see p. 119) and leather star (p. 133). Species is found on northern Atlantic coasts as well as Pacific Northwest.

BROODING ANEMONE

Epiactis prolifera Verrill, 1869.
Alternate name: Proliferating anemone.
Size: To 4" (10 cm) high; crown to 2" (5 cm) diameter.
Range: Southern Alaska to southern California.
Habitat: On rocks, on coralline algae, intertidal and shallow subtidal.
Description: Low and squat with variable colour: pink, green, brown, orange. Light radiating lines on disk, lines on column. Bears up to 30 young of various sizes, mostly in a ring.
Comments: This is the most common of several *Epiactis* species.

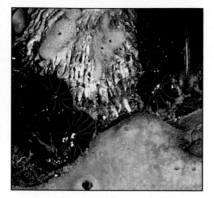

LINED ANEMONE

Haliplanella lineata Verrill, 1869.
Alternate name: *Haliplanella luciae.*
Size: To 1¹/₄" (3 cm) high; crown to 1¹/₂" (4 cm) diameter.
Range: BC to southern California.
Habitat: In crevices or tidepools, high intertidal and subtidal.
Description: Olive-green column with pale orange, yellow to white lengthwise stripes.
Comments: Uses threads of stinging cells for protection or aggression. Species is also found in Japan and along Atlantic coasts, and may have been introduced to this area from Japan.

GIANT GREEN ANEMONE

Anthopleura xanthogrammica (Brandt, 1835).
Size: To 12" (30 cm) high; 10" (25 cm) diameter.
Range: Alaska to Panama.
Habitat: On completely exposed rocky shores, intertidal and shallow subtidal.
Description: Column green-olive, tentacles and oral disc uniform bright green. Solitary.
Comments: Green colour comes from symbiotic algae living in the tissues.

AGGREGATE GREEN ANEMONE

Anthopleura elegantissima (Brandt, 1835).
Alternate name: Elegant anemone.
Size: To 6" (15 cm) high, 3¹/₈" (8 cm) diameter or more.
Range: Alaska to Baja California.
Habitat: On rocks and hard surfaces, intertidal and shallow subtidal.
Description: Budding colonies, which frequently accumulate sand, gravel and shell. Lengthwise rows of tubercles on green column. Green disk often with dark bands, tentacles with pink tips.
Comments: Clear boundaries are established between colonies (clones) by the use of stinging cells.

BURIED GREEN ANEMONE

Anthopleura artemisia (Pickering, in Dana, 1848).
Alternate name: Moonglow anemone.
Size: To 4" (10 cm) diameter, column buried to 10" (25 cm).
Range: Alaska to southern California.
Habitat: Buried in sand–shell, base attached to a rock or shell. Intertidal and shallow subtidal, to 35' (10.5 m).

Description: Long, slender tentacles, sometimes pink or orange, usually white bands on green-grey to brown or black. Tubercles at top of column. Typically only crown of tentacles is exposed.
Comments: Symbiotic algae in upper, exposed tissues.

PAINTED ANEMONE

Urticina crassicornis (O.F. Müeller, 1776).
Alternate names: Northern red anemone; Christmas anemone; *Tealia crassicornis*.
Size: To 5" (12.5 cm) high, 3" (7.5 cm) diameter.
Range: Circumpolar; Pribilof Islands, Alaska to south of Monterey, California.
Habitat: On rocks, intertidal to shallow subtidal.
Description: Column variable in colour with green, red and yellow patches; rings of short, thick, blunt tentacles of varying colours; light bands, usually with white tips; disk is same colour as tentacles.
Comments: Species is also found on north Atlantic coasts.

WHITE-SPOTTED ANEMONE

Urticina lofotensis (Danielssen, 1890).
Alternate names: *Tealia lofotensis*; strawberry anemone.
Size: To 6" (15 cm) diameter, column to 6" (15 cm) high.
Range: Southeast Alaska to San Diego, California.
Habitat: On exposed coasts, intertidal to 50' (15 m).
Description: Squat scarlet column, white tubercles in vertical rows, long yellow tentacles with pink-red tips.

Comments: Shell fragments may stick to tubercles. The juvenile painted greenling (p. 169) is often found associated with this anemone and, when larger, often sleeps at the base at night. Species is also found on northern Atlantic coasts.

FISH-EATING ANEMONE

Urticina piscivora (Sebens & Laakso, 1977).
Alternate name: *Tealia piscivora*.
Size: To 10" (25 cm) high, 8" (20 cm) diameter.
Range: Polar seas to La Jolla, California.
Habitat: On prominences, subtidal to 100' (30 m) and more.
Description: Tall, smooth maroon column; oral disk often has red lines and many short, slender tentacles, white, sometimes tipped with red or pink.

Comments: Captures and eats small fish. Note broken-back shrimp (*Heptacarpus*) at base of anemone. Caution: Severe stings can be caused by handling this anemone.

BURIED ANEMONE

Urticina coriacea (Cuvier, 1798).
Alternate names: Stubby rose anemone; leathery anemone; red beaded anemone; *Tealia coriacea*.
Size: To 6" (15 cm) high, 6" (15 cm) diameter.
Range: Alaska to Monterey, California.
Habitat: Usually partially buried in sand–shell, intertidal to 50' (15 m).
Description: Red column, green-olive disk with short, blunt, banded tentacles varying in colour: green, pink, red or blue.
Comments: There may be several species of burying *Urticina* in Pacific Northwest waters, as yet undescribed.

COLUMBIA SAND ANEMONE

Urticina columbiana (Verrill, 1922).
Alternate names: Sand anemone;
Tealia columbiana.
Size: To 6" (15 cm) high, 3' (1 m) diameter or more.
Range: Vancouver Island to Baja California.
Habitat: Partially buried in sand–mud–shell, subtidal to 150' (45 m) or more.
Description: Column encircled by rough tubercles. Long, slender tentacles.
Comments: One of the largest anemones in the world. Candy stripe shrimp (see p. 82) are often found associated with this and other anemones.

TUBE-DWELLING ANEMONE

Pachycerianthus fimbriatus McMurrich, 1970.
Alternate name: Burrowing anemone.
Size: To 14" (35 cm) long, crown to 8" (20 cm) diameter.
Range: BC to southern California.
Habitat: Secretes tube to 3' (1 m) long in mud.
Description: 2 sets of banded golden-brown to purple-black tentacles, short inner circle over mouth, longer delicate outer ring. Secretes a mucous-like tube.
Comments: Giant dendronotid nudibranch (see p. 116) feeds on this anemone and lays egg masses attached to tube.

SNAKELOCK ANEMONE

Cribrinopsis fernaldi Siebert & Spaulding, 1976.
Alternate name: Crimson anemone.
Size: Column to 8" (20 cm) high.
Range: Aleutian Islands to Puget Sound.
Habitat: On rocks, subtidal to 1,000 (300 m) or more.
Description: Crown with long, slender, drooping tentacles that drape over column and have distinctive raised zigzag lines. Colour varies from white to pink to red. Upper column has longitudinal rows of tubercles; oral disk has lines radiating from the mouth.
Comments: Shrimp species *Lebbeus* (see p. 82) and *Heptacarpus* (p. 82) live under the protective canopy of the tentacles. The heart crab (see p. 72) also shelters under the canopy, when moulting.

SWIMMING ANEMONE

Stomphia didemon Siebert, 1973.
Size: To 4" (10 cm) high, 5" (12.5 cm) diameter.
Range: BC and Washington.
Habitat: On rocks, subtidal to 65' (20 m) or more.
Description: Cream to bright orange, sometimes mottled column with orange, white or banded tentacles. Squat animal, sometimes with white oral disc.
Comments: This anemone can swim as an escape response to leather star (see p. 133).

SPOTTED SWIMMING ANEMONE

Stomphia coccinea (O.F. Müeller, 1776).
Size: To 1¼" (3 cm) high, 1¼" (3 cm) diameter.
Range: Pt. Barrow, Alaska to Washington.
Habitat: Often attached to shells of horsemussels.
Description: Pale orange to brown-orange. Tentacles with white spots at bases, whitish column, sometimes mottled.
Comments: There is a similar Atlantic species.

Jellyfish Class Hydrozoa

Jellyfish are members of two classes. The hydromedusae, of the class Hydrozoa, are reproductive stages of hydroids (see pp. 29–34) which are typically smaller than 4" (10 cm) in diameter. "True" jellyfish (scyphomedusae), of the class Scyphozoa, are usually larger than 4" (10 cm) in diameter and differ in internal structures (see moon jellyfish, and sea blubber, p. 48). Most scyphomedusae have an attached polyp stage too. Much of the time jellyfish drift with currents, and they can also move deliberately by pulsing their bodies.

Class Hydrozoa

Hydromedusae Order Siphonophora

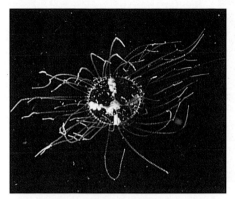

CLINGING JELLYFISH
Gonionemus vertens A. Agassiz, 1862.
Alternate names: Orange-striped jellyfish; angled hydromedusa.
Size: To 1¼" (3 cm) diameter.
Range: Alaska to southern California.
Habitat: Attached to kelp, eelgrass and other substrates in spring and summer.
Description: Transparent bell with cross-shaped gonads coloured red, violet, orange or yellow-brown. Long tentacles with adhesive pads.
Comments: When attached, tentacles form an angle at the sucker. Species is also found in Russia, Japan, and in the Arctic to Cape Cod.

SAIL JELLYFISH
Velella velella (Linnaeus, 1758).
Alternate name: By-the-wind-sailor.
Size: To 3" (7.5 cm) wide.
Range: Worldwide in temperate and tropical waters.
Habitat: Typically offshore, blown onto beaches.
Description: Dark blue floating hydroid colony with an upright sail.
Comments: The floating hydroid produces hundreds of these tiny jellyfish.

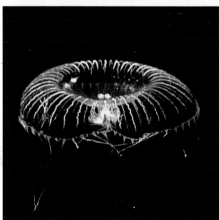

WATER JELLYFISH
Aequorea spp.
Alternate names: *Aequoreus aqueuorea A. flava, A. forskalea, A. victoria.*
Etymology: L. *Aequoreus* = smooth, even surface, calm sea.
Size: To 5" (12.5 cm) wide, 1½" (4 cm) high.
Range: Southeast Alaska to southern California.
Habitat: Coastal waters.
Description: Numerous white radial canals, thick gelatinous bell.
Comments: Luminescent in the dark. May be more than one species.

RED-EYE MEDUSA
Polyorchis pencillatus (Eschscholtz, 1829).
Size: To 1¹/₂" (4 cm) high.
Range: Alaska to San Diego, California.
Habitat: Coastal waters and bays of outer coast.
Description: Hydromedusa with a high bell. As many as 120 tentacles with single red eye-spots around margin.
Comments: Species alternately swims and drifts. It feeds in the water column and preys on worms and crustaceans by bouncing off the bottom.

"True Jellyfish" Class Scyphozoa

Order Semaeostomeae

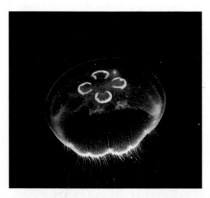

MOON JELLYFISH
Aurelia labiata Chamisso and Eysenhardt, 1820.
Alternate name: Often in error *Aurelia aurita.*
Size: To 3" (7.5 cm) high, 8" (20 cm) diameter or more.
Range: SE Alaska to Newport Beach, CA.
Habitat: Coastal waters, bays and harbours.
Description: 4 horseshoe-shaped gonads in translucent grey to blue bell; bell scalloped into 8 pairs of lobes. Short marginal tentacles.
Comments: Typically lives 1 year. Caution: tentacles can cause a rash. *Aurelia aurita* has 8 lobes.

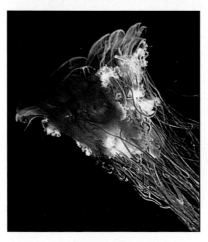

SEA BLUBBER
Cyanea capillata (Linnaeus, 1758).
Size: Bell typically to 20" (50 cm) or more; tentacles trail to 30' (9 m).
Range: Pt. Barrow, Alaska to southern California; Arctic to Florida and Mexico.
Habitat: Coastal waters.
Description: Margin of 8 pairs of lobes. Combination of colours: red-brown to yellow, rose, violet, to white body. Numerous long tentacles.
Comments: Beware—tentacles cause burning and blistering! Large bell hosts a number of juvenile pollock and other fish. *Cyanea* species also live in the Atlantic Ocean, where specimens 8' (2.5 m) across have been reported.

STALKED MEDUSA
Manania handi Larson and Fautin, 1989.
Size: To 1 1/2" (4 cm) long, including tentacles.
Range: West coast of Vancouver Island to Puget Sound.
Description: Green or yellowish green. Shaped like a wine goblet with a flexible stalk. 8 short arms, in pairs, each with 15–25 small tentacles, outermost tentacles with enlarged basal pads.
Habitat: On eelgrass (see p. 212) and algae in semiprotected subtidal habitats.
Comments: Found from late summer through early spring. May be found with another common stalked jellyfish (*Haliclystus*). Feeds especially on amphipods.

PHYLUM CTENOPHORA

Comb jellies (sea combs, sea gooseberries, ctenophores)

The comb jellies resemble jellyfish but differ in internal structure and do not have stinging cells. These animals are usually small, oval to elongated and growing to 3–4" (7.5–10 cm) long. They have 8 rows of beating cilia, or combs, that run down the body. About 100 species of comb jellies are distributed worldwide.

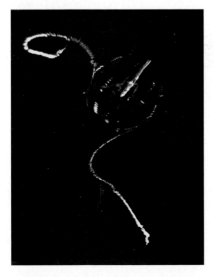

CAT'S EYE COMB JELLY
Pleurobrachia bachei A. Agassiz, 1860.
Size: To 1/2" (1 cm) high, tentacles to 6" (15 cm) or more.
Range: Alaska to Baja California.
Habitat: Near shore, usually in swarms.
Description: Round to egg-shaped body with combs of cilia that show a rainbow of colours and 2 long, trailing tentacles.
Comments: Common in shallow waters in spring, summer and early autumn.

CHAPTER 3

Worms

Segmented Worms, Ribbon Worms, Flatworms

PHYLUM ANNELIDA

Segmented Worms

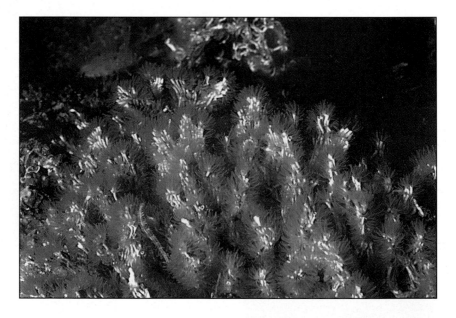

Thisis phylum takes its name from the Latin *annelis*, or "little ring," referring to the grooves that encircle the worm's body, dividing it into segments. Of the approximately 9,000 species of worms in this phylum—which also includes earthworms, freshwater worms and leeches—the marine worms or class Polychaeta comprise 6,000 to 8,000.

Class Polychaeta

The mostly marine, elongated, segmented worms in this class are known as polychaetes or bristleworms (*polychaete* means "many bristles"), because some segments of the various species bear bristles or paddle-like appendages. Segmentation is not superficial but internal, so that functions often take place in several sections of the worm at once. The polychaetes are divided into two subclasses, Sedentaria (body is fixed in a tube with the head visible, modified as a plume) and Errantia (free-swimming or burrowing, but not in a tube).

PREY–PREDATORS

Some polychaetes are herbivores and others are carnivores. Among the free-swimming worms, those that prey on human food sources such as clams are considered pests. A number of scale worms live in the protected habitat of mussel beds, or in the body grooves of hosts such as keyhole limpets, sea cucumbers, sea stars and hermit crab shells.

REPRODUCTION

Most polychaetes have separate sexes and fertilization usually occurs externally. Some species engage in nighttime swarming behaviour on the surface of the water, as the wriggling female worms shed their eggs and the males discharge sperm.

Many polychaetes can replace their own head or tail sections.

Sedentary Segmented Worms

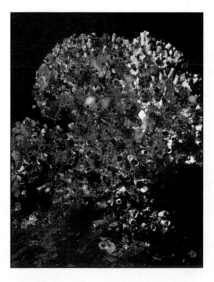

FRINGED TUBE WORMS
Dodecaceria fewkesi Berkeley & Berkeley, 1954.
Alternate names: Fewke's fringed worm; *D. pacifica*; *D. fistulicola*.
Size: 1⁵/₈" (4 cm) long, ¹/₈" (3 mm) wide.
Range: BC to southern California.
Habitat: In rocky, current-swept areas, intertidal to 65' (20 m).
Description: Short limy tube from clusters over 3' (1 m) across. Dark brown or green to black body with 11 pairs of dark filaments from the head end.
Comments: Tubes are often covered over by encrusting coralline algae. Other *Dodecaceria* species burrow into dead shells.

CORALLINE FRINGED TUBE WORMS

Dodecaceria concharum Oerstad, 1843.
Size: 1⁵/₈" (4 cm) long, ¹/₈" (3 mm) wide.
Range: BC to southern California.
Habitat: Bores into calcareous substrata, in rocky, current-swept areas, intertidal to 65' (20 m).
Description: Dark filaments from the head end.
Comments: Often in encrusting coralline algae, may burrow into dead shells.

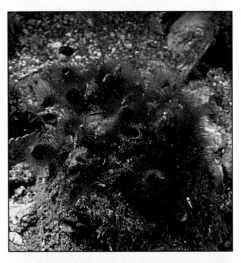

CEMENTED TUBE WORMS

Sabellaria cementarium Moore, 1906.
Alternate name: California honeycomb worm.
Size: Individual tubes to 3" (7.5 cm) long; worm to 2³/₄" (7 cm) long; forms reefs of tubes to 330' (100 m) long, 100' (30 m) high.
Range: Alaska to southern California.
Habitat: On and under rocks, intertidal to 265' (80 m).
Description: Deposits hard, dark grey tubes of cemented sand grains. Typically in clusters over 3' (1 m) across, sometimes extending to form reefs.

NORTHERN FEATHER DUSTER WORMS

Eudistylia vancouveri (Kinberg, 1867).
Size: Tubes to 24" (60 cm) high, ¹/₂" (1 cm) diameter; worm to 6" (15 cm) long; plumes to 2" (5 cm) across.
Range: Alaska to central California.
Habitat: On floats and rocks, intertidal to 65' (20 m) and more.
Description: Aggregated in large clumps. Distinctive banded maroon and green plumes from long, light grey, parchment-like tubes.
Comments: Often has hairysnails and anemones (see pp. 40–46) feeding at tops of tubes.

CALCAREOUS TUBE WORMS

Serpula vermicularis Linnaeus, 1767.

Alternate name: Red tube worm.

Size: Limy tubes to 4" (10 cm) long; worm to 4" (10 cm) long, 1/4" (6 mm) wide; plume to 3/4" (2 cm) long.

Range: Alaska to southern California.

Habitat: Tubes attached to rocks, pilings or floats, often on the underside, intertidal to more than 330' (100 m).

Description: White calcareous tubes, coiled or rambling. 1 or 2 red conical stoppers (opercula) close off the tube as the worm withdraws into it. Stoppers and fringe of tentacles (cirri) usually red, often with white bands.

Comments: Species is also found in Atlantic and Indian Oceans.

ORANGE TUBE WORMS

Salmacina tribranchiata (Moore, 1923).

Alternate name: Fragile tube worm.

Etymology: *Salmacina* = fountain; *tribranchiata* = three-gilled.

Size: Large clumps to 8" (20 cm) across; tube less than 1/16" (1 mm) diameter; worms to 1/4" (6 mm) long.

Range: BC to southern California.

Habitat: On rocks on open coast, intertidal to 70' (21 m) or more.

Description: Small, fragile white tubes with brilliant orange-red or pink worm plumes.

FIBRE-TUBE WORM

Pista elongata Moore, 1909.

Alternate name: Basket-top worm.

Size: Tube to 3" (7.5 cm) high; worm to 8" (20 cm) long.

Range: BC to San Diego, California.

Habitat: In crevices in current-swept areas; in the roots of surfgrass (see p. 213), intertidal to 40' (12 m) and more.

Description: Solitary. Opening of tube is a globular, woven hood of fibres that loosely forms a plug.

Comments: Species is also found in Japan.

SLIME TUBE WORMS

Myxicolla infundibulum (Renier, 1804).
Alternate name: Slime feather duster.
Etymology: *Myxi/colla* = slime/glue; *infundibul* = funnel.
Size: Worm to 8" (20 cm) long, 1¼" (3 cm) wide.
Range: Along entire Pacific coast.
Habitat: Wedged into crevices between rocks, intertidal to 1,400' (427 m).
Description: Transparent mucous-like tube, tentacles (cirri) partially united.
Comments: Worms retract rapidly into mucous-like collar, in response to shadows.

Free-Swimming Segmented Worms

A number of worm species move about freely in sand, gravel, temporary burrows, or mussel beds and other compact marine growth. Some, particularly scale worms, live on the surface of sea cucumbers or in the grooves of sea stars (leather star, painted star, bat star), the giant chiton (*Cryptochiton*) or other animals such as the rough keyhole limpet (*Diodora*).

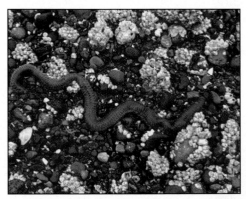

CLAM WORM

Nereis vexillosa Grube, 1851.
Alternate names: Pile worm; mussel worm.
Size: 6–12" (15–30 cm) long, to ⅜" (9 mm) wide.
Range: Alaska to San Diego, California.
Habitat: In a variety of habitats, often in mussel beds or burrowed in sand–gravel. Intertidal and subtidal.
Description: Iridescent greenish, blue and grey tones. Large paddle-like feet.
Comments: Often found by clam diggers. Species uses its large, black pincer-like jaws to tear algae, and everts jaws when disturbed. Species used as bait by sport fishers.

BLOOD WORM

Glycera americana Leidy, 1855.
Size: To 13" (33 cm) long.
Range: BC to Baja California.
Habitat: Under rocks, in mudflats, in the roots of eelgrass; intertidal and subtidal to 1,035' (315 m).
Description: Head tapers to a point, unlike head of clam worm (above), and body tapers toward rear. Iridescent green-blue to green-brown back.
Comments: Can burrow in sand quickly. Often mistaken for large clam worms (above) found on mud flats. When cut, species releases a bright red fluid resembling blood.

BAT STAR WORM

Ophiodromus pugettensis (Johnson, 1901).
Size: To 1 1/2" (4 cm) long, 1/8" (3 mm) wide.
Range: Along entire Pacific coast.
Habitat: Free-living among algae on muddy sand and in the tube feet of bat stars and other sea stars.
Description: Long, thin, red-brown to purple-black body. Segments have filaments.
Comments: As many as 20 of these worms can be found on one bat star (see p. 133) and as many as 20,000 per square metre on the bottom of Bamfield Inlet, BC.

SCALE WORM

Halsydna brevisetosa Kinberg, 1855.
Size: To 2 3/8" (5.9 cm) long.
Range: Kodiak Island, Alaska to Baja California.
Habitat: Free-moving, on floats, in mussel beds, in encrusting growths; intertidal to 1,790' (545 m).
Description: Slender brown-grey body. Black-spotted dorsal scales in 18 pairs.
Comments: Species is carnivorous and feeds on a variety of small invertebrates.

RUFFLED SCALE WORM

Arctonoe fragilis (Baird, 1863).
Size: To 3" (7.5 cm) long, sometimes longer.
Range: Alaska Peninsula to San Francisco Bay, California.
Habitat: Free-living; often commensal on painted sea stars (see p. 137, 138) and mottled sea stars (p. 135).
Description: 29–34 dorsal scales with 2 rows of ruffled margins. Pale colours match host.

PHYLUM NEMERTEA
Ribbon Worms

This phylum is named for the worms' practice of attacking with the proboscis (*Nemertea* means "unerring").

Nemertean worms are long (to 65'/20 m or more), thin, often colourful worms often referred to as ribbon worms or proboscis worms. The unique proboscis can be shot out to strike and capture prey. Several species of these mostly free-swimming worms are common and conspicuous along Pacific shores. Some have ringed markings, but nemerteans are not segmented. Field identification can be made by the unique coloration and characteristics of the head.

GREEN AND YELLOW RIBBON WORM
Emplectonema gracile (Johnson, 1837).
Size: To 6" (15 cm), rarely to 20" (50 cm) long.
Range: Aleutian Islands to Ensenada, Baja California.
Habitat: Among barnacles and mussels, intertidal and shallow subtidal.
Description: Slender worm. Dark green back, white to yellow underside, pale head region.
Comments: Sometimes tangled in groups. Species is also found in Atlantic and Mediterranean waters.

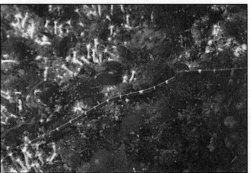

LINED RIBBON WORM
Tubulanus sexlineatus (Griffin, 1898).
Alternate name: *Carinella sexlineata*.
Size: Typically to 8" (20 cm) long, rarely to 3' (1 m).
Range: Sitka, Alaska to southern California.
Habitat: Among mussels, algae and growths on rocks or floats, intertidal and shallow subtidal.
Description: Brown body with 5-6 white longitudinal stripes and white rings, wide in the mid-body region.

PRIMITIVE RIBBON WORM
Tubulanus polymorphus Renier, 1804.
Alternate names: *Carinella rubra* Griffin;
C. speciosa.
Size: To 10' (3 m) long when extended.
Range: Aleutian Islands to central California.
Habitat: Common under rocks in the intertidal and subtidal.
Description: Long, thin, soft-bodied, often coiled. Bright orange. Head is broad and rounded and pinched off from the body.

PHYLUM PLATYHELMINTHES

Flatworms

The marine flatworms, members of the class Turbellaria, are thin, oval, compressed and inconspicuous worms. They are free-moving predators, not parasites.

Their flat bodies allow them to travel along crevices and to enter body openings to feed on other animals. They are considered pests to aquaculture, as they attack and destroy growing shellfish, oysters and scallops. They also feed on limpets, barnacles and a variety of other organisms. Some are commensal, living in a close relationship with other animals but not harming them.

Approximately 3,000 species of Turbellaria have been described. Two of the larger flatworms are included here. By turning over rocks or looking closely, divers and tidepool explorers can see them.

Polyclad Flatworms

Usually found on or under rocks, and occasionally in the open. Numerous species of polyclad flatworms inhabit the Pacific Northwest, and are difficult to identify positively to species level in the field—microscopic examination of the reproductive organs is often required. The flatworm *Eurylepta leoparda* has been identified feeding on the transparent sea squirt (see p. 153).

BIVALVE FLATWORM
Pseudostylochus ostreophagus Hyman, 1955.
Size: To 1 1/4" (3 cm) long.
Range: BC to Puget Sound.
Habitat: Settles in oyster beds, on floats and on hanging bags of scallop seed.
Description: Elongated oval shape, about half as wide as long.
Comments: Species is also found in the north Pacific off the coast of Asia, and was introduced to this area with oyster seed from Japan. It is a pest to shellfish growers, as it eats oyster and scallop seed (shown at left).

CHAPTER 4

Moss Animals
Bryozoans

PHYLUM BRYOZOA (Ectoprocta)

The phylum Bryozoa, sometimes called Ectoprocta, comprises moss-like colonies of animals occurring in encrusting forms, erect branching growths, and sometimes leaf-like or coral-like lobes. They are common and abundant but are often overlooked or confused with hydroids (see Chapter 2). The encrusting forms may be mistaken for colonial tunicates (Chapter 8) or sponges (Chapter 1).

There are about 6,000 living species of bryozoans in the world, in marine and freshwater habitats, and many more fossil species. Approximately 230 living marine species occur in the Pacific Northwest.

PHYSICAL FEATURES

Most bryozoans are partially or wholly calcified. Individuals, called zooids, are small (1/32"/1 mm long) and cased in box-like or tubular units made of limy, chitinous or other materials. A "crown" of ciliated tentacles protrudes from the individual pores. Collectively the animals form a colony that may measure several feet (1–2 m) across. There may be specialized individuals for feeding, reproduction, attachment and other purposes.

Most bryozoans have to be examined under a microscope to be identified positively. Included here are 11 commonly occurring bryozoans that can be identified in their natural habitat.

PREY–PREDATORS

A bryozoan eats by drawing in water, and filtering out algal detritus and bacteria coating the detritus. Long tentacles with cilia surround the mouth. The animal's U-shaped gut empties from an anus outside the ring of tentacles, hence the term "ecto-proct."

Bryozoans are eaten by crabs, including the kelp crab (see p. 79), and the encrusting forms are grazed by various snails and nudibranchs.

REPRODUCTION

Colonies grow by asexual budding, and new colonies are formed by sexual means. Some species are hermaphroditic.

Class Stenolaemata

Many individuals in this class are tubular in shape and have limy circular openings for the tentacles. Some have encrusting forms.

Order Cyclostomata

WHITE BRANCHING BRYOZOAN
Diaperoecia californica (d'Orbigny, 1852).
Alternate names: Coralline bryozoan; southern staghorn bryozoan.
Etymology: *Diaperoecia* = perforated dwelling.
Size: Masses to 1" (2.5 cm) high, 10" (25 cm) wide.
Range: BC to San Benitos Islands, Baja California; to Costa Rica.
Habitat: On rocks, shells and giant kelps, just below low tide to >600 ft. (180 m).
Description: White to dark yellow coral-like colony, flattened branches erect and often fusing and becoming attached to the bottom.

STAGHORN BRYOZOAN
Heteropora magna O'Donahughe, 1923.
Alternate name: Northern staghorn bryozoan.
Etymology:
Hetero/pora = different/pore;
magna = great.
Size: Colony to 2" (5 cm) high, 4–6" (10–15 cm) wide.
Range: BC to southern California.
Habitat: On rocks.
Description: Greenish colonies, with branches with rounded yellow tips. Branches do not unite.
Comments: More common and abundant in the northern range, BC to Oregon. A different form or species, *Heteropora pacifica* Borg, 1933, has branches that unite.

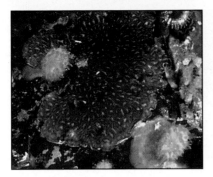

PURPLE ENCRUSTING BRYOZOAN
Disporella separata Osburn, 1953.
Size: Crust to 1/8" (3 mm) thick; colonies to 4" (10 cm) or more wide.
Range: BC and southern California.
Habitat: On rocks.
Description: Hard, colourful dark purple with patches of lighter purple.

Class Gymnolaemata

Individuals in this class are tube-shaped, encrusting, membranous, or limy.

Order Ctenostomata

LEATHER BRYOZOAN
Flustrellidra corniculata (Smitt, 1871).
Alternate names: Seaweed bryozoan; branched-spine bryozoan; *Flustrella corniculata*.
Etymology: *corniculata* = bearing little horns.
Size: Colony with larger stems to 4" (10 cm) long.
Range: Alaska to southern California.
Habitat: On rocks and shells, intertidal to 245' (75 m) or more.
Description: Rubbery tan colony; erect, flattened branches that may branch again, with short, sometimes branched dark brown spines at the margin.
Comments: May be confused with algae. Also found in northern Europe.

Order Cheilostomata

KELP LACE BRYOZOAN
Membranipora membrancea (Linnaeus, 1767).
Alternate name: Lacy-crust bryozoan.
Size: Thin crusts to 1/32" (1 mm) high, more than 3" (7.5 cm) diameter.
Range: Alaska to Baja California.
Habitat: On kelps and algae in shallow waters.
Description: Circular crust of small boxes, white to silver, colonial patches often merging.
Comments: Common and abundant late spring to fall. May be a number of species. Several small cryptic nudibranchs, including *Doridella steinbergae* and *Corambe pacifica*, feed on this bryozoan.

STICK BRYOZOAN

Microporina borealis (Busk, 1855).
Size: To 3" (7.5 cm) high or more.
Range: Circumpolar, Arctic to Washington.
Habitat: On rocks, often on vertical faces; shallow subtidal to 1320' (400 m).
Description: Jointed, short segments, elliptical in cross-section. Yellow-cream to tan.
Comments: Similar species, with longer segments and a circular cross-section, are *Cellaria* spp. See specimen in background (at right) of photo of leather bryozoan (page 61).

SPIRAL BRYOZOAN

Bugula californica Robertson, 1905.
Size: One to many spiral colonies, to 2³/4" (7 cm) or more high.
Range: BC to Galapagos Islands.
Habitat: On rocks and shells, shallow subtidal to 200' (60 m).
Description: Spiral whorls of branches, whitish-tan to orange.
Comments: Species is eaten by the clown dorid nudibranch (see p. 113).

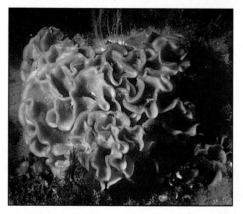

SCULPTURED BRYOZOAN

Hippodiplosia insculpta (Hincks, 1882).
Alternate name: Fluted bryozoan.
Etymology: *Hippo/diplosia* = double/horse; *insculpta* = carved.
Size: Colony of layered frills to 2" (5 cm) or more high, 4" (10 cm) or more diameter.
Range: Alaska to Gulf of California; to Costa Rica.
Habitat: On rocks and a variety of other hard surfaces in currents. Subtidal to 770' (230 m).
Description: Double layered folds and frills, "curled-leaf" shape, light yellow or pale tan to orange.
Comments: The channeled topsnail *Calliostoma canaliculatum* feeds on this bryozoan.

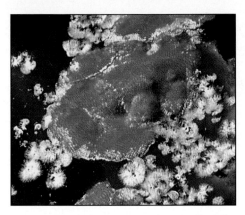

ORANGE ENCRUSTING BRYOZOAN

Schizoporella unicornis (Johnson, 1847).
Size: Colonies to 2" (5 cm) diameter.
Range: BC to South America.
Habitat: On rocks, shells, floats and other hard surfaces. Intertidal to 200' (60 m).
Description: Orange, brown or golden yellow crust, with fine pattern of pores.
Comments: Species was introduced with oyster seed from Japan, and is also found in Mediterranean waters. It is the dominant orange encrusting bryozoan in the shallows of the Pacific Northwest. The sometimes orange, derby hat bryozoan, *Eurystomella bilabiata*, is also common on rocks, shells and algae. Another white bryozoan, *Lichenopora* sp., with elevated tubular portions is also shown in this photograph.

LACY BRYOZOAN

Phidolorpora labiata (Gabb & Horn, 1862).
Alternate names: Lace coral; lattice-work bryozoan; formerly *Phidolopora pacifica*.
Etymology: *Phidolopora* = sparse pores.
Size: Colony to 2 1/2" (6 cm) high, 8 1/2" (22 cm) wide.
Range: Gulf of Alaska to Peru.
Habitat: Attached to rocks, intertidal to 660' (200 m), often on offshore reefs.
Description: Stiff, brittle and delicate lattice formation, salmon-pink to orange, to white.
Comments: Observed eaten by leather star (see p. 133) and purple-ring topsnail (p. 103).

RUSTY BRYOZOAN

Costazia ventricosa (Lorenz, 1886).
Size: To 1" (2.5 cm) high, 6" (15 cm) or more wide.
Range: Bering Sea to northern California.
Description: Colony encrusting and rising up to form stout protuberances. Dark orange to pale peach.
Comments: Species is also found in Japan, and in Arctic and Atlantic waters.

CHAPTER 5

Crabs, Shrimp, Isopods, Amphipods, Barnacles

Crustaceans

PHYLUM ARTHROPODA

Subphylum Crustacea

The classification of these marine animals is complex. The phylum Arthropoda ("jointed legs") comprises more than 900,000 living species, making up more than three-quarters of all known species. Understandably there are many opinions on how the animals should be grouped: for example the crustacea are considered by some zoologists to be a subphylum or class of arthropods, and by others to be a separate phylum. (See pp. 14–15), for a listing of classifications used in this book.) Some 30,500 species of crustacea are described worldwide, with more than 1,570 species of intertidal or shallow water species of crabs, shrimp, barnacles and other crustaceans in the region between Alaska to Baja California.

LOCOMOTION

As it says in the old song, "Crabs walk sideways and lobsters walk back." Usually the leading legs pull by flexing and the trailing legs push by extending. Many species swim, using legs which are often flattened or modified for swimming, and may travel great distances both vertically and horizontally. Shrimp escape predators by rapidly flexing the tail fan.

PREY–PREDATORS

Crabs and shrimp have a number of mouth parts for biting and grinding. Barnacles, which are fixed, sweep particles out of the water.

EXTERNAL ANATOMY OF A TRUE CRAB

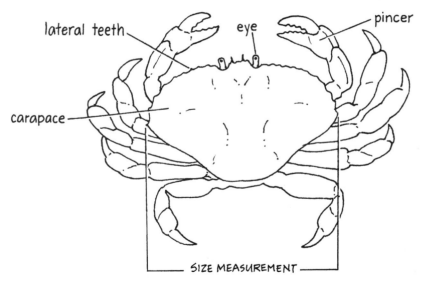

Measurements and physical features of "true crabs."

Crabs feed on barnacles, worms and small bivalves, including clams and mussels. Many crabs, shrimp and barnacles live in association with other organisms, and some are parasites.

REPRODUCTION

Crustaceans have diverse and complex life cycles. Reproduction is typically sexual, with mating and internal fertilization. Many groups, including crabs, have separate sexes, with clearly identifiable features.

Some shrimps begin life as males, then undergo transformation into females and bear eggs. A female shrimp (or crab) usually carries a cluster of eggs for some weeks before the eggs hatch and drift off as planktonic larvae. Some crabs, such as the Dungeness (see p. 78), can store packets of sperm and fertilize several clusters of eggs from one mating.

Barnacles are typically hermaphrodites (having both male and female reproductive organs in one individual) but must grow in clusters to reproduce. Males cross-fertilize adjacent barnacles. Females brood eggs and release many small shrimp-like larvae to drift and settle, adjacent to other barnacles if possible.

Shrimp, Crabs, Isopods, Amphipods
Class Malacostracea

This class contains the largest group of crustaceans, the order Decapoda (suborder Pleocyemata, includes the various shrimp and crabs), the order Isopoda (isopods) and the order Amphipoda (amphipods).

Mud Shrimp, Ghost Shrimp, Infraorder Thassinidea

BLUE MUD SHRIMP
Upogebia pugettensis (Dana, 1852).
Size: Body to 6" (15 cm) long, 1/2" (1 cm) high.
Range: Southern Alaska to Baja California.
Habitat: Permanent burrows in sand–mud and mud–gravel, intertidal.
Description: Speckled body, tan-grey to blue-grey. First pair of legs unequal, modified with small claws. Hairy legs and claws, large fan-tail.
Comments: A common intertidal species, whose burrows are inhabited by clams, worms, shrimp and others. Often has a commensal wrinkled bivalve (*Pseudopythina rugifera*) attached to the underside. Considered a pest to oyster growers, undermining the substrate and covering oyster seed with silt.

BAY GHOST SHRIMP

Neotrypaea californiensis (Dana, 1854).
Alternate name: *Callianassa californiensis.*
Size: Body to 4 5/8" (12 cm) long, 3/4" (2 cm) high.
Range: Southern Alaska to Baja California.
Habitat: Common in burrows to 24" (60 cm) deep in intertidal sand–mud.
Description: Smooth, slender body coloured pink, orange and yellow. White claws unequal, not hairy. Male has huge claw.
Comments: A number of shrimp, crabs and other animals cohabit the burrows. Often harvested for bait by fishers. Considered a pest to oyster growers, undermining the substrate and covering oyster seed with silt.

Hermit Crabs, King Crabs, Lithodid Crabs, Galatheid Crabs, Porcelain Crabs Infraorder Anomura

Hermit crabs (family Paguridae) are common surprises, inhabiting snail shells in tidepools. As a hermit grows, it must move to successively larger shells, and it must often fight other hermit crabs to secure them.

ORANGE HERMIT CRAB

Elassochirus gilli (Benedict, 1892).
Alternate name: Pacific red hermit.
Size: Carapace to 1 1/2" (4 cm) long.
Range: Bering Sea to Puget Sound.
Habitat: In rocky areas, low intertidal to 655' (200 m).
Description: Smooth claws and legs, brilliant uniform orange-red coloration, white spots at joints.
Comments: A common species, found west to Sea of Japan.

WIDEHAND HERMIT CRAB

Elassochirus tenuimanus (Dana, 1851).
Alternate name: *Pagurus tenuimanus.*
Size: Carapace to 1 1/2" (4 cm) long.
Range: Aleutian Islands to Puget Sound.
Habitat: Mud, sand, gravel and shell bottom, intertidal to 1,275' (388 m).
Description: Large flattened right claw with a "wide hand."
Comments: The large hand acts as a block when crab retreats into shell. Inhabits large hairy Oregon triton (see p. 107) shells. Hermit crabs often fight for larger shells as they grow.

BLACKEYED HERMIT

Pagurus armatus (Dana, 1851).
Size: Carapace to 15/8" (4.2 cm) long.
Range: Dutch Harbor, Alaska to San Diego, California.
Habitat: Sand bottom, intertidal to 480' (146 m).
Description: Large oval black eyes stand out. Alternating orange and white bands on legs, spiny claws.
Comments: A large and common hermit which occupies the shells of Lewis's moonsnail (see p. 108).

BERING HERMIT CRAB

Pagurus beringanus (Benedict, 1892).
Size: Carapace to 1" (2.5 cm) long.
Range: Bering Sea and Aleutian Islands to Monterey, California.
Habitat: In rocky areas, intertidal to 1,195' (364 m).
Description: Walking legs pale blue-grey with red bands and spots. Brown claws with red bumps and spines.
Comments: Prefers a large, heavy shell. Often found in the shell of the frilled dogwinkle (see p. 109), sometimes in hermit crab sponge (p. 23).

GOLD RING HERMIT CRAB

Pagurus hemphilli (Benedict 1892).
Alternate name: Maroon hermit.
Size: Carapace to 5/8" (1.5 cm) long.
Range: Klokachef Island, Alaska to San Miguel Island, California.
Habitat: On open coast only, among algae on rocks.
Description:: Distinctive gold rings in black eyes. Walking legs and hands of claws red with white or blue granules.
Comments: Usually found in topsnails (shown here and on pp. 103–4) or turban snails (pp. 102–3).

HAIRY HERMIT CRAB

Pagurus hirsutiusculus (Dana, 1851).
Size: Carapace to 3/4" (2 cm) long.
Range: Pribilof Islands, Alaska to
Monterey, California.
Habitat: In tidepools in cover of
coralline and other algae; intertidal,
rarely subtidal, but found to 365' (110
m).
Description: Variable coloration.
Conspicuous white band at outer seg-
ment of walking legs.
Comments: Commonly occurs in
great numbers in tidepools. Shown
here in hermit crab sponge (see p. 23).

ALASKAN HERMIT CRAB

Pagurus ochotensis Brandt, 1851.
Alternate name: Formerly *Pagurus
alaskensis*.
Size: Carapace to 13/4" (5 cm) long.
Range: Pribilof Islands, Alaska to
Point Arena, California.
Habitat: Mud or sand bottom, intertidal to 1,275' (388 m).
Description: Green-yellow eyes.
Granular claws and legs with iridescent sheen.
Comments: Similar to the blackeyed
hermit (see p. 68), other than the
eyes. This large hermit also occupies
the shells of Lewis's moonsnail (p. 108). The common name "Alaskan hermit" has been retained
from the earlier Latin species name *alaskensis*. Confusion can often occur when geographical references are used for Latin or common names.

STEVEN'S HERMIT CRAB

Pagurus stevensae Hart, 1971.
Size: Carapace to 5/8" (1.5 cm)
long.
Range: Akun Island, Bering
Sea to Puget Sound.
Habitat: Mud, sand or gravel
bottom, often in sponge-covered
shell, 16' (5 m) to 650' (195 m).
Description: Fairly uniform
red-brown in colour. Right claw
unusually long and slender with
granular surface.
Comments: Often found in hermit crab sponge (see p. 23) and similar in colour.

What distinguishes these typically spiny, hairy crabs (family Lithodidae) from others is the three pairs of walking legs with the fourth pair reduced or absent. The north Pacific has more lithodid species than any other region of the world. The Latin *Lithodes* translates as "rock-like."

RED FUR CRAB

Acantholithodes hispidus (Stimpson, 1860).
Alternate names: Spiny crab; fuzzy crab.
Etymology: *hispidus* = hairy, bristly.
Size: Carapace to 2¹/₂" (6 cm) wide.
Range: Aleutian Islands to Monterey, California.
Habitat: Sand–mud, in rocky areas; intertidal to 540' (164 m).
Description: Spiny, hairy body, brown, red and white. Rostrum (horn) studded with spines. Claws bright red-orange.
Comments: Often taken in prawn traps.

UMBRELLA CRAB

Cryptolithodes sitchensis Brandt, 1853.
Alternate name: Turtle crab.
Etymology: *Crypto/lithodes* = cryptic/rock-like.
Size: Carapace to 4" (10 cm) wide.
Range: Sitka, Alaska to Point Loma, California.
Habitat: On rocks, low intertidal to 60' (18 m).
Description: Oval carapace extending to cover legs and smooth claws. Rostrum (horn) flares at tip. Colours and patterns variable with orange, red, grey and white markings.

BUTTERFLY CRAB

Cryptolithodes typicus Brandt, 1849.
Alternate names: Umbrella crab; turtle crab.
Size: Carapace to 3" (7.5 cm) wide.
Range: Sitka, Alaska to Santa Rosa Island, California.
Habitat: On rocks, low intertidal to 150' (45 m).
Description: Oval-elongated carapace extending to cover legs and rough claws. Rostrum (horn) narrows at tip. Colour and patterns variable with white, black and shades of grey, pink and brown.
Comments: Cryptic (well camouflaged and often overlooked). Grazes on bryozoans, coralline algae and other organisms.

HAIRY LITHODID

Hapalogaster mertensii Brandt, 1850.
Size: Carapace to 1¹/₂" (4 cm) wide.
Range: Alaska to Puget Sound.
Habitat: Often under rocks in currents, intertidal to 180' (55 m).
Description: Flattened, hairy brown body. Soft abdomen flattened out.
Comments: A similar species, *Hapalogaster grebnitzkii*, with blue-black on the claws, occurs in the northern range.

BROWN BOX CRAB

Lopholithodes foraminatus (Stimpson, 1859).
Alternate names: Box crab; Oregon queen crab.
Size: Carapace to 8" (20 cm) wide.
Range: Southern Alaska to central California.
Habitat: Sand–mud habitats near rocks; intertidal to 1,800' (550 m).
Description: Bumpy, box-shaped, tan to red-brown body. Short, stubby legs. When crab is buried, first walking leg and circular holes formed between claws are exposed, allowing water to pass for respiration.
Comments: Species has been harvested commercially in Oregon.

PUGET SOUND KING CRAB

Lopholithodes mandtii Brandt, 1849.
Alternate names: Box crab; red box crab.
Size: Carapace to 12" (30 cm) wide.
Range: Sitka, Alaska to Monterey, California.
Habitat: On rock reefs in currents, shallow subtidal to 450' (137 m).
Description: 4 large bumps on top of box-like body. Short, stubby legs. Colour a mix of bright red, purple, orange. Juveniles are a uniform brilliant red-orange.

GRANULAR CLAW CRAB

Oedignathus inermis (Stimpson, 1860).
Size: Carapace to 1½" (4 cm) wide.
Range: Dutch Harbor, Alaska to Pacific Grove, California.
Habitat: In crevices, in giant barnacle shells; intertidal to 60' (18 m).
Description: Pear-shaped carapace with abdomen flattened rather than folded under. Large right claw has dark blue circular granules.
Comments: Species is also found in Japan.

HEART CRAB

Phyllolithodes papillosus Brandt, 1849.
Alternate names: Heart lithodid; papilla crab; flat spined triangle crab.
Size: Carapace to 3½" (9 cm) wide.
Range: Dutch Harbor, Alaska to southern California.
Habitat: On rocky reefs with currents, shallow subtidal to 600' (180 m).
Description: Grey to brown body with orange markings. Triangular carapace, raised heart-shaped outline. Legs have long, flattened spines and white "socks."
Comments: After moulting, crab shelters under the tentacle canopy of the snakelock anemone (see p. 45).

SCALY LITHODID

Placetron wosnessenskii Schalfeew, 1892.
Size: Carapace to 3" (7.5 cm) wide; overall size, including legs, to 15" (37.5 cm).
Range: Pribilof Islands, Alaska to Puget Sound.
Habitat: In rocky areas, shallow subtidal to 365' (110 m).
Description: Carapace and legs have scaly appearance. Tan to orange to grey coloration.
Comments: A large, fast-moving crab.

GOLF-BALL CRAB
Rhinolithodes wosnessenskii Brandt, 1849.
Alternate name: Rhinoceros crab.
Size: Carapace to 2¹/₂" (6 cm) wide.
Range: Aleutian Islands to northern California.
Habitat: On rock walls, subtidal 20–240' (6–72 m).
Description: Triangular carapace has golf ball-like protrusion formed by semicircular depression. Body with orange and white markings. Claws and legs spiny, with long brown hair.

Galatheid Crabs

Galathei is Greek for "sea nymph."

SQUAT LOBSTER
Munida quadraspina Benedict, 1902.
Alternate name: Galatheid crab.
Size: Carapace to 3" (7.5 cm) long, body to 5" (12.5 cm) long.
Range: Sitka, Alaska to Baja California.
Habitat: On or swimming above mud bottom, subtidal 40–4,800' (12–1440 m).
Description: Lobster-like crab with very long slender claws.
Comments: Sometimes taken in prawn traps. This is our only representative of the family Galatheidae.

Porcelain Crabs

These crabs (family Porcellanidae) get their names from their practice of releasing legs when they are disturbed—they appear to break as easily as porcelain. In fact, lost limbs regenerate in weeks. Their claws are broad and flat.

PORCELAIN CRAB
Petrolisthes eriomerus Stimpson, 1871.
Alternate name: Flattop crab; blue-mouth crab.
Size: Carapace to ³/₄" (2 cm) wide.
Range: Northern Alaska to southern California.
Habitat: Under rocks, low intertidal to 280' (85 m).
Description: Flattened, dark brown body, brown-red to blue. Bright blue on broad claws.

Comments: Most common in BC and Washington. To the south, a similar species, the flat porcelain crab (*Petrolisthes cinctipes*), which has orange-red mouth parts, is more common.

HAIRY PORCELAIN CRAB

Pachycheles pubescens Holmes, 1800.
Alternate name: Pubescent porcelain crab.
Etymology: *pubesc* = downy.
Size: Carapace to 7/8" (2.2 cm) long.
Range: Queen Charlotte Islands, BC to Thurloe Head, Baja California.
Habitat: On open coasts, intertidal in rocky areas but usually subtidal to 180' (55 m).

Description: 5 plates on abdominal section. Short, thick, dense brown hairs on claws.

THICKCLAW PORCELAIN CRAB

Pachycheles rudis Stimpson 1858.
Etymology:
Pachy/cheles = thick/claws; *rudis* = wild, rough.
Size: Carapace to 3/4 x 3/4" (2 x 2 cm); females slightly smaller.
Range: Kodiak Island, Alaska to Bahia de la Magdalena, Baja California.
Habitat: Intertidal; in shallows, under rocks, in holdfasts of kelp and in crevices near strong currents.

Description: 7 plates on abdominal section. Large, unequal claws with tubercles and scattered hairs. Colour variable, with grey, brown and white markings.
Comments: Species is a filter feeder.

"True Crabs" Infraorder Brachyura

The brachyuran crabs are the common and familiar "true crabs," including shore crabs, spider crabs and cancer crabs. This crab has 10 legs, 2 of which are modified with claws. It has a hard upper shell (carapace), larger in males than in females. The crab grows through a series of moults, discarding its old shell and hardening a new one by extracting nutrients from the water and sometimes by eating the old shell. At the front of the carapace are small eyes, antennae, 2 horns (the nose, or rostrum), and tooth-like projections along the front margin of the shell, called the lateral teeth.

The female crab has a broad U-shaped abdomen to carry eggs, and the male has a sharp V-shaped abdomen.

Shore Crabs

The familiar shore crabs of the family Grapsidae and Xanthidae are found by overturning rocks in the intertidal zone.

"PURPLE" SHORE CRAB

Hemigrapsus nudus (Dana, 1851).
Size: Carapace to 2¼" (5.5 cm) wide.
Range: Yakobi Island, Alaska to Mexico.
Habitat: Under rocks, intertidal.
Description: Square carapace. Body typically purple with dark spots on claws, but may be olive or red-brown. Walking legs not hairy.
Comments: Eats barnacles in the intertidal. Uncommon in southern California.

HAIRY SHORE CRAB

Hemigrapsus oregonensis (Dana, 1851).
Alternate name: Yellow shore crab.
Size: Carapace to 2" (5 cm) wide.
Range: Resurrection Bay, Alaska to Baja California.
Habitat: Under rocks, intertidal.
Description: Hairy legs, body grey to dark green, white or mottled.
Comments: Very abundant and widespread.

BLACK-CLAWED SHORE CRAB

Lophopanopeus bellus bellus (Stimpson, 1860).
Size: Carapace to 1½" (4 cm) wide.
Range: Resurrection Bay, Alaska to Point Sur, California.
Habitat: Under rocks or partially buried in gravel–sand, intertidal.
Description: Thick, heavy, smooth, dark claws. Body colour variable from purple, grey to red-brown.
Comments: A similar subspecies has tubercles on the claws, and is subtidal in sand, mud or gravel.

The family Majidae includes the long-legged spider crabs, decorator crabs and kelp crabs. Many species can be identified just by their carapaces, which have distinctive outlines.

TANNER CRAB

Chionoecetes bairdi Rathburn, 1893.
Alternate name: Snow crab.
Etymology:
Chionoe/cetes = snow/dweller.
Size: Carapace to 6" (15 cm) wide.
Range: Bering Sea to Winchester Bay, Oregon.
Habitat: Mud to bedrock, shallow subtidal to 1,640' (490 m).

Description: Oval carapace, light brown to pink when newly moulted. Long, slender, flattened walking legs. Short claws with iridescent sheen.

Comments: Fished commercially in Alaska with pots. The male carries the female in his claw prior to moulting and mating.

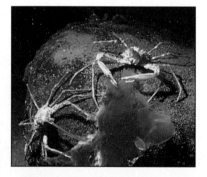

LONGHORN DECORATOR CRAB

Chorilia longipes Dana, 1851.
Size: Carapace to 1³/4" (4.5 cm) wide.
Range: Kodiak, Alaska to Mexico.
Habitat: On rocks and boulders, shallow subtidal 30–3,900' (9–1,170 m).
Description: Spiny, pear-shaped carapace with 2 divergent horns. Pale orange, often with banded legs.
Comments: Often decorated and confused with the smaller slender decorator crab (below).

SLENDER DECORATOR CRAB

Oregonia gracilis Dana, 1851.
Etymology: *gracilis* = slender.
Size: Carapace to 1¹/2" (4 cm) wide.
Range: Bering Sea to Monterey, California.
Habitat: On rocks, intertidal to 1,430' (435 m).
Description: Triangular carapace with 2 equally long horns. Long, slender walking legs. Grey or tan colour but typically very "decorated" with available sponges, hydroids, algae and other growths.

SLENDER KELP CRAB

Pugettia gracilis Dana, 1851.
Alternate name: Spider crab; graceful kelp crab.
Etymology: *gracilis* = slender.
Size: Carapace to 1³/₈" (3.4 cm) wide.
Range: Aleutian Islands to Monterey, California.
Habitat: In eelgrass and kelp on rocky shores, intertidal to 460' (138 m).
Description: Smooth, clean carapace, brown, yellow or red. Front margin indented between lateral teeth. Long, slender legs end in points; a key identifying feature is the blue claw ends with red tips.
Comments: Carapace may be lightly decorated with algae and other organisms.

NORTHERN KELP CRAB

Pugettia producta (Randall, 1839).
Alternate name: Spider crab.
Size: Carapace to 3¹/₂" (9 cm) wide.
Range: Prince of Wales Island, Alaska to Baja California.
Habitat: In kelp beds and on pilings, intertidal to 240' (73 m).
Description: Smooth, typically clean carapace, red to olive. Front margin straight or slightly curved between lateral teeth. Underside yellow or scarlet. Long, slender legs end in sharp points.
Comments: Favourite food of sea otters. Has sharp spines and strong claws.

CRYPTIC KELP CRAB

Pugettia richii Dana, 1851.
Alternate name: Spider crab.
Size: Carapace to 1⁵/₈" (4.2 cm) wide.
Range: Prince of Wales Island, Alaska to Baja California.
Habitat: On rocky shores of exposed outer coast, intertidal to 320' (96 m).
Description: Bumpy, spiny carapace, brown to red. Shell outline has more lateral teeth than the slender kelp crab (see above). A key identifying feature is the violet to reddish claw ends with white tips.
Comments: Often confused with the smoother slender kelp crab (above), which is less common on outer coasts.

SHARP-NOSED CRAB

Scyra acutafrons Dana, 1851.
Etymology: *acutafrons* = sharp nose.
Size: Carapace to 1¾" (4.5 cm) wide.
Range: Cook Inlet, Alaska to San Carlos Point, Mexico.
Habitat: In rocky areas, low intertidal to 720' (216 m).
Description: 2 flattened leaf-like horns. Short walking legs and large, long claws.
Comments: Usually has some decoration, is sometimes covered completely. Species is also found in Japan.

Bristly Crabs

The small family Cheiragonidae is a group of odd, bristly crabs.

HELMET CRAB

Telmessus cheiragonus (Telsius, 1815).
Size: Carapace to 4" (10 cm) wide.
Range: Alaska to Monterey, California.
Habitat: In eelgrass beds or algae, buried in sediment, intertidal to 360' (110 m).
Description: Hairy crab, with 6 large teeth on both sides of the carapace. Yellowish-green with red, orange or brown marks.
Comments: Buries in sediment. Not common south of Washington. Species is also found in Japan.

Cancer Crabs

The family Cancridae is one of the most familiar and commercially important crab families.

DUNGENESS CRAB

Cancer magister Dana, 1852.
Alternate names: Pacific edible crab; commercial crab.
Size: Carapace to 10" (25 cm) wide; females to 7" (18 cm) wide.
Range: Pribilof Islands, Alaska to Santa Barbara, California.
Habitat: In sand–mud or eelgrass beds, intertidal to 750' (225 m).
Description: Grey-brown with purple carapace widest at tenth and largest tooth. Underside yellow; claws yellow with white tips. Female has a broad U-shaped abdomen to carry the eggs (see photo, left); male has a sharp V-shaped abdomen.
Comments: Important commercial, recreational and Native food fisheries along the coast. Moulted crab skeletons washed up on the beach often trigger reports of dead crabs.

RED ROCK CRAB

Cancer productus Randall, 1839.
Size: Carapace to 8" (20 cm) wide;
female to 6¼" (15.5 cm) wide.
Range: Kodiak, Alaska to Isla San
Martin, Baja California.
Habitat: In eelgrass, gravel and
rocky areas, intertidal to 260' (78 m).
Description: Brick red fan-shaped
carapace, black-tipped pincers.
Juvenile colour varies from white to
dark with or without a white-
lined pattern.
Comments: Important
recreational and Native food
fisheries. Less favoured than
Dungeness crab (see p. 78) in
terms of abundance and meat
recovery.

SLENDER CANCER CRAB

Cancer gracilis Dana, 1852.
Etymology: *gracilis* = slender.
Size: Carapace to 4½" (11 cm)
wide.
Range: Prince William Sound,
Alaska to Mexico.
Habitat: In sand-mud, inter-
tidal to 470' (142 m).
Description: Teeth outlined in
white on margin of carapace,
which is widest at ninth tooth.
Legs purple, claws purple with
white tips.

Comments: Often mistaken for Dungeness crab (see p. 78). This species is released, as it does not reach legal size of Dungeness crab.

HAIRY CANCER CRAB

Cancer oregonensis (Dana, 1852).
Alternate names: Oregon cancer
crab; pygmy cancer crab.
Size: Carapace to 2" (5 cm) wide.
Range: Pribilof Islands, Alaska to
Palos Verdes, California.
Habitat: In small holes, often in
giant barnacle shells; low intertidal to
1,335' (400 m).
Description: Dull red, circular cara-
pace with short hairy legs. Claws have
black-tipped pincers.

Shrimp Infraorder Caridea

Approximately 1,700 species of shrimp live in the world's oceans, in the intertidal zone to depths exceeding 16,500' (5000 m). At least 85 species of shrimp have been observed in BC waters.

Edible/Commercial Shrimp

All commercially harvested shrimps along Pacific Northwest shores—and many others throughout the world—are "pandalids," members of the family Pandalidae. Approximately 20 pandalids are found between Alaska and California, at least 7 of which are important to sport and commercial fisheries.

SPINY PINK SHRIMP

Pandalus borealis eous Kroyer, 1838.
Alternate names: *Pandalus borealis*; *P. eous* Makarov. Alaskan pink shrimp; northern pink shrimp; deepsea prawn.
Size: Carapace to 1" (2.5 cm) wide, body to 6" (15 cm) long.
Range: Bering Sea to Oregon.
Habitat: Soft sand-mud bottom, 55–4,535' (16–1,360 m). Typically 165–1,970' (50–590 m), but occasionally seen by divers at 35' (10.5 m) or less. In BC, usually found in mainland inlets and protected waters.

Description: Spines on dorsal (back) and at posterior of third and fourth body segments. Fine red dots over translucent body make it appear uniformly pink to bright red.

Comments: Species is the most important shrimp taken in Alaskan waters. It differs from the smooth pink shrimp (*Pandalus jordani*). It was described as *P. eous*, a species distinct from the shrimp found in the North Sea and Atlantic, but is currently considered a subspecies of *P. Borealis*. It is also found in Korea and the Sea of Japan. This shrimp lives on the sea bottom and at times moves away from it vertically. Females carry 1,600 to 2,150 eggs, or more.

COONSTRIPE SHRIMP

Pandalus danae Stimpson, 1857.
Alternate names: Dock shrimp (American Fisheries Society); coon-striped shrimp; Dana's all-shining shrimp.
Size: Carapace to 1 1/4" (3 cm) long, body to 5 1/2" (14 cm) long.
Range: Resurrection Bay, Alaska to Point Loma, California.
Habitat: On pilings and floats, intertidal to 605' (182 m).
Description: Translucent body with red-brown irregular stripes, thin white lines and many fine blue spots. Telson (tail section) has 6 pairs of small lateral spines.

Comments: Species is harvested in recreational and commercial winter trap fisheries. It is the pandalid shrimp most likely to be found on pilings, and most often encountered by divers.

HUMPBACK SHRIMP

Pandalus hypsinotus Brandt, 1851.
Alternate names: Coon-striped shrimp (American Fisheries Society); king shrimp.
Size: Carapace to 1¹/₂" (4 cm) long, body to 7¹/₂" (19 cm) long.
Range: Norton Sound, Alaska to Puget Sound.
Habitat: On both soft and rocky bottom, 15–1,510' (5–453 m).
Description: Strongly arched profile. Light tan with reddish bands; carapace and lower body marked with conspicuous white spots.

Comments: Taken commercially in both trawls and traps, usually a by-catch. Due to the sweet taste of this large shrimp and the high potential value, there is significant interest in directed fisheries for this species.

PRAWN

Pandalus platyceros Brandt, 1851.
Alternate names: Spot shrimp; spot prawn.
Size: Carapace to 2³/₈" (5.9 cm) long, body to 10" (25 cm) long (females largest).
Range: Unalaska Island, Alaska to San Diego, California.
Habitat: Rocky bottom, intertidal to 1,600' (480 m).

Description: Red body with conspicuous white spots paired on the first and fifth abdominal sections. Carapace has white bars down the entire length.

Comments: The largest of the northern shrimp species, and the most important shrimp taken in traps or pots from California to Alaska.

SIDESTRIPE SHRIMP

Pandalopsis dispar Rathburn, 1902.
Alternate name: Giant red shrimp.
Size: Carapace to 1¹/₂" (4 cm) long, body to 8" (20 cm) long (females largest).
Range: Pribilof Islands, Alaska to Manhattan Beach, Oregon.

Habitat: Soft bottom, 150–2,130' (45–640 m).

Description: Antennules are about twice as long as carapace (head section). Body is reddish-orange with rows of longitudinal white bars; irregular white patches and bars on posterior of carapace.

Comments: Rarely taken in traps; often landed in trawl catches from 240' (73 m) and deeper. From Pribilof Islands to Queen Charlotte Islands, species is found with a barnacle parasite, *Sylon hippolytes*.

STOUT COASTAL SHRIMP

Heptacarpus brevirostris (Dana, 1852).
Size: Carapace less than 5/8" (1.5 cm) long, body to 2³/8" (5.9 cm) long.
Range: Aleutian Islands to Santa Cruz, California.
Habitat: On rocky shores, intertidal to 420' (126 m).
Description: Short pointed rostrum (horn), to eye only. Variable colour and markings, typically browns and greens with white patches or stripes.

Comments: One of the most common intertidal shrimp along the BC coast.

BROKEN-BACK SHRIMP

Heptacarpus kincaidi (Rathburn, 1902).
Alternate name: Kincaid's shrimp.
Size: Carapace to 1/4" (6 mm) long, body to 13/8" (3.4 cm) long.
Range: Queen Charlotte Strait, BC to San Padre, California.
Habitat: On rocks, at base of snakelock anemone (see p. 45) or painted anemone (p. 43), 33–600' (10–180 m).

Description: Transparent body with red and yellow marks; prominent hump on back. Rostrum (horn) has a white midrib.

Comments: Found with candy stripe shrimp (below) as well as anemones.

CANDY STRIPE SHRIMP

Lebbeus grandimanus (Brazhnikov, 1907).
Alternate name: Clown shrimp.
Size: Carapace to 3/8" (9 mm) long, body to 13/4" (4.5 cm) long.
Range: Bering Sea to Puget Sound.
Habitat: At base of snakelock anemone (see p. 45), painted anemone (p. 43), fish-eating anemone (p. 44) and Columbia sand anemone (p. 45); at depths of 20–590' (6–180 m).
Description: Transparent with uniquely brilliant bands of red, yellow and blue.

HORNED SHRIMP

Paracragnon echinata Dana, 1852.
Alternate name: Spike shrimp.
Etymology: *echinata* = horned, spiked.
Size: Carapace to 1/2" (1 cm) long, body to 25/8" (6.7 cm) long.
Range: Port Etches, Alaska to La Jolla, California.
Habitat: Soft bottom, in algae; subtidal 23–660' (7–200 m).
Description: Spiny carapace and sharp rostrum (horn). Yellow to tan, with brown or black spots. Defensive posture with head and tail up is characteristic.

Comments: Common along the coast.

Isopods Order Isopoda

Isopods ("equal foot") are crustaceans with 7 pairs of legs typically adapted for crawling. Some isopods are parasitic. They are commonly found hiding in kelp and algae, under rocks and on floats.

KELP ISOPOD

Idotea wosnesenskii (Brandt, 1851).
Alternate name: *Idotea (Pentidotea) wosnesenskii.*
Size: Body to 13/8" (3.4 cm) long.
Range: Alaska to Estero Bay, California.
Habitat: In mussel beds, kelp and under rocks; mid-intertidal to 50' (15 m).
Description: Elongated, not tapered. Dark to black, tan, red and green colours. Pink when in association with coralline algae.
Comments: Species is also found in Russia.

Amphipods Order Amphipoda

The amphipods are common on seaweed, sand, wharves and pilings.

BEACH HOPPER

Traskorchestia traskiana (Stimpson, 1857).
Alternate name: *Orchestia traskiana.*
Size: To 3/4" (2 cm) long.
Range: Aleutian Islands to Baja California.
Habitat: Gravel, rocky and sand beaches in seaweed drift; high intertidal.
Description: Dark grey; antennae transparent.
Comments: Eaten by stalked medusa (see p. 49), and by foxes foraging on the beach.

Most barnacles have calcareous shells that attach to rocks and other hard surfaces. Gooseneck barnacles attach with flexible stalks. The shrimp-like animal housed inside the shell is protected by a series of plates.

Some barnacles are found attached to whales; some are parasitic on shrimp, crab and sea star species; others burrow into the shells of mollusks, corals and other barnacles. The barnacle eats small plants, animals and organic matter, sweeping it up with its appendages or legs (cirri).

About 65 of the world's 900 species of barnacles live in the Pacific Northwest.

GIANT BARNACLE

Balanus nubilus Darwin, 1854.
Alternate name: Giant acorn barnacle.
Etymology: *Balanus* = acorn; *nubilus* = cloudy.
Size: Individuals to 5" (12.5 cm) high, to 4" (10 cm) wide; clusters to 12" (30 cm) and more high and across.
Range: Alaska to southern California.
Habitat: On rocks and other hard surfaces, intertidal to 300' (90 m).
Description: Often found growing on one another, forming clusters. 2 of the 4 closing plates are hooked.

Comments: Common and abundant. Can be roasted and eaten. One of the world's largest barnacles. Shell often has yellow boring sponge (see p. 22) attached.

ACORN BARNACLE

Balanus glandula Darwin, 1854.
Size: To 3/4" (2 cm) high and wide.
Range: Aleutian Islands to Mexico.
Habitat: On rocks, floats and pilings.
Description: White, volcano-shaped. Inner plates close tight to seal the animal. Plates have a jet black lining.
Comments: The most common of several intertidal barnacles. Eaten by the barnacle nudibranch (see p. 115).

THATCHED BARNACLE

Semibalanus cariosus (Pallas, 1788).
Size: Individuals to 2" (5 cm) high, 2³/₈" (5.9 cm) diameter.
Range: Alaska to southern California.
Habitat: On rocks, intertidal and shallow subtidal.
Description: Ribbed wall has downward-pointing finger-like projections.
Comments: May live 15 years.

GOOSE BARNACLE

Pollicipes polymerus Sowerby, 1833.
Alternate names: *Mitella polymerus*; leaf barnacle, goose neck barnacle.
Size: Stalk to 3¹/₄" (8 cm) high; to 1¹/₈" (2.9 cm) diameter at crown.
Range: BC to Baja California.
Habitat: On open ocean coasts, intertidal and occasionally in currents to 100' (30 m) or more.
Description: Found growing in clumps; individuals topped with 5 large plates and numerous small plates.
Comments: Often clumped with California mussel (see p. 89).

PELAGIC GOOSE BARNACLE

Lepas anatifera Linnaeus, 1758.
Alternate name: Common goose barnacle, goose neck barnacle.
Etymology: *anatifera* = goose bearer.
Size: To 6" (15 cm) long, 2³/₄" (7 cm) wide at top.
Range: Pacific and Atlantic waters.
Habitat: Attached to objects floating on the high seas.
Description: Plates have fine striations.
Comments: Often found on driftwood washed ashore.

CHAPTER 6

Bivalves, Snails, Limpets, Nudibranchs, Octopus, Squid, Chitons, Lampshells

Mollusks & Brachiopods

PHYLUM MOLLUSCA

The phylum Mollusca ("soft-bodied") comprises more than 50,000 living species worldwide, and 35,000 fossil species described. In number of species, only the phylum Arthropoda is larger. Mollusks live on land and in fresh water, but most species live in marine environments. Some 800 species inhabit the waters and intertidal areas of the Pacific Northwest; the 83 species seen most often and identified most easily are included here. (For more detailed information on the mollusks with shells, see Rick Harbo's *Shells and Shellfish of the Pacific Northwest: A Field Guide*, 1997.)

The soft body of a mollusk is usually not segmented and is usually protected by a shell. The animal has a head, often with a rasping file-like "tongue" (radula) for feeding, a gut and other internal organs, a protective skin covering the body (mantle), and typically a muscular foot.

Mollusks are usually divided into seven classes, four of which include commonly found species: the bivalves, **Class Bivalvia** (see p. 87), gastropods, **Class Gastropoda** (p. 100), cephalopods, **Class Cephalopoda** (p. 121) and chitons, **Class Polyplacophora** (p. 123).

LOCOMOTION

Mollusks exhibit a variety of movement abilities, from the slow crawling of the many snails and other gastropods, to the jumping escape response of cockles, to the fast swimming of octopus and squid.

PREY–PREDATORS

Mollusks have many predators. Most bivalves (mussels, oysters, scallops, cockles, clams, shipworms), many gastropods (abalone, whelks) and cephalopods (squid and octopus) are essential food for humans and a large variety of other animals and birds.

REPRODUCTION

Reproductive strategies and patterns vary greatly among the mollusks. Many species have separate sexes, and fertilization usually takes place externally as eggs and sperm are discharged into the water. Other species lay eggs in capsules, still others brood their young.

Class Bivalvia

The bivalves ("two shells") comprise about 12,000 living species. Bivalves are exclusively aquatic and are found in a variety of habitats from moist sediments to submerged sediments in rivers, lakes and marine waters.

CAUTION: If you are harvesting bivalves, be aware of bag limits and marine protected areas or marine parks where harvest is prohibited. And you must check with the local fisheries authorities for information on closures due to pollution or toxic algal blooms, which can cause paralytic shellfish poisoning (PSP) and have other severe toxic effects.

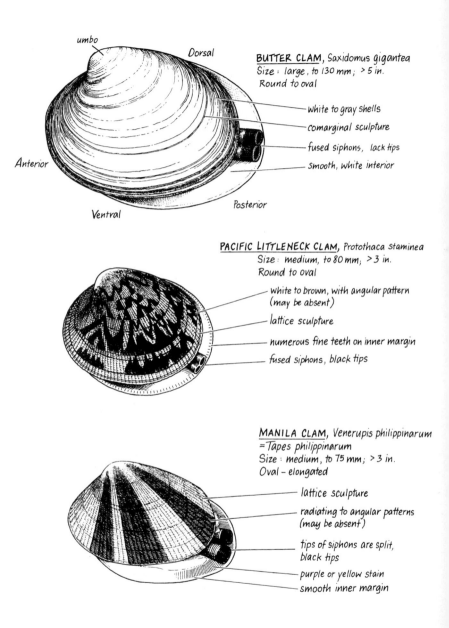

BUTTER CLAM, Saxidomus gigantea
Size: large, to 130 mm; > 5 in.
Round to oval

umbo

Dorsal

Anterior

Ventral

Posterior

white to gray shells
comarginal sculpture
fused siphons, lack tips
smooth, white interior

PACIFIC LITTLENECK CLAM, Protothaca staminea
Size: medium, to 80 mm; > 3 in.
Round to oval

white to brown, with angular pattern
(may be absent)
lattice sculpture
numerous fine teeth on inner margin
fused siphons, black tips

MANILA CLAM, Venerupis philippinarum
= Tapes philippinarum
Size: medium, to 75 mm; > 3 in.
Oval - elongated

lattice sculpture
radiating to angular patterns
(may be absent)
tips of siphons are split,
black tips
purple or yellow stain
smooth inner margin

Bivalve measurements and comparative features of butter, littleneck and Manila clams.

Mussels

Many common intertidal mussels and several less common, subtidal mussels are found in the Pacific Northwest. A mussel has two shells of equal size and shape, is typically elongated, and attaches to surfaces by strong, thin threads (byssus, beard or byssal threads) which grow from the foot. Groups of common mussels form beds by attaching to rocks, pilings and other hard surfaces.

PACIFIC BLUE MUSSEL

Mytilus edulis (Linnaeus, 1758) complex.

Alternate names: Edible mussel; bay mussel.

Size: To 6" (15 cm).

Range: 71°N–19°N; Arctic to Mexico.

Habitat: Typically in quiet, sheltered locations, intertidal to 16' (5 m). Common and dominant, forming dense masses on hard surfaces attached by strong byssal threads.

Description: Blue to black, sometimes tan to brown shells (in spite of common name "blue mussel"), triangular to elongate. Beak is blunt and flared, or curved and pointed.

Comments: Blue mussels, found worldwide, were once thought to be one species, but are now considered to be several species or subspecies: *Mytilus edulis* (Linnaeus, 1758) complex, which cannot be distinguished by the shells alone. The blue mussel species in the Pacific Northwest are considered to include the species or subspecies of *Mytilus edulis* and the foolish blue mussel *Mytilus trossulus* (A.A. Gould, 1850). The Mediterranean blue mussel *Mytilus galloprovincialis* (Lamarck, 1819) is considered an exotic that has hybridized with native species. Blue mussels live only 1–2 years in this region, compared to other locations such as Sweden, where they may live to 17 years and reach shell lengths to 4$^{1/2}$" (11 cm) or more.

CALIFORNIA MUSSEL

Mytilus californianus (Conrad, 1837).

Alternate names: Sea mussel; ribbed mussel.

Size: To 10" (25 cm).

Range: 60°N–18°N; Cook Inlet, Alaska to Punta Rompiente, Baja California; in Mexico.

Habitat: In extensive beds on surf-exposed rocks, wharves and sea mounts, intertidal to 330' (100 m).

Description: Thick shells pointed at anterior end; strong radial ribs, often worn on larger specimens. Heavy blue-black periostracum. Blue-grey interior, iridescent at margins; bright orange meat. Shells are held fast by thread-like byssus secreted at the foot.

Comments: Often hosts pea crabs. May contain tiny pearls of various shapes. Native peoples once used these mussels extensively for food and for tools.

Oysters

There are more than 200 species of oysters worldwide. Three species are commonly found in this region: the introduced Pacific (Japanese) oyster, the Olympia oyster and the Atlantic oyster. The green false-jingle, commonly called the rock or jingle oyster (below), is a member of the family Anomiidae, and differs greatly from the true oysters.

PACIFIC OYSTER
Crassostrea gigas (Thunberg, 1793).
Alternate name: Japanese oyster.
Size: To 12" (30 cm) or more.
Range: 61°N–34°N; Prince William Sound, Alaska to Newport Bay, California.
Habitat: On firm or rocky beaches, intertidal to 20' (6 m).
Description: Shape varies from long and thin to round and deep. Fluted shell; grey-white exterior with new growth often purple-black, smooth white interior.

Lower (left) valve is usually cupped; upper valve is flattened and smaller than other valve.
Comments: This oyster, introduced as seed from Japan in the early 1900s, is the most important culture species on the west coast. It may live 20 years or longer, and often harbours irregular pearls, without lustre. It is preyed upon by snails, oyster drills and sea stars.

Jingle/Rock Oysters, or False-Jingles

"Jingle shells," flattened shells which grow to fit the contours of the sea bottom, are typically anchored with a plug-like byssus.

GREEN FALSE-JINGLE
Pododesmus macroschisma (Deshayes, 1839).
Alternate names: Rock oyster; jingle shells; blister shells; may be two species or subspecies (see Comments).
Size: To 5 1/4" (13 cm).
Range: 58°N–28°N; Bering Sea to southern Baja California, and in Gulf of California.
Habitat: Attached to rocks and other solid objects, intertidal to 295' (90 m).
Description: Circular shell grows to shape of substrate. Upper (left) shell exterior is grey-white with light radiating lines; lower shell has a pear-shaped hole near the hinge for a short, thick byssus with a calcareous attachment. Polished interior; upper valve often iridescent green.
Comments: Painted star (see p. 137) has been observed feeding on abundant jingle oysters on a shallow, rocky reef. There may be a second subspecies, *P. macroschisma cepio*, or a second species, *P. cepio*, confined to a portion of Alaska.

Scallops

A scallop shell typically has strong radial ribs and wing-like hinges (called "ears"). When the shells gape, eyes can be seen between sensory tentacles, around the edge of the mantle. The eyes do not perceive images but can detect shadows. Unlike most bivalves, scallops are often free-swimming animals that move through the water by clapping their shells to expel water. An exception is the rock scallop which, after a brief free-swimming stage, cements its shell to hard objects. Both types of scallops are typically encrusted with sponges.

Four of the common scallops can be seen in the shallow waters of the Pacific Northwest.

ROCK SCALLOP
Crassadoma gigantea (Gray, 1825).
Alternate names: Purple-hinged or giant scallop; *Hinnites giganteus* (Gray, 1825).
Etymology: *crassadoma* = big house.
Size: To 10" (25 cm) high.
Range: 60°N–27°N; Prince William Sound, Alaska to southern Baja California.
Habitat: On rocky bottoms, in crevices and under boulders, intertidal to 260' (78 m).

Description: Thick, round shells often infested with boring sponge (see p. 22); irregular exterior has ribs, many with spiny projections. Orange mantle bears numerous blue eyes.
Comments: Typically encrusted with various plants and animals. The juvenile, to 1³/4" (4.5 cm), is usually orange, sometimes cream and brown. It is free-swimming, then the lower (right) valve attaches. The juvenile shape and pattern are retained at the umbo, but the colours are lost.

The weathervane scallop is the largest scallop in the world, but rock scallops have thick shells and are heavier by weight. Rock scallops were harvested for food by coastal native peoples, and the shells were used as pendants. The species is not abundant enough for a commercial fishery.

If harvesting, please consider that this is a slow-growing species that can live longer than 20 years. An area can be quickly depleted of large scallops.

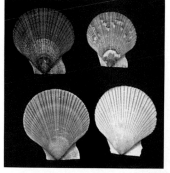

SMOOTH PINK SCALLOP
Chlamys rubida (Hinds, 1845).
Alternate names: Hind's scallop; swimming scallop.
Size: To 2¹/2" (6 cm) high.
Range: 57°N–33°N; Kodiak Island, Alaska to San Diego, California; not common south of Puget Sound.
Habitat: On gravel–mud bottom, 3–655' (1–200 m).
Description: Circular shells have prominent radial ridges; front ears are about 2 times the length of hind ears; byssal notch almost triangular. Upper (left) valve exterior is pink to red-purple, white or yellow; lower (right) valve is paler. Smooth, more than 30 prominent radial ribs, more than the spiny pink scallop (below), and small narrower riblets between.
Comments: Shells are typically encrusted with sponges. Species is not as common, abundant or large as the spiny scallop, but is often mixed in catches of other species by commercial and sport fishers.

SPINY PINK SCALLOP

Chlamys hastata (Sowerby, 1843).
Alternate names: Pink scallop; Pacific pink scallop; swimming scallop.
Size: To 3¼" (8 cm) high.
Range: 60°N–33°N; Gulf of Alaska to San Diego, California.
Habitat: On rocky reefs in shallow water, 7–495' (2–150 m).
Description: Almost circular shells; margin broadly fluting or undulating. Variable in colour and sculpture. Coarse, wide primary ribs with strong spines and several riblets between; deep, squarish byssal notch. Typically encrusted with sponges.

Comments: Species can swim when disturbed, or threatened by predators.
Edibility: Abundant on rocky reefs at 60' (18 m) and deeper, and is fished commercially by divers and fishers using drags from a small vessel. The scallop is usually steamed open and served whole like a clam.

Cockles

There are several hundred living species of cockles in the world. In this region, one large, common cockle is found in the intertidal zone and several less common species are found in subtidal areas. The distinguishing feature of cockles is the pattern of prominent radiating ribs.

NUTTALL'S COCKLE

Clinocardium nuttallii (Conrad, 1837).
Alternate names: Basket cockle; heart cockle.
Size: To 5½" (14 cm).
Range: 60°N–33°N; Southern Bering Sea to San Diego, California.
Habitat: In sand–gravel in sheltered waters, intertidal to 100' (30 m).
Description: Shells as high as or slightly higher than long; 34–38 strong ribs with wavy lines across ribs at margins. Short siphons (see photo, below) show at surface. Yellow-brown, young often mottled with russet and brown patterns.
Comments: Species may live 16 years. It exhibits a stunning leaping escape response to the sunflower star (see p. 135) and spiny pink star (p. 136). Traditionally, aboriginal peoples harvested cockles intertidally and subtidally from canoes, using sticks.

Clams

Horse Clams (Gaper Clams)

These large, smooth clams are recognized by the small spoon-shaped socket (chondrophore) holding the interior ligament in the centre of the hinge. Horse clams (*Tresus* spp.) are fished commercially by divers in BC and taken by recreational diggers. The largest shells were used by Native peoples as bowls and ladles.

FAT GAPER

Tresus capax (Gould, 1850).
Alternate names: Alaskan gaper; summer clam; otter clam.
Etymology: *capax* = roomy, spacious.
Size: To 7" (17.5 cm) long.
Range: 55°N–35°N; Cook Inlet, Gulf of Alaska to Oceano, California.
Habitat: In sand–mud, intertidal to 100' (30 m). More common at northern latitudes.
Description: Oval shells, length typically 1 1/2 times the height; lower margin more deeply rounded than Pacific gaper (below).
Comments: When exposed at low tide, species can be seen spitting jets of water when disturbed. The fat gaper almost always has a pair of pea crabs in its mantle.
Edibility: This clam was traditionally harvested and dried by Native peoples. It is taken for sport by digging with forks in the intertidal zone. Commercial divers harvest it by loosening the sand with a high-pressure jet of water, then pulling the clam free (see geoduck, p. 98). The neck meat is removed, blanched and frozen.

PACIFIC GAPER

Tresus nuttallii (Conrad, 1837).
Alternate names: Summer clam; otter clam.
Size: To 9" (22.5 cm) long. Whole wet weight to 3 lbs. (1.4 kg).
Range: 58°N–25°N; Kodiak Island, Alaska to southern Baja California.
Habitat: Buries deeper (3'/1 m in sand) or lower on the tide than the fat gaper (above), to avoid freezing. Usually in sandier substrate than fat gaper. Intertidal to 165' (50 m).
Description: Shell length at least 1 1/2 times the height. Gaping elongated shells cannot contain the large siphon; siphon has thick leather-like plates at tip.
Comments: Unlike fat gaper (above), species rarely hosts pea crabs.

PACIFIC RAZOR-CLAM

Siliqua patula (Dixon, 1788).
Alternate name: Northern razor clam.
Size: To 7" (18 cm).
Range: 59°N–35°N; Cook Inlet, Gulf of Alaska to Morro Bay, California.
Habitat: On surf-exposed sandy beaches, intertidal to 180' (55 m).
Description: Thin, brittle, long, narrow shells, rounded at anterior end, slightly truncated at posterior. Shiny, smooth periostracum, olive to brown. Short white siphons fused except at tips. Shell interior white with purple, with rib slanting to anterior end.

Comments: Species has a strong muscular foot and smooth, streamlined shell which allow it to burrow to depths of 24" (60 cm) within a minute. Harvested on the lowest spring tides.

Edibility: Species supports Native, commercial and sport fisheries. Harvesters should check with local fisheries offices for red tide and pollution closures before harvesting.

Tellin Clams, Macoma Clams

This family is known worldwide for its colourful clams. They are abundant and common in the intertidal zone and shallow waters, and they are also found to depths of 660' (200 m). The shells often have a twist at the posterior end. The pallial line and pallial sinus are key characters of the *Macoma* spp. on the inside of the shells and do not show well in photographs.

BALTIC MACOMA

Macoma balthica (Linnaeus, 1758).
Alternate name: *M. inconspicua.*
Size: To 1 1/2" (4 cm).
Range: 70°N–38°N; Panarctic and Circumboreal; Beaufort Sea to San Francisco Bay, California.
Habitat: Buried to 8" (20 cm) in sand–mud bays or estuaries, intertidal to 130' (40 m). Often abundant.
Description: Small, oval shells varying in colour from pink, blue, yellow to orange.

Comments: A small, colourful clam commonly found on sand beaches. Populations in the southern range may have been introduced from the Atlantic.

POINTED MACOMA
Macoma inquinata (Deshayes, 1855).
Alternate names: Polluted, fouled macoma; *Macoma iris*.
Size: To 2¹/₂" (6 cm).
Range: 57°N–34°N; Pribilof Islands, Alaska to Santa Barbara, California.
Habitat: In sand–mud in bays and offshore, intertidal to 165' (50 m).
Description: Wedge-shaped shell posterior (at right in photo) has slight but distinctive indentation. Cream exterior with concentric striations; marginal brown periostracum. Large, prominent external ligament.

Hind end more round than bent-nose macoma (below). Internal pallial line and pallial sinus joined at muscle scar.

BENT-NOSE MACOMA
Macoma nasuta (Conrad, 1837).
Size: To 3" (7.5 cm).
Range: 60°N–22°N; Cook Inlet, Alaska to southern Baja California; reports to Cabo San Lucas.
Habitat: Buried 4–6" (10–15 cm) beneath the surface, common in intertidal sand to 165' (50 m).
Description: Thin white shells, bending sharply to the right near pointed posterior end. Separate orange siphons collect detritus off sea bottom.

Comments: A shell is often found on the surface of the water with a perfect small hole, usually near the hinge, drilled by a moonsnail.

WHITE SAND-MACOMA
Macoma secta (Conrad, 1837).
Size: To 4" (10 cm).
Range: 54°N–25°N; Queen Charlotte Islands, BC to southern Baja California.
Habitat: Buried 8–18" (20–46 cm) in sand in sheltered waters, intertidal to 165' (50 m).
Description: Thin white shell with ridge from umbo to posterior ventral margin. Separate white siphons.

BIVALVES

DARK MAHOGANY-CLAM

Nuttallia obscurata (Reeve, 1857).
Alternate name: Varnish clam.
Size: To 2¼" (5.5 cm).
Range: Strait of Georgia and Barkley Sound, BC to Puget Sound.
Habitat: Buried to 8" (20 cm) in sand–gravel in the high to mid-intertidal, often in areas of freshwater seepage.

Description: Thin, oval, flat shells. Shiny brown periostracum, worn white at the hinge. Shell interior purple. Long, separate siphons.
Comments: Recently (since the 1980s) introduced from Japan. Has multiplied quickly in the protected waters of the Strait of Georgia, Puget Sound and in Barkley Sound, BC, since the mid-1990s. Species hosts pea crabs.

Venus Clams, Hardshell–Steamer Clams

Extensive sport and commercial fisheries operate for harvest of the hardshell butter and steamer (manila and littleneck) clams. The colour and markings of the manila and littleneck clams may vary, but all three varieties have internal teeth in the hinges (see p. 88).

PACIFIC LITTLENECK

Protothaca staminea (Conrad, 1837).
Alternate names: Rock cockle; native littleneck.
Size: To 3" (7.5 cm).
Range: 54°N–23°N; Aleutian Islands south to southern Baja California.
Habitat: Buried to 4" (10 cm) or more in gravel–sand–mud bottom; mid-intertidal to 35' (10.5 m).
Description: Round to oval inflated shells, white to brown, sometimes with dark, angular patterns. Lattice sculpture. Interior margin of shell has numerous fine teeth visible to the eye and easily felt (key character). Short, fused siphons. External hinge ligament.
Comments: Shells bearing holes drilled by moonsnails are often found.
Edibility: Species is less abundant than Manila or butter clam (see p. 97), and is harvested as a steamer and for chowders. It is fast-growing, reaching a legal size in the commercial fishery of 1½" (4 cm) in 3–4 years in many areas. Life span can reach 8–14 years.

MANILA CLAM
Venerupis philippinarum (A. Adams & Reeve, 1850).
Alternate names: Japanese littleneck; *Tapes philippinarum* Adams & Reeve, 1850. The scientific name has changed frequently.
Size: To 3" (7.5 cm).
Range: 54°N–37°N; Central northern coast of BC to Elkhorn Slough, California.
Habitat: Buried to 4" (10 cm) in gravel–sand–mud, high intertidal.
Description: Elongated oval shells have lattice sculpture with strong radial ribs. Ribs are stronger at posterior end. Exterior colour varies from grey to brown, often with streaked patterns, occasionally with angular pattern similar to the native littleneck. Short siphons with split tip. Interior of shell often has purple or yellow coloration; inside edge is smooth to the touch.

Comments: Species was introduced accidentally with Pacific oyster seed from Japan. Local populations were first recorded in BC in 1936. Species is fast-growing, reaching a legal size in the commercial fishery of 1¹/4" (4 cm) in 3–4 years in many areas. Life span can reach 8–14 years.

Edibility: This is the only clam for which there has been extensive development of aquaculture in recent years in BC and Washington. It has been the main species of the intertidal clam fishery in BC through the 1980s and 1990s, for the fresh steamer clam market. Some argue that the Manila is sweeter than the Pacific littleneck. It is gathered with rakes and remains fresh long after harvest. Species opens quickly when steamed. Harvesters should check with local fisheries offices for red tide and pollution closures before harvesting.

BUTTER CLAM
Saxidomus gigantea (Deshayes, 1839).
Alternate name: Smooth Washington clam; *Saxidomus giganteus*.
Size: To 5¹/4" (13 cm).
Range: 60°N–37°N; Southeast Bering Sea to central California.
Habitat: Buried to 12" (30 cm) in gravel–sand–mud of protected bays; mid- to lower intertidal to 130' (40 m).
Description: Large oval to square shells only have comarginal lines or grooves. Typically white to grey shells; gape at posterior end. Smooth but not glossy interior; large, deeply marked muscle scars.

Comments: Species forms abundant populations in the lower intertidal. It grows to a minimum legal size of 2¹/2" (6 cm) in 4–5 years in southern areas of BC but takes 8–9 years in northern areas, and may live to 20 years or more. The butter clam is typically harvested with a garden fork.

Edibility: This clam is considered the best for chowders. All of the meat is edible, but recreational harvesters should remove the black siphon tips, where PSP toxin may accumulate.

Softshell Clams (Gaper Clams)

SOFTSHELL CLAM

Mya arenaria (Linnaeus, 1758).
Alternate name: Mud clam.
Size: To 4" (10 cm).
Range: 70°N–37°N; Icy Cape, Alaska to Elkhorn Slough, California.
Habitat: Buried 4–8" (10–20 cm) in sand–mud, often in estuarine conditions; intertidal.
Description: Thin, brittle, elongated shells. Large spoon-shaped chondrophore at hinge of left valve and large "shelf" projection (myophore) on right shell are distinguishing features of softshell clams. White to grey exterior, with brown or yellow-orange periostracum obvious at edges. Dark siphons.

Comments: Because this shell is not found in middens of coastal aboriginal people, it is believed to have been introduced from the Atlantic coast, probably in the late 1800s.

Giant Clams: Geoducks (King Clams)

All clams of this family gape: they cannot retract fully into the shell. Some are buried deep in the substrate to 12" (30 cm); others burrow as deep as 36" (1 m). The smaller clams of this family nestle in rock burrows or kelp holdfasts.

PACIFIC GEODUCK CLAM

Panopea abrupta (Conrad, 1849).
Alternate names: King clam; *Panope generosa.*
Etymology: *Geoduc* = a native American term for "dig deep."
Size: To 7 3/4" (19.5 cm) or more.
Range: 58°N–34°N; Kodiak Island, Alaska to Newport Bay, California.

Habitat: Buried in gravel–sand–mud, lowest intertidal to 330' (100 m) or more.
Description: Shells are rounded at anterior, truncated at siphon end, gaping at all sides due to large body and neck. Species cannot draw siphons or neck into shell. White shell; thin patches of periostracum at edges. Both shells have a cardinal tooth at the hinge; this may be broken off by a sea otter. White interior with continuous pallial line, unlike false geoducks.
Comments: This is the largest intertidal clam in the world, reaching weights greater than 10

lbs (4.5 kg). It is among the oldest animals in the world, reported to live as long as 146 years.
Edibility: Species has been occasionally harvested for food by Natives and recreational harvesters. It is found only on the lowest tides of the year, and buried to 3' (1 m) in the substrate, making it a challenge to capture.

The geoduck supports an important subtidal commercial fishery in Alaska, BC and Washington. Divers detect the siphon or show (see photo at left), then loosen the substrate with a high-pressure water jet and pull the clam free.

Shipworms (Woodborers, Teredos)

The shipworm is a worm-like bivalve with a modified and reduced shell used for drilling in wood. This family of bivalves creates extensive damage to untreated wood in the marine environment, including wharves, pilings and the hulls of ships, and a great deal of effort has gone into preventing larval settlement. Shipworm larvae burrow into wood surfaces as soon as they settle there. One reason logs are so often stored in rivers or estuaries is to reduce shipworm infestation.

FEATHERY SHIPWORM
Bankia setacea (Tryon, 1863).
Size: Shell to 3/4" (2 cm), worm-like body to 3.3' (1 m).
Range: 57°N–33°N; Bering Sea to San Diego, California.
Habitat: In wood only, in burrows lined with a calcareous secretion; intertidal to 295' (90 m).
Description: Worm-like body with separate posterior siphons, protected by feather-like "pallets" of cones that may stopper the burrow. Siphons (shown in photo) take in plankton, as well as wood, for food.
Comments: Called the "termite of the sea," species bores through wood with anterior cutting edge of toothed shells.

PHYLUM BRACHIOPODA

Lampshells Class Articulata

The lampshells, or brachiopods, look like bivalve mollusks but they are actually members of a different group of animals, belonging to the phylum Brachiopoda. Brachiopod, meaning "arm-foot," refers to the lopophores, arm-like structures which were once thought to be used for locomotion but are now known to be used for gathering food. The animal's two shells are not the same size and shape, as they are in bivalves.

The lampshell attaches to the sea bottom by means of a fleshy stalk (pedicel), but unlike bivalves that attach, such as the rock oyster and jingle oyster, it is not capable of detaching and "swimming."

There are more than 30,000 fossil species but only about 325 living species of brachiopods, all marine. Lampshells occur intertidally to great depths, 7,920' (2,400 m) and more. Bernard (1971) described 11 species found in BC waters.

LAMPSHELL
Terebratalia transversa (Sowerby, 1846).
Size: To 1¹/4" (3 cm).
Range: 57°N–33°N; Kodiak Island, Alaska to Ensenada, Mexico.
Habitat: On rocks and rock faces, intertidal to 5,575' (1,672 m).
Description: Shells are typically wider than long; surface varies from smooth to prominently ribbed with tan to brown periostracum. Broader anterior margin has pronounced undulations.
Comments: The most common intertidal brachiopod in Pacific Northwest waters.

LAMPSHELL
Laqueus californianus (Koch, 1848).
Size: To 1¹/4" (3 cm).
Range: Queen Charlotte Islands, BC to California.
Habitat: Under intertidal rocks, often abundant on subtidal rock faces to 1,620' (486 m).
Description: Thin, rounded, inflated shells, varying from smooth to prominently ribbed, with a tan to brown periostracum. Attached by a long, slender stalk.
Comments: Most common and abundant subtidally in Pacific Northwest waters. Also found in Sea of Japan.

PHYLUM MOLLUSCA

Gastropods Class Gastropoda

The gastropods ("stomach-foot") comprise some 50,000 marine, freshwater and terrestrial species. About 37,500 of these are living species; about 15,000 are fossils. The gastropods, named for the "stomach-foot" on which they travel, occur in diverse forms. Many species have a single shell, including snails, abalone and limpets. The nudibranchs (sea slugs) do not have shells.

Abalone

NORTHERN ABALONE

Haliotis kamtschatkana (Jonas, 1845).
Alternate names: Japanese abalone; Pinto abalone.
Etymology: *Hali/otis* = of the sea/ear.
Size: To 7" (17.5 cm).
Range: Sitka, Alaska to Point Conception, California.
Habitat: Found in kelp and rocks, lower intertidal to 50' (15 m).
Description: Thin, oval-elongated shell with irregular surface. Exterior mottled greenish and reddish-brown; 3 to 6 open holes have raised edges. Interior is iridescent white, lacking the prized colours of other abalone.
Comments: Traditionally, abalone was harvested from the intertidal zone by coast Natives. The practice of diving for abalone came later. Today, there are many closures to harvest of abalone for conservation reasons. Check with local fisheries authorities before harvesting.

Keyhole Limpets

This family is characterized by a hole at or near the top (*apex*) of the shell, which distinguishes them from the "true" limpets (see p. 104). Many feed on algae or detritus, but a few are carnivorous, feeding on sponges and other animals. The keyhole limpet extends its mantle to cover the shell and prevent predatory sea stars from getting a strong hold.

ROUGH KEYHOLE LIMPET

Diodora aspera (Rathke, 1833).
Etymology: *Diodora* = with a passage through; *aspera* = rough, referring to rough surface of the shell.
Size: To 2³/4" (7 cm).
Range: Alaska to Baja California.
Habitat: On rocks, low intertidal and shallow subtidal.
Description: Ovate shell, narrow in front, grey-white with 12–18 radial colour bands of purple-brown. Shell has lattice sculpture and circular opening to anterior of centre.
Comments: Species has escape response to predatory starfish—painted star (see p. 137), sunflower star (p. 135), six ray star (p. 136)—in which mantle is extended to cover the shell. It also hosts a commensal scale worm which bites at the tube feet of the ray of the sea star and can cause it to retreat.

Snails

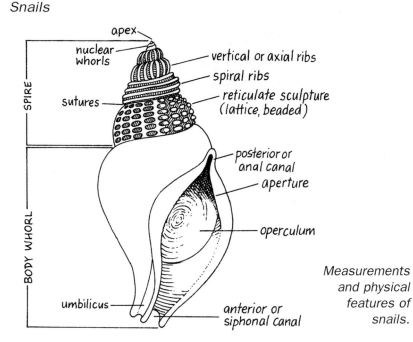

apex

nuclear whorls

vertical or axial ribs

spiral ribs

reticulate sculpture (lattice, beaded)

sutures

SPIRE

posterior or anal canal

aperture

operculum

BODY WHORL

umbilicus

anterior or siphonal canal

Measurements and physical features of snails.

Turban Snails

RED TURBAN

Astraea gibberosa (Dillwyn, 1817).
Alternate name: *Lithopoma gibberosum.*
Etymology: *Astraea* = starry; *gibberosa* = hunched.
Size: To 3" (7.5 cm).
Range: Southeast Alaska to Baja California; not common between Washington and northern California.
Habitat: On rocks on open coast; sometimes the shell is covered with coralline algae; intertidal to 260' (78 m).
Description: Reddish-brown shell with brown periostracum. Flat base of shell is lined with furrows; whorls have prominent wavy, bumpy ridge. Thick, oval, white pearly operculum.
Comments: A common and sometimes abundant species. The pearly operculum was used for decoration in wooden bentboxes made by the Haida and Natives of southeast Alaska.
Edibility: There has been interest in harvesting this species commercially.

BLACK TURBAN

Tegula funebralis (A. Adams, 1855).
Etymology: *Tegula* = roof or covering; *funebralis* = funereal, referring to dark colour.
Size: To 1¼" (3 cm) diameter.
Range: Vancouver Island to Point Conception, California, and reports to central Baja California.
Habitat: Common and abundant aggregations under rocks, intertidal.
Description: Thick shell with strong, low cone of 4 whorls; umbilicus closed, 2 teeth in aperture. Dark black-purple shell, often worn to pearly white at the top. Pearly interior; black body.

Comments: Species often has a black limpet (*Lottia asmi*) or white slippersnails growing on the shell. It has been estimated to live as long as 80 to 100 years.

PURPLE-RING TOPSNAIL

Calliostoma annulatum (Lightfoot, 1786).
Alternate name: Purple top shell.
Etymology: *annulatum* = ringed.
Size: To 1¼" (3 cm) high.
Range: Alaska to Baja California.
Habitat: On open coast, feeding on kelp and animals on rocks, intertidal to 100' (30 m).
Description: Orange-yellow shell has bright purple-violet bands, beaded ribs and 8–9 whorls. Soft body is pinkish-orange with black.
Comments: Species has been observed feeding on sponges.

BLUE TOPSNAIL

Calliostoma ligatum (Gould, 1849).
Alternate names: Western ridged top shell; formerly known as costate top shell (*C. costata*).
Size: To 1" (2.5 cm) diameter.
Range: Northern BC to California.
Habitat: In rocky areas and kelp beds, intertidal to 100' (30 m) and deeper. Common and abundant.
Description: Brown shell with light tan spiral ridges; worn patches show pearly blue inner layer. Well-rounded whorls and round aperture..
Comments: Common species exhibits an escape response to the ochre star (see p. 136). It is known to eat lobed ascidian (p. 155), and feeds on sponges.

SPINY TOPSNAIL

Cidarina cidaris (Carpenter, 1864).
Alternate names: Adam's spiny margarite; *Lischkeia cidaris* (Fischer, 1879).
Size: To 1 1/2" (4 cm) high.
Range: Alaska to Baja California.
Habitat: On offshore rocky–rubble bottom, 50' (15 m) and deeper. Moderately common.
Description: Shell has rounded, beaded whorls with a deep suture line. Beaded spiral chords at base. Round aperture. Grey exterior with beads and ridges worn white; pearly interior.

"True" Limpets

These one-shelled animals are typically cone-shaped. They are found in a number of habitats, on rocks, kelp, eelgrass and snail shells. They are classified as Patellogastropoda, a separate order from that of the snails and keyhole limpets. Several unrelated families, the siphon shells or falselimpets and the cup-and-saucer shells, produce uncoiled limpet-shaped shells.

Some limpets in the Pacific Northwest are less than 5/8" (15 mm) long, and the largest in the region is likely the mask limpet, which can reach 2" (5 cm) or more in length. The limpet's life span is estimated at 5 to 16 years.

Most limpets feed by scraping algae from rock surfaces. The subtidal limpets tend to forage and move great distances; the intertidal species are typically highly territorial and defend their space aggressively. Many limpets exhibit escape responses to predatory sea stars and carnivorous snails. They are also preyed upon by a number of marine birds and small fishes such as surf perch.

WHITECAP LIMPET

Acmaea mitra Rathke, 1833.
Alternate name: Dunce-cap limpet.
Etymology: *Acmaea* = pointed; *mitra* = cap.
Size: To 1 3/8" (3.4 cm) long, 1 1/4" (3 cm) high.
Range: Alaska to Baja California.
Habitat: On rocks with encrusting coralline algae, intertidal and shallow subtidal. Shells are often washed up on surf beaches.
Description: Round shell with smooth, thick margin; apex is central. White exterior, usually covered by a pink, knobby coralline alga that is its major food.

Family Lottidae

SHIELD LIMPET
Lottia pelta (Rathke, 1833).
Alternate name: *Collisella pelta.*
Etymology: *pelta* = small shield.
Size: To 2¹/₄" (5.5 cm) long, ⁵/₈" (1.5 cm) high.
Range: Alaska to Baja California.
Habitat: Often associated with brown algae, including sea palm (see p. 207), and common in mussel beds.
Description: Oval shell with central apex, irregular ribbing. Greyish exterior with irregular white radial stripes that form a net pattern. Bluish-white interior with brown spot.
Comments: Species exhibits a running escape response to predatory sea stars.

RIBBED LIMPET
Lottia digitalis (Rathke, 1833).
Alternate names: Finger limpet; *Collisella digitalis.*
Etymology: *digitalis* = finger, referring to the finger-like ribbing of the shell.
Size: To 1¹/₄" (3 cm) long.
Range: Aleutian Islands to southern tip of Baja California.
Habitat: In cracks and crevices in high intertidal and splash zones, on vertical or overhanging rock faces, sometimes on shells of goose barnacles (see p. 85).
Description: Apex of shell is near anterior margin. Olive-green to brown exterior with white blotches or dots. Interior has brownish central patch.
Comments: Species is one of the most common limpets. It grazes on algae.

PLATE LIMPET
Tectura scutum (Rathke, 1833).
Alternate names: Pacific plate limpet; *Notoacmaea scutum.*
Etymology: *scutum* = shield, referring to the flattened profile.
Size: To 2" (5 cm) or more.
Range: Alaska to California.
Habitat: Common in mid- to low inter-tidal and shallow subtidal.
Description: Low, flattened shell with rounded off-centre apex, smooth oval margin. Green-grey exterior with light and dark streaks, blotches or checkerboard pattern. Bluish interior with banded dark marginal rim and often a brown centre.
Comments: Species is the only Pacific limpet with brown tentacles. It exhibits a running escape response to several sea stars.

MASK LIMPET

Tectura persona (Rathke, 1833).
Alternate names: Speckled limpet; *Notoacmaea persona*; *Acmaea persona*.
Etymology: *persona* = mask, referring to the dark interior stain.
Size: To 2" (5 cm) long.
Range: Alaska to Monterey, California.
Habitat: Common in deep cracks and depressions, high on beach often in area of freshwater seepage and in shade of overhanging trees, sheltered from the heaviest wave action.

Description: Oval shell with smooth margin; apex to front. Mottled blue-grey exterior with brown or black, speckled with white dots at top. Bluish-white interior with dark margin, sometimes spotted with white and a dark mask-like stain behind the apex.

Periwinkles (Littorines)

These two small snails are often found together, high in the intertidal zone.

SITKA PERIWINKLE

Littorina sitkana (Philippi, 1845).
Etymology: *littorina* = of the earth, referring to the habitat high in the intertidal.
Size: To 7/8" (2.2 cm).
Range: Alaska to Puget Sound.
Habitat: In sheltered waters on rocks among rockweed and other algae; in eelgrass, high to low intertidal.
Description: Squat shell with diameter almost equal to height. Sculpture varies from smooth to strong spiral threads; colour varies from light brown to red-brown, grey or black, some with yellow, orange or white bands. Large, circular aperture; brown or orange interior.

CHECKERED PERIWINKLE

Littorina scutulata (Gould, 1849).
Size: To 5/8" (1.5 cm) high.
Range: Alaska to Baja California.
Habitat: In sheltered waters on rocks, intertidal.
Description: Somewhat slender shell with height greater than diameter; about 4 whorls thick; no umbilicus. Dark brown to black-purple, often checkered with white, sometimes with spiral bands of orange crossed with bars or white spots. Purplish interior.

Hornsnails

MUDFLAT SNAIL
Batillaria cumingi (Crosse, 1862).
Alternate names: False cerith snail; *Batillaria zonalis*; *B. attramentaria* (Sowerby, 1855). **Size:** To 1¼" (3 cm). **Range:** Introduced from Japan along with oyster seed. **Habitat:** Common and abundant on protected sand–mud shores, mid- to high intertidal. **Description:** Small, elongated shell; 8–9 whorls with beaded spiral ridges. Teeth on inner margin of outer lip of the aperture. Grey with brown beads.

Hairysnails

OREGON TRITON
Fusitriton oregonensis (Redfield, 1848).
Alternate name: Hairy triton.
Size: To 6" (15 cm) high.
Range: Bering Sea to San Diego, California.
Habitat: Intertidal to 295' (90 m). Common and abundant in some areas. **Description:** Shell has about 6 whorls; axial riblets crossed by spiral pairs of threads. Long siphon canal is about one-third as long as aperture. Exterior has thick, shaggy, grey-brown periostracum.
Comments: Species is the largest intertidal snail in the Pacific Northwest region. It is carnivorous, feeding on tunicates and even sea urchins, which sometimes bear black scars where they were attacked by the triton. White eggs are laid in distinctive coils of translucent capsules, resembling kernels of corn, attached to the bottom. Shells of this species are in much demand by the largest hermit crabs, which occupy shells of other species and must fight for larger shells as they grow.

Moonsnails

Several hundred moonsnail species are found throughout the world, living on sandy bottoms and feeding on clams. In England they are called "necklace-shells" because of the sand collars of eggs. Each species has its own characteristic egg collar shape.

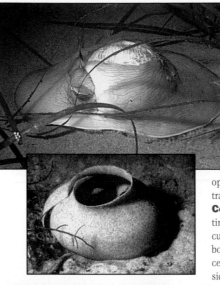

LEWIS'S MOONSNAIL

Euspira lewisii (Gould, 1847).
Alternate names: *Polinices lewisii* (Gould, 1847); *Lunatia lewisii*.
Size: To 5¹/₂" (14 cm) high.
Range: Southeastern Alaska to southern California.
Habitat: Common on sand, intertidal to 165' (50 m).
Description: Large globular shell. Cream exterior with thin brown periostracum; wide, flaring aperture; open umbilicus; tan to brown horny operculum. Brown interior. Soft body is translucent brown with no spots or blotches.
Comments: Species lays its eggs in a distinctive sand collar, moulded by the shell curvature as it is released from the snail's body. Many small eggs are distributed in a central jelly layer, coated with sand on both sides. They are found in the intertidal zone and deeper, generally from April to September with a peak in May–June. The eggs hatch out of the collar in 6 weeks.

The moonsnail burrows and feeds on clams, drilling into shells and cutting the flesh of the clam with its tooth-like radula. An adult moonsnail consumes about one clam every 4 days. Littleneck, butter, truncated softshell (*Mya truncata*) and Pacific gaper clams (shown here), are among the species whose shells are often found with the characteristic hole drilled by the moonsnail. Cockles are rarely drilled by moonsnails. Moonsnail shells are much in demand by larger hermit crabs, which live in other species' shells and must compete for the rarer large shells as they grow.
Edibility: Species is massive but not particularly edible.

Rocksnails (Dwarf Tritons)

LEAFY HORNMOUTH

Ceratostoma foliatum (Gmelin, 1791).
Alternate names: Leafy, foliated thorn purpura.
Size: To 3¹/₂" (8.5 cm).
Range: Alaska to San Pedro, California.
Habitat: On barnacles and bivalves, intertidal to 200' (60 m).
Description: Large tooth projecting from aperture; 3 wing-like projections or frills; canal closed and turned and twisted at the end.
Comments: Species feeds on barnacles and bivalves. When the snail is dislodged by a fish, its frills help it land with the aperture down, to avoid being picked. Leafy hornmouth snails cluster to lay yellow egg cases, often in late February and March. Each case contains 25–80 eggs, and eggs are sometimes guarded while they hatch. Larvae develop in the egg case and emerge as small snails.

Whelks, Dogwinkles

The names of the families and genera of these snails have changed several times, as they are extremely variable in shape and they occur in a variety of marine environments. Species in the Pacific Northwest area have been assigned to the genus *Nucella*; the genus *Thais* appears to comprise species that are exclusively tropical. Whelks and dogwinkles are found drilling and feeding on barnacles in the intertidal zone and are determining factors in the vertical distribution of barnacles.

FRILLED DOGWINKLE
Nucella lamellosa (Gmelin, 1791).
Alternate name: Wrinkled dogwinkle.
Size: To 3¹/₄" (8 cm) high.
Range: Alaska to central California.
Habitat: On rocks, in crevices, intertidal to shallow subtidal.
Description: Shells vary from smooth (often in exposed areas) to ornamented with up to 12 axial frills (in sheltered areas). Uniform colour ranges from grey to white to pale brown, sometimes banded. Outer lip is broadly flared with 3 rounded teeth.
Comments: A large number of snails gather in winter and lay stalked yellow egg cases in spring and summer. Researchers at Bamfield, BC have observed smooth-shelled animals to grow axial frills when in the presence of their major predator, the red rock crab (see p. 79).

CHANNELLED DOGWINKLE
Nucella canaliculata (Duclos, 1832).
Size: To 1¹/₂" (4 cm).
Range: Alaska to central California.
Habitat: On rocks and barnacles.
Description: Shell may be slightly more slender than other whelks; short spire, 14–16 spiral ridges separated by deep furrows. Exterior white-grey.
Comments: Species is often found feeding on barnacles.

STRIPED DOGWINKLE

Nucella emarginata (Deshayes, 1839).
Alternate names: Emarginate or ribbed dogwinkle; *Thais emarginata*.
Size: To 1¹¹/₁₆" (2.7 cm).
Range: Bering Sea to northern Baja California.
Habitat: On semi-protected and exposed rocky beaches. Feeds on mussels.
Description: Thick, plump shell with alternating thick and thin ribs, which often have white bands. Exterior varies from grey to black, brown or yellow. Interior of aperture often purple; width of opening less than half the diameter of the shell.
Comments: Two or more species of striped dogwinkles may be included in *N. emarginata*.

Whelks

DIRE WHELK

Lirabuccinum dirum (Reeve, 1846).
Alternate names: Spindle whelk; *Searlesia dira*.
Etymology: *dirum* = ominous, probably referring to the dull grey colour.
Size: To 2" (5 cm) high.
Range: Alaska to central California.
Habitat: On wave-washed rocks, intertidal.
Description: Thick, strong shell with 9–11 low, rounded axial ribs, numerous unequal-size spiral threads. Tan-coloured aperture, more than half as long as shell. Dull grey exterior. White body.

Olive Shells

PURPLE OLIVE

Olivella biplicata (Sowerby, 1825).
Size: To 1¹/₄" (3 cm) high.
Range: Vancouver Island to Baja California.
Habitat: In sand on open coast, burrowing quickly into sand when the tide goes out.
Description: Elongated, somewhat globular, highly polished shell. Blue-grey exterior with violet around lower part of aperture.
Comments: Species is a carnivorous scavenger. Its glossy shells have been highly prized throughout human history. Illustrations made by early Spanish explorers show that coastal Natives made necklace strings of olive shells and used them to decorate their clothing.

Nudibranchs: Order Nudibranchia

Nudibranchs ("naked gills"), or sea slugs, are known to divers and naturalists as one of nature's wonders, because so many species are so spectacular in their colours and markings. Nudibranchs feed on a variety of sponges, bryozoans, hydroids, colonial ascidians, and even barnacles, and the animal's colour is often changed by the food it takes in. The Pacific Northwest is home to more than 200 species of nudibranchs (for a comprehensive treatment, see Behrens 1991); the most common and abundant species are included here.

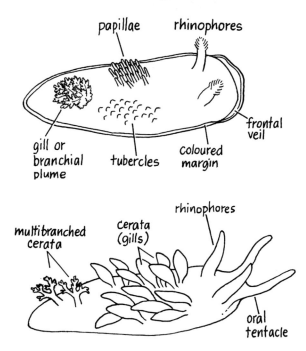

Physical features of nudibranchs, with retractable gill or plume, papillae and tubercles (top); with gills in clusters of single or multibranched cerata and with or without oral tentacles (bottom).

The nudibranch has paired sensory projections on the head, often stalked, called rhinophores. For breathing, it has a retractable plume-like (branchial) gill projection with many tufts, or numerous dorsal processes (cerata) shaped like fingers, clubs or paddles. The cerata often drop off and are replaced. Other finger-like projections, the papillae, provide additional respiration and may help camouflage the nudibranch by changing its outline. Small rounded bumps called tubercles increase the surface area of the body, or contain sharp rods (spicules) for protection.

Dorids

The dorids are the largest group of nudibranchs on the Pacific coast. They have a flattened shape, and most have a retractable gill plume. They are commonly found eating a variety of sponges. Many of the dorids that eat sponges are very species-specific due to the arrangement of the spicules in the sponge.

SEA LEMON
Anisodoris nobilis (MacFarland, 1905).
Size: To 8" (20 cm) long.
Range: Kodiak Island, Alaska to Mexico.
Habitat: On rocks and sponges, intertidal to 750' (225 m).
Description: Yellow to orange with dark spots between tubercles. White branchial plume.
Comments: Species is common. It feeds on tennis ball, yellow encrusting, peach ball and other sponges (see pp. 17–28), and lays ribbons of yellow eggs.

MONTEREY SEA LEMON
Archidoris montereyensis (Cooper, 1863).
Size: To 6" (15 cm).
Range: Alaska to San Diego, California.
Habitat: On and under rocks, intertidal to 165' (50 m).
Description: Yellow to orange with dark tubercles.
Comments: Species is common. It eats crumb of bread sponges and other sponges.

RED SPONGE NUDIBRANCH
Rostanga pulchra MacFarland, 1905.
Size: To 5/8" (1.5 cm).
Range: Point Craven, Alaska to Baja California; Chile.
Habitat: On red-orange sponges, intertidal and shallow subtidal to 60' (18 m).
Description: Oval. Uniform orange to red, sometimes with brown to black spots. Rings of similarly coloured eggs are often seen nearby.
Comments: Species is often found feeding on the velvety red sponge (see p. 24) in intertidal areas. It is well camouflaged against the sponge.

GIANT WHITE DORID

Archidoris odhneri (MacFarland, 1966).
Alternate name: White knight dorid.
Size: To 8" (20 cm).
Range: Kenai Peninsula, Alaska to Point Loma, California.
Habitat: On rocks and sponges, intertidal to 75' (23 m).
Description: Bright white body with many small tubercles.
Comments: Species eats sponges, including bread crumb sponges (see p. 24) and *Myxilla* spp. (see pp. 22, 24).

LEOPARD DORID

Diaulula sandiegensis (Cooper, 1863).
Alternate names: San Diego dorid; ring-spotted dorid; tar spot nudibranch.
Size: To 3" (7.5 cm).
Range: Unalaska Island, Alaska to Baja California.
Habitat: On rocks and sponges, intertidal to 115' (35 m).
Description: Oval-elongated white body with very fine tubercles; light to dark brown rings, occasionally without spots.
Comments: Species eats sponges: bread crumb (see p. 24), purple encrusting (p. 23) and *Neoesperiopsis* spp. (p. 26). Also found in Japan.

CLOWN DORID

Triopha catalinae (Cooper, 1863).
Alternate names: *Triopha carpenteri; Catalina triopha.*
Size: To 6" (15 cm).
Range: Aleutian Islands to Baja California.
Habitat: On rocks, intertidal to 115' (35 m).
Description: Slender white body with orange on rhinophores, front veil of tubercles, body tubercles and gills.
Comments: Species eats spiral bryozoans (see p. 62). It is also found in Japan.

HUDSON'S (YELLOW-MARGIN) DORID

Acanthodoris hudsoni MacFarland, 1905.
Size: To 3/4" (2 cm).
Range: Three Entrance Bay, Alaska to San Diego, California.
Habitat: On rocks, intertidal and shallow subtidal.
Description: Yellow margin, yellow-tipped papillae. Long rhinophores.
Comments: Species feeds on bryozoans (see p. 58).

NANAIMO (RED GILLED) DORID

Acanthodoris nanaimoensis O'Donoghue, 1921.
Size: To 1 1/4" (3 cm).
Range: Alaska to Santa Barbara, California.
Habitat: On rocks, intertidal to shallow subtidal.
Description: White body, sometimes speckled; yellow margin; long yellow-tipped papillae; maroon colour on branchial plume and rhinophores.
Comments: Species eats soft colonial bryozoans, *Alcyonidium*.

YELLOW MARGIN DORID

Cadlina luteomarginata MacFarland, 1966.
Size: To 1 3/4" (4.5 cm).
Range: Lynn Canal, Alaska to Point Eugenia, Mexico.
Habitat: On rocks and sponges, intertidal to 150' (45 m).
Description: White body with yellow margin; large low tubercles tipped with yellow.
Comments: Species feeds on a wide variety of sponges.

BARNACLE NUDIBRANCH

Onchidoris bilamellata (Linnaeus, 1767).
Alternate name: Rough-mantled doris.
Size: To 3/4" (2 cm).
Range: Alaska to Baja California.
Habitat: On rocks and barnacles, intertidal to shallow subtidal.
Description: Oval; cream-coloured with pale to dark brown pattern on rough back.

Comments: Species has been found in large numbers on barnacles, feeding and laying ribbons of eggs.

Dendronotids

Dendronotids have numerous branching cerata or gill tufts along the margins (*Dendronotus* means "tree-back"). The rhinophores on the head are covered by a cup-like sheath.

WHITE DENDRONOTID

Dendronotus albus MacFarland, 1966.
Size: To 1 3/8" (3.4 cm).
Range: Kenai Peninsula, Alaska to Los Coronas Islands, Baja California.
Habitat: On rocks and hydroids, intertidal to 100' (30 m).
Description: White body; all processes are white at base and tipped with white or orange. A white stripe runs down back and tail, from the fourth pair of tufts, through the last pair of gill tufts, of which there are up to 7 pairs.

DALL'S DENDRONOTID

Dendronotus dalli Bergh, 1879.
Etymology: Named in honour of William Healy Dall.
Size: To 5 1/2" (14 cm).
Range: Bering Sea to Puget Sound.
Habitat: On rocks and stalked bryozoans (see p. 58).
Description: White to pale pink body with branched appendages tipped with white.

Par姐

VARIABLE DENDRONOTID
Dendronotus diversicolor Robillard, 1970.
Size: To 2" (5 cm).
Range: Ketchikan, Alaska to Point Loma, California.
Habitat: On rocks and hydroids, shallow subtidal.
Description: White to lilac body; top third of gill tufts and other appendages tipped with white, orange or both. A white stripe runs down the tail only, from last pair of gill tufts.

Comments: Species is very similar to white dendronotid (see p. 115), but larger and with fewer (4) rows of cerata.

GIANT DENDRONOTID
Dendronotus iris (Cooper, 1863).
Size: To 10" (25 cm).
Range: Unalaska Island, Alaska to Coronados Island, Baja California.
Habitat: In sand–mud, shallow subtidal to 655' (200 m).
Description: Large, with long branched processes on back; frontal veil of 4 paired appendages. Colour varies from white to grey, orange or red. A white line runs along foot margin.
Comments: Species feeds on the tentacles of tube-dwelling anemone (see p. 45), often lays loosely looped eggs on the tube and is sometimes pulled into it. The animal can swim if disturbed.

GIANT RED DENDRONOTID
Dendronotus rufus O'Donoghue, 1921.
Size: To 11" (28 cm).
Range: Auke Bay, Alaska to Puget Sound.
Habitat: On rocks and algae, in shallows.
Description: White, often with red-maroon dots; all appendages have red-maroon tips.
Comments: Species is found in winter. It lays coils of eggs in the shallows.

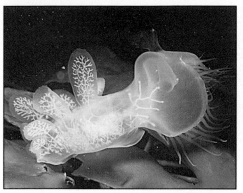

HOODED NUDIBRANCH

Melibe leonina (Gould, 1852).
Alternate name: Lion nudibranch.
Etymology: *leonina* = lionine, referring to hood tentacles resembling a lion's mane.
Size: To 4" (10 cm).
Range: Kodiak, Alaska to Baja California.
Habitat: On rocks, eelgrass and kelp, intertidal to shallow subtidal.
Description: Translucent, yellow-brown to green-brown and spotted. Slender body has paddle-like appendages and large hood with 2 fringes of tentacles to capture prey.
Comments: Species feeds on small crustaceans. It swims when disturbed.

ORANGE PEEL NUDIBRANCH

Tochuina tetraquetra (Pallas, 1788).
Size: To 12" (30 cm).
Range: Alaska to Los Angeles, California.
Habitat: On rocks, shallow subtidal.
Description: Brilliant yellow with white tubercles and a margin of white branchial tufts.
Comments: Species feeds on various hydroids, soft coral and orange sea pens. It is also found in Russia, where it is called *tocni* and eaten raw or cooked. This is the largest nudibranch in the world.

PINK TRITONIA

Tritonia diomedea Bergh, 1894.
Size: To 8 3/4" (22 cm).
Range: Aleutian Islands to Panama.
Habitat: In sand–mud, shallow subtidal.
Description: Pale to dark pink, broad-bodied. Gill tufts around the margin.
Comments: Species cuts down white sea pen (see p. 36) with scissor-like jaws. Also feeds on the orange sea pen (p. 36).

DIAMOND BACK TRITONIA

Tritonia festiva (Stearns, 1873).
Alternate name: Festive nudibranch.
Size: To 4" (10 cm).
Range: Kachemek Bay, Alaska to Coronados Island, Baja California.
Habitat: On rocks, hydroids and sponges, low intertidal to 165' (50 m).
Description: Slender, white, pink with fine white diamond pattern on the back, sometimes not visible. Head veil and branchial tufts along the side.
Comments: Species feeds on soft coral (see p. 37), orange sea pen (p. 36) and other cnidarians. Also found in Japan.

Arminacea

Most nudibranchs in this group have cerata, frontal veils and rhinophores without sheaths.

STRIPED NUDIBRANCH

Armina californica (Cooper, 1863).
Alternate name: California armina.
Size: To 2³/₄" (7 cm).
Range: Gulf of Alaska to Panama.
Habitat: On or partially buried in sand–mud, shallow subtidal to 755' (226 m).
Description: Smooth, brown body with raised white longitudinal ridges. No visible branchial appendages.
Comments: Individuals and groups are often found feeding on orange sea pens (see p. 36).

WHITE-LINED DIRONA

Dirona albolineata MacFarland, 1905.
Alternate names: Alabaster nudibranch; chalk-line dirona.
Etymology: *albolineata* = white line.
Size: To 7" (17.5 cm).
Range: Kachemak Bay, Alaska to San Diego, California.
Habitat: On rocks and occasionally on mud, intertidal to 115' (35 m).
Description: Grey, white to purple translucent body with white lines; large, flattened, pointed cerata. Eggs are coiled.
Comments: Species feeds on stalked bryozoans, snails (it cracks the shells with its jaws) and other organisms. It is also found in Russia and Japan.

GOLD DIRONA

Dirona aurantia Hurst, 1966.
Alternate name: Orange dirona.
Etymology: *aurantia* = golden,
referring to orange colour.
Size: To 5" (12.5 cm).
Range: Norton Sound, Alaska to
Puget Sound.
Habitat: On rocks, kelp and mud,
shallow subtidal.
Description: Orange body with
white lines and tips on bulbous cera-
ta; white spots on body.
Comments: Species feeds on bry-
ozoans and other organisms.

Aeolids

These nudibranchs typically have long oral tentacles, pairs of long, fleshy rhinophores, and many cerata on the back containing branches of the digestive gland. The animal preys on hydroids and anemones, stores the stinging capsules of its prey in the cerata, then uses the capsules as a defence.

SHAGGY MOUSE (AEOLID) NUDIBRANCH

Aeolidia papillosa (Linnaeus, 1761).
Size: To 2³/8" (5.9 cm).
Range: Cosmopolitan, worldwide.
Habitat: On rocks, pilings and mudflats, intertidal to 2,500' (750 m).
Description: Bare back, numerous
crowded cerata along the sides. Grey-
brown body, usually with large, triangular white patch at front of head region.

Comments: Species feeds on short plumose (see p. 41) and other anemones.

PEARLY (AEOLID) NUDIBRANCH

Flabellina japonica Volodchenko, 1941.
Alternate names: *Coryphella
salmonacea*; salmon aeolid.
Size: To 3" (7.5 cm).
Range: Circumboreal; Arctic to
Vancouver.
Habitat: On rocks, shallow subtidal.
Description: Pearly cream to pink
with bare back and densely packed
cerata on margins.
Comments: This nudibranch is a
winter species. It sheds its cerata

when disturbed. Also found in Russia and Sea of Japan.

Red Aeolids

A number of aeolid nudibranchs have maroon to red cerata, with white tips. Those in the genus *Flabellina* have the front of the foot expanded into lateral tentacles which separates them from similarly coloured species.

THREE-LINED (AEOLID) NUDIBRANCH
Flabellina trilineata (O'Donoghue, 1921).
Alternate name: Formerly known as *Coryphella trilineata*.
Size: To 1³/₈" (3.4 cm).
Range: Lisianski Inlet, Alaska to Baja California.
Habitat: On rocks and hydroids (see pp. 29–34), low intertidal to 65' (20 m) or greater.
Description: Very slender. 3 lines run down the back. Light orange to red cerata in well-spaced clusters. Rhinophores have distinct rings.
Comments: Species is common. It feeds on pink mouth hydroids (see pp. 32–33) and others.

RED FLABELLINA
Flabellina triophina (Bergh, 1894).
Alternate name: Formerly known as *Coryphella fusca*.
Etymology: *fusc* = dusky, brown.
Size: To 4" (20 cm).
Range: Port Valdez, Alaska to Oregon.
Habitat: On rocks, mud or hydroids (see pp. 29–34), shallow subtidal.
Description: Long, pointed head; translucent white body has pinkish cerata with white tips, inserted continuously on flanges along the sides. Faint bars on rhinophores. Eggs are coiled.
Comments: Species' head is longer and thicker than that of the verrucose aeolid (below).

VERRUCOSE AEOLID
Flabellina verrucosa (M. Sars, 1829).
Alternate name: Formerly known as *Coryphella rufibranchialis*.
Etymology: *verrucosa* = studded with wart-like protuberances, referring to wrinkly rhinophores.
Size: To 4" (20 cm).
Range: Port Valdez, Alaska to Oregon.
Habitat: On rocks, hydroids (see pp. 29–34) and various other habitats, shallow subtidal.
Description: Short, rounded head; translucent white body. Cerata in ill-defined clusters; brick-red with white tips.
Comments: Species' head is shorter and rounder than that of the red flabellina (above). Its rhinophores are wrinkly.

OPALESCENT (AEOLID) NUDIBRANCH

Hermissenda crassicornis (Eschscholtz, 1831).
Size: To 2" (5 cm).
Range: Kodiak Island, Alaska to Baja California.
Habitat: On rocks, eelgrass beds, floats and various other habitats, intertidal to 115' (35 m).
Description: Slender; numerous cerata topped with orange band and white tips. Orange areas on back, bordered by blue, but colours vary.
Comments: Species is common and abundant. It feeds on a variety of organisms, including hydroids. It is also found in Japan.

Octopus, Squid Class Cephalopoda

This class of marine species—about 600 to 650 altogether—includes the octopus, squid and some species with external shells, such as the nautilus. The cephalopod's head has a mouth with a beak—like a parrot's beak—for feeding. Its foot is developed into a number of arms, equipped with suckers, surrounding the mouth. Squid have two additional long appendages, called tentacles. Cephalopods are well known for their colour-changing abilities. Many experts believe these are the most advanced invertebrates, capable of learning complex behaviours.

GIANT PACIFIC OCTOPUS

Octopus dofleini (Wülker, 1910).
Size: Mantle to 8" (20 cm), arm span to 30' (9 m).
Range: Bering Sea to California.
Habitat: On sandy and rocky shores, intertidal to 330' (100 m).
Description: 8 arms of equal length; species changes colour from pale to dark reddish-brown or mottled patterns. Large, globular body; head has no fins.
Comments: This is the largest octopus in the world, reported to weigh up to 600 lbs (272 kg). It is also found in Japan. The female guards strings of eggs attached to the roof of the den (left).

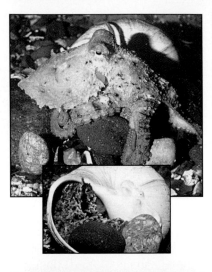

RED OCTOPUS

Octopus rubescens (Berry, 1953).
Size: Mantle to 4" (10 cm).
Range: Alaska to Baja California; Gulf of California.
Habitat: In sand and rocky areas; intertidal to 660' (200 m).
Description: Arms are four times body length. Dull red to red-brown, mottled with white. Rough skin; not folded as in giant Pacific octopus (see p. 121).
Comments: Species is often found in prawn traps. Some use old bottles or moonsnail shells as dens.

STUBBY SQUID

Rossia pacifica Berry, 1911.
Alternate name: Short squid.
Size: Mantle to 1¹/₂" (4 cm), 8 arms and 2 tentacles about mantle length.
Range: Bering Sea to California.
Habitat: In sand–mud and shrimp grounds, subtidal, 50–1,215' (15–364 m).
Description: Short; reddish-brown with pale underside. Mantle to twice as long as wide; small semicircular fins.
Comments: Eggs are laid singly or in small clusters, from shallow to deep water. Species is also found in Japan.

OPAL SQUID

Loligo opalescens Berry, 1911.
Alternate name: Market squid.
Size: Mantle to 8" (20 cm), total length to 11" (28 cm).
Range: Northern BC to Mexico.
Habitat: In coastal waters; in shallow waters in sandy bays where species returns to spawn.
Description: 8 long arms with 2 short tentacles. Elongate; mantle has prominent fins. Colours change from translucent white to mottled brown and gold.
Comments: Species schools in large numbers in shallows to lay eggs. A commercial fishery has operated in California for some years. Minor fisheries are located in BC and elsewhere.

Chitons Class Polyplacophora

The class Polyplacophora ("bearing many plates") comprises 800 to 1,000 living marine species. Chitons (pronounced KY-tons) are oval, flattened animals comprised of 8 overlapping shell plates, or valves, bound together by a leathery girdle (polyplacophora means "bearing many plates"). The valves are jointed so that the chiton can roll up into a ball when disturbed, hence the common name "sea cradle." The valves of dead chitons often wash up on the shore, and are known to beachcombers as butterfly shells.

Chitons are strictly marine animals. There are approximately 500 to 600 species of chitons worldwide and more than 100 species (intertidal and subtidal) along the Pacific coast between the Aleutian Islands and Baja California.

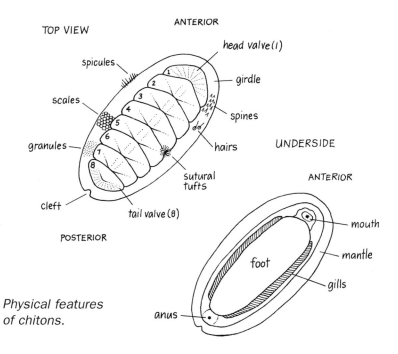

Physical features of chitons.

The chiton does not have eyes or tentacles, but its shell contains light-sensitive organs. Many species prefer very low light and are nocturnal, living only in crevices and on the undersides of rocks or embedded under rocks in sand. With its muscular foot, much like the foot of a snail, the chiton attaches to surfaces and moves along the contours of the sea bottom, scraping algae and animal life from rocks with its radula (a rasping tongue-like strap). It moves very slowly: some chitons have been observed at the same site for 25 years.

The sexes are separate in chitons. Gametes are released into the water, where fertilization takes place, and a few species brood their eggs in grooves along the foot.

The black Katy chiton and the giant Pacific chiton (see p. 125) were important foods to Native peoples living along the coast. The experience of collecting, preparing and eating chitons was culturally significant to many communities, and chitons play a part in local traditional stories and legends.

LINED CHITON

Tonicella lineata (Wood, 1815).
Size: To 2" (5 cm).
Range: Aleutian Islands to Channel Islands, California.
Habitat: On rocks, grazing on encrusting coralline algae (see pp. 210–11). Often in depressions under purple sea urchins (see p. 145).
Description: Smooth, dark girdle, often banded with whitish, yellowish or orange blotches; red to orange-red to pink valves with dark zigzag lines edged with white.
Comments: Species is relatively common and distinct with bright colour patterns. It is often eaten by the ochre star (see p. 136) and six ray star (p. 136).

BLUE-LINE CHITON

Tonicella undocaerulea (Sirenko, 1973).
Alternate name: Often misidentified as the lined chiton, *T. lineata*.
Size: To 2" (5 cm).
Range: 57°N–34°N; Kodiak Island, Alaska to central California.
Habitat: On rocks grazing on coralline algae, intertidal and shallow subtidal.
Description: Light orange to pink valves with concentric white zigzag lines; brilliant blue zigzag lines in live specimens.

HAIRY CHITON

Mopalia ciliata (Sowerby, 1840).
Size: To 3" (7.5 cm).
Range: Alaska to Baja California.
Habitat: In protected areas, under rocks and sometimes in mussel beds, mid- to low intertidal.
Description: Elongated-oval; wide girdle bristly with soft hairs and clearly notched at rear end, varies in colour from dark to light. Valves, reduced in size, vary in colour, often with brilliant patterns of blotches and streaks.
Comments: Species feeds on algae, sponges, hydroids and bryozoans.

MOSSY CHITON
Mopalia muscosa (Gould, 1846).
Size: To 2³/4" (7 cm).
Range: Alaska to Isla Cedros, Baja California.
Habitat: Often in tidepools or on top of rocks, not affected by accumulations of silt.
Description: Oval; girdle has small, shallow notch at rear; stout, stiff hairs. Head valve has 10 beaded ribs; valves are dull, dark brown, grey to black, sometimes with white stripes. Light blue interior.

Comments: Species is common in intertidal areas, and moves only at night when submerged or wet. Its valves often bear barnacles, seaweeds or other growths. It feeds on algae.

BLACK KATY CHITON
Katharina tunicata (Wood, 1815).
Alternate names: Leather chiton; black chiton; aboriginals referred to it as sea prune or "small Chinese slippers."
Size: To 3" (7.5 cm).
Range: Alaska to southern California.
Habitat: Common in exposed wave-swept and current areas, mid-intertidal.
Description: Oval to elongated; smooth, black to brownish-black girdle covers about two-thirds of the white plates. Foot on underside is pink-red.

Comments: The female lays greenish eggs in the summertime. Species is not extremely sensitive to light and is often found in the open, feeding on algae. These chitons were eaten traditionally by Native people and are the subjects of many legends. The Haida believed they originated from the black beetle while the Manhousat on the west coast of Vancouver Island told of the transformation of a land slug to the black chiton.

GIANT PACIFIC CHITON
Cryptochiton stelleri (Middendorff, 1847).
Alternate names: Gumboot chiton; giant red chiton; moccasin chiton; butterfly shells. The Haida name for large specimens, SGIIDAA, translates to "lying face down forever."
Size: To 13" (33 cm) and more. This is the largest chiton in the world.
Range: Alaska to Channel Islands, California.
Habitat: Intertidal to 65' (20 m).
Description: Oval-elongated; brown to reddish brown granular girdle completely covers plates. Yellow underside with large broad foot. Juveniles, smaller than 1/2" (1 cm), are yellow and a tiny portion of the valves may be exposed.

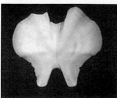

Comments: Species' radular teeth are covered with magnetite, to the extent that it can be picked up by a magnet. The snail *Ocinebrina lurida* eats and leaves yellow pits into the dorsal (upper) body surface. This species is edible and its large plates (left) are often found in middens.

CHAPTER 7

Sea Stars, Brittle Stars, Sea Cucumbers, Sea Urchins, Sand Dollars, Feather Stars

PHYLUM ECHINODERMATA

The phylum Echinodermata ("spiny-skinned") comprises 6,000 living marine species of sea stars, brittle stars, sea cucumbers, sea urchins, sand dollars and feather stars (sea lilies), among other animals. Approximately 180 species of echinoderms live in the Pacific Northwest region. They are prolific, with impressive numbers of both species and individuals.

PHYSICAL FEATURES

Echinoderms come in a variety of body shapes, but all exhibit both a radial symmetry and a five-part symmetry, and all have tubular appendages called tube feet. Many sea stars have very small jaw-like appendages (pedicellariae) that keep the upper surface clean of small settling organisms. Sea cucumbers have tiny crystals of calcium carbonate (ossicles), feature that can help in identifying species.

The mouth of the sea star, brittle star, sea urchin and sand dollar is on the underside; the mouth of the sea cucumber is at one end; and the mouth of the feather star is on the upper surface.

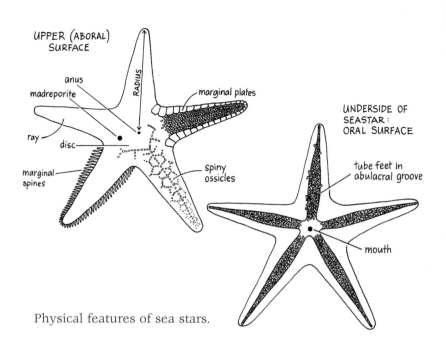

UPPER (ABORAL) SURFACE

anus

madreporite

RADIUS

marginal plates

ray

disc

marginal spines

spiny ossicles

UNDERSIDE OF SEASTAR: ORAL SURFACE

tube feet in abulacral groove

mouth

Physical features of sea stars.

PREY–PREDATORS

Echinoderms, especially sea stars and sea urchins, play an important part in the ecology of the seashore, affecting species distribution by their voracious predation.

Some echinoderms forage for live or dead animals, seaweed drift or bottom sediments. Others feed on particles drifting by in the water. Aquaculturists growing mussels, clams, oysters and scallops often regard sea stars as significant pests. At one time in Britain, fishermen were fined for not treading on or throwing ashore a "five-finger," which ate the favoured oysters. Sea urchins consume algae to such an extent that heavily grazed areas are sometimes referred to as "sea urchin barrens."

The major predators of echinoderms are the sea stars themselves, sea birds, sea otters and human beings—who take sea stars for ornaments, and who operate commercial sea urchin and sea cucumber fisheries all over the world. In the Pacific Northwest, there are fisheries for the purple sea urchin, red sea urchin, green sea urchin and California sea cucumber.

ATTACHMENT AND LOCOMOTION

Many echinoderms take water into the body through a sieve plate (madreporite), and an internal hydraulic system operates the tube feet. The tips of the sea stars attach and release with a duo-gland system of adhesion and release, not suction. Brittle stars do not use the tube feet for locomotion, but move by a writhing motion of the rays. Sea cucumbers use both the tube feet and muscles in the body wall to move around, to anchor in a position, and to activate escape responses to predators. Feather stars attach to the sea bottom with a stalk.

REPRODUCTION

Sexes are separate for most species, and gametes are discharged into the water for external fertilization. A few species reproduce by division of the parent body into new individuals. Some sea stars brood their young around the mouth. A few species are hermaphroditic.

Sea stars exhibit remarkable regeneration: with a portion of the central disc intact, the animal can recover and grow a full new body.

Sea Stars Class Asteroidea

There are some 2,000 species of sea stars inhabiting the intertidal to 24,000' (7,245 m) worldwide, and approximately 150 species between Point Barrow, Alaska and San Diego, California. Lambert (1981) describes 36 species in BC from the near shore to the outer edge of the continental shelf, 650' (200 m).

Many sea stars have 5 "arms," or "rays," but the number of arms is variable by species. The sun stars (*Solaster* spp.) have 7–14 rays, while the sunflower star has as many as 15–24 rays. The arm radius is measured from the centre of the disk to the tip of the arm (see figure, p. 127).

SPINY MUDSTAR
Luidia foliolata Grube, 1866.
Alternate name: Sandstar.
Size: Arm radius to 12" (30 cm).
Range: Southeast Alaska to San Diego, California.
Habitat: On mud and sand, often half-buried, intertidal to 2,010' (603 m).
Description: Disc and 5 long, flattened rays. Upper surface dull grey to brown, white marginal spines. Underside tube feet yellow to orange.
Comments: Pointed tube feet are typical of sea stars found on mud to sand. Those on rocks have strong flat discs on tips of tube feet. The mudstar in the photo is regenerating a ray.

MUDSTAR

Ctenodiscus crispatus (Verrill, 1909).
Size: Arm radius to 2" (5 cm).
Range: Circumpolar, Arctic to Panama; possibly to Chile.
Habitat: On soft mud, sand to rock, 35' (10.5 m) to 6,200' (1,860 m).
Description: Almost pentagonal with distinct marginal plates, elevated cone in centre. Grey to yellow-white.
Comments: Species eats mud as well as organisms in the mud, such as small bivalves and worms, and absorbs organic compounds from them.

COOKIE STAR

Ceramaster patagonicus (Sladen, 1889).
Size: Arm radius to 3" (7.5 cm).
Range: Bering Sea to Cape Horn, South America.
Habitat: On rocks and mud, often in inlets, 33–800' (10–240 m).
Description: Often slightly swollen and soft to the touch. Creamy orange to red-orange.

ARCTIC COOKIE STAR

Ceramaster arcticus (Verrill, 1909).
Size: Arm radius to 2 1/4" (5.5 cm).
Range: Bering Sea to southern Vancouver Island; more common north of Kodiak Island, Alaska.
Habitat: On shallow rocks to mud in deeper waters, intertidal to 610' (183 m).
Description: Flattened, stiff and firm to the touch. Pale orange, often with red patches.
Comments: Relatively rare south of Alaska. Smaller than cookie star (above).

SPINY RED STAR

Hippasteria spinosa Verrill, 1909.
Size: Arm radius to 6⅝" (17 cm).
Range: Kodiak Island, Alaska to southern California.
Habitat: On sand, mud, shell and rock, 33–1,680' (10–504 m).
Description: 5 rays; large prominent tapering spines over body. Red to orange.
Comments: Feeds primarily on orange sea pen (see p. 36), but also white plumose anemones (p. 41), zoanthids (p. 40), tunicates and worms.

VERMILION STAR

Mediaster aequalis Stimpson, 1857.
Alternate name: Equal-arm star.
Size: Arm radius to 4" (10 cm).
Range: Chagnik Bay, Alaska to southern California.
Habitat: Often on rocks, intertidal to 960' (288 m).
Description: Large flat disc and 5 broad rays. Vermilion.
Comments: Similar to gunpowder star (below), but different in colour.

GUNPOWDER STAR

Gephyreaster swifti (Fisher 1905).
Size: Arm radius to 8" (20 cm).
Range: Aleutian Islands to Washington; more common in northern BC and Alaska.
Habitat: On rock and sand, 15' (4 m) to 1130' (344 m).
Description: 5 rays outlined by conspicuous marginal plates. Pale pink-orange. Distinctive odour similar to gunpowder.
Comments: Larger and paler than vermilion star (above). Feeds on anemones, particularly plumose anemone (see p. 41) and sometimes spotted swimming anemone (p. 46).

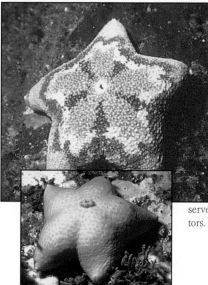

CUSHION STAR

Pteraster tesselatus Ives, 1888.
Alternate name: Slime star.
Size: Arm radius to 4³/4" (12 cm).
Range: Bering Sea to Monterey Bay, California.
Habitat: On broken or solid rock at 30–1,435' (9–435 m).
Description: 5 short stubby rays; slightly elevated central pore, rather than closed sieve plate (madreporite) on topside. Yellow to tan and grey, sometimes with checkered patterns.
Comments: Species releases copious amounts of thick, gelatinous mucus that serves as protection against fish and other predators. Has been observed feeding on sponges.

WRINKLED STAR

Pteraster militaris (O.F. Müller, 1776).
Alternate name: Slime star.
Size: Arm radius to 3" (7.5 cm).
Range: Circumpolar, Arctic to Oregon.
Habitat: On rocks in shallows to mud at depths, 30–3,630' (9–1,100 m).
Description: Soft, fleshy wrinkled surface with large pore in top centre. Cream to yellow to pink.
Comments: Feeds on sponges and hydrocorals. Broods 30–40 juvenile sea stars internally.

STRIPED SUNSTAR

Solaster stimpsoni Verrill, 1880.
Etymology: *Sol/aster* = sun/star.
Alternate name: Stimpson's sunstar.
Size: Arm radius to 10" (25 cm).
Range: South Bering Sea to Oregon.
Habitat: On rocks and other surfaces, to 2,000' (600 m); often intertidal.
Description: Typically 10 (sometimes 9) long, slim, tapering rays. Each ray has dark purple-blue stripe bordered by blue, pink, red or orange.
Comments: The most common sunstar and one of the most beautiful intertidal stars. Feeds on a variety of sea cucumbers, sea squirts and other invertebrates. Does not appear to feed on other sea stars.

MORNING SUNSTAR

Solaster dawsoni Verrill, 1880.
Alternate name: Dawson's sea star.
Size: Arm radius to 8" (20 cm).
Range: Point Franklin, Alaska to Monterey Bay, California.
Habitat: Typically on rocks but also on gravel and sand, intertidal to 1,380' (414 m).
Description: Broad disc and 8–15 long tapering rays. Brown-orange, occasionally red or mottled brown-orange.
Comments: A common species. Often preys on other sea stars, even its own species, and elicits escape responses. It is also known to eat sea cucumbers and the diamond back nudibranch (see p. 118).

NORTHERN SUNSTAR

Solaster endeca (Linnaeus, 1771).
Alternate name: Smooth sunstar.
Size: Arm radius to 8" (20 cm).
Range: Alaska to Puget Sound.
Habitat: Shallow rocky areas to deeper pebbles and mud, intertidal to 1,567' (475 m).
Description: Broad disc and 7–13 (usually 9–11) short, "fat," quickly tapering rays. Typically red-orange, occasionally with purple at tips or purple stripe down the ray similar to striped sunstar (see p. 131).
Comments: Uncommon. Does not elicit escape responses of the morning star or sunflower star.

ORANGE SUNSTAR

Solaster paxillatus Sladen, 1889.
Size: Arm radius to 7¹/₂" (19 cm).
Range: Bering Sea to northern Oregon.
Habitat: On rock, gravel and mud, 35–2,100' (10.5–630 m).
Description: 8–10 broad, quickly tapering rays. Orange to yellow.
Comments: A relatively rare find in BC.

ROSE STAR

Crossaster papposus (Linnaeus, 1767).
Alternate names: Spiny sunstar;
snowflake star.
Etymology: *Cross/aster* = fringed/star;
papposus = downy.
Size: Arm radius to 7" (18 cm).
Range: Circumpolar, Arctic to
Washington.
Habitat: Often on rocks, intertidal to
1,080' (324 m).
Description: 8–16 rays. Typically has
concentric rings of bright red, orange,
white or yellow on a purple background.
White underside.

Comments: Eats anemones, sea pens and sometimes small sea stars whole.

BAT STAR

Asterina miniata Sladen, 1889.
Alternate names: Sea bat; broad disc
sea star; *Patiria miniata* (Brandt, 1835).
Etymology: *Aster* = star; *miniata* = ver-
milion; *Patir* = from *pater* = dish.
Size: Arm radius to 4" (10 cm).
Range: Sitka, Alaska to Gulf of
California.
Habitat: On rocks, sand and mud, on
exposed coasts, not in surf; intertidal to
990' (300 m).
Description: 3–8 rays, typically 5–6.
Rough granular surface and web-footed
appearance. Red, blue, yellow, green
and/or brown, solid or in patterns.

Comments: Abundant and common. Hosts a number of polychaete worms (see p. 55) on the underside.

LEATHER STAR

Dermasterias imbricata (Grube, 1857).
Alternate name: Garlic star.
Size: Arm radius to 6" (15 cm).
Range: Sitka, Alaska to La Jolla, California.
Habitat: On rocks in protected waters, intertidal
to 300' (90 m).
Description: Smooth, slick leather-like surface.
Garlic-like odour. Upper surface grey with patches
of red, brown and purple.
Comments: Feeds on many and various
animals, including sea pens, anemones, sea
cucumbers and sea urchins. The anemone
Stomphia (see p. 46) has a dramatic escape
response to the touch of the leather star: it
will release its hold and actually swim away
in a thrashing fashion.

BLOOD STAR

Henricia leviuscula (Stimpson, 1857).
Alternate name: Pacific Henricia.
Size: Arm radius to 6¹/₄" (15.5 cm).
Range: Aleutian Islands to Turtle Bay, Baja California.
Habitat: On rocky surfaces, intertidal to 1,435' (435 m).
Description: Disc often has grey patch. Long, thin arms compared to most other sea stars; orange to brick red. 3 rows of plates along lower side of each ray.
Comments: Most common blood star of BC, of which there are likely several subspecies. It feeds primarily on sponges.

FAT HENRICIA

Henricia sanguinolenta (O. F. Müller, 1776).
Alternate names: Atlantic blood star; blood star.
Size: Arm radius to 9¹/₄" (23 cm).
Range: Circumpolar, Arctic to Washington.
Habitat: On rock to mud, 50–7,875' (15–2,360 m).
Description: Long rays, fat and often creased where they leave disc. Often nearly white, sometimes lavender or pale orange. Small marginal plates along lower side of each ray do not form a distinct series.
Comments: Similar to blood star (above), but with a heavier body, and the rays are thickened at the base, forming a crease.

RIDGED BLOOD STAR

Henricia aspera Fisher 1906.
Size: Arm radius to 6¹/₄" (15.5 cm).
Range: Bering Sea south to Santa Barbara, California.
Habitat: On mud to sand to rock, typically in fjords of British Columbia, 20–2,970' (6–890 m).
Description: 5 long tapering rays. Distinctive lacy, net-like pattern forms ridges on upper surface. Yellow to purple or brown-red.
Comments: Rays are usually wider than those of the blood star (see p. 134).

SUNFLOWER STAR

Pycnopodia helianthoides (Brandt, 1835).
Etymology: *Pycno/podia* = Many-legged; *helianthoides* = sunflower.
Size: Arm radius to 18" (46 cm).
Range: Alaska to southern California.
Habitat: On rocky shores and many other surfaces, intertidal to 1,435' (435 m).
Description: Broad disc with up to 24 rays; juveniles typically start with 5 rays. Soft, flexible body, abundant surface spines, pincers and gills. Orange to mottled red-orange, purple and purple-grey.
Comments: Largest, softest and having the most rays of any northern Pacific species. Very fast-moving, up to 360' (110 m) per hour. Elicits escape responses from northern abalone (see p. 101) and swimming responses from swimming scallops (pp. 91–92), the California sea cucumber (p. 142) and giant dendronotid (p. 116). Often digs out butter clams and leaves pits in sandy areas.

MOTTLED STAR

Evasterias troschelii (Stimpson, 1862).
Alternate name: False ochre star.
Size: Radius to 11" (28 cm).
Range: Alaska to Monterey, California; less common south of Puget Sound.
Habitat: On rocks and cobble, sometimes on sand, intertidal to 230' (70 m).
Description: Similar to ochre star but smaller disc; 5 longer and more tapered arms; less pronounced spines on upper surface. Colour variable from rust, brown and orange to blue-grey.
Comments: Elicits escape response from the plate limpet and the keyhole limpet. Scale worms (see p. 55) often live in the underside grooves of the rays.

135

SIX RAY STAR

Leptasterias hexactis (Stimpson, 1862).
Alternate names: Six-armed star; brooding star; = *Leptasterias aequalis*.
Size: Arm radius to 2" (5 cm).
Range: Alaska to Washington.
Habitat: Under rocks and in crevices, intertidal to 150' (45 m).
Description: Highly variable in appearance. Species is the only small 6-ray star in BC–Washington waters, except for the occasional juvenile ochre star. Rays are broad at the base and quickly taper to blunt tips. Colour ranges from grey, green, pink, purple to orange.
Comments: Females raise their bodies in a hunched posture to brood golden-yellow eggs, December to March. Species is highly variable in appearance and the taxonomy of it is uncertain: there may be more than one species, and not all have 6 rays.

OCHRE STAR

Pisaster ochraceus (Brandt, 1835).
Alternate names: Purple sea star; common sea star.
Size: Arm radius to 7" (18 cm).
Range: Sitka, Alaska to Cedros Island, Baja California.
Habitat: Often in clusters, intertidal in mussel beds or on rocks, to 290' (87 m).
Description: 5 rays, thick and very stiff body. Shorter, thicker rays than mottled star (see p. 135). Purple, orange, yellow to brown with a network of white spines.
Comments: Common, obvious and abundant. Feeds on mussels, barnacles, limpets and snails. With its life span of 20 years or more, this may be the longest-living sea star in the region.

SPINY PINK STAR

Pisaster brevispinus (Stimpson, 1857).
Alternate name: Short-spined sea star.
Etymology: *brevi/spinus* = short/spined.
Size: Arm radius to 12 1/2" (32 cm).
Range: Sitka, Alaska to Santa Barbara, California.
Habitat: On soft surfaces, intertidal to 335' (102 m).
Description: 5 large, stiff rays. Pink to grey.
Comments: Can stretch tube feet to excavate and capture bivalves. Commonly takes butter clams, littlenecks and ribbed clams. The purple olive snail (p. 110) exhibits a strong escape response to this star.

PAINTED STAR

Orthasterias koehleri (de Loriol, 1897).
Alternate names: *O. columbiana* Verrill, 1914; long-armed sea star; rainbow star.
Size: Arm radius to 10" (25 cm).
Range: Yakutat Bay, Alaska to Santa Rosa Island, California.
Habitat: On sand–shell to rock, intertidal to 770' (230 m).
Description: 5 long rays. Prominent white or purple spines, reddish banding between white-cream patches.

Comments: Often feeds on the ribbed clam and on rock oysters (false-jingles) (see p. 90). Hosts commensal worms, usually in the underside grooves of the rays.

LONG RAY STAR

Stylasterias forreri (de Loriol, 1887).
Alternate names: Black star; fish-eating star.
Size: Arm radius to 13" (33 cm).
Range: Southeast Alaska to San Diego, California.
Habitat: On rocky surfaces to shell–gravel, 20–1,745' (6–520 m).
Description: Species is the only long-rayed black sea star in Pacific Northwest waters. 5 very long rays, black to grey with grey wreaths of pincers (pedicellariae) and white spines.
Comments: Species feeds on gastropods and chitons; moves as fast as 62' (19 m) per hour; captures fish when they accidentally land on the surface and get snared by the pedicellariae (jaw-like appendages).

Brittle Stars, Basket Stars Class Ophiuroidea

There are more than 2,000 species of brittle stars, or ophiuroids (*ophus* means "snake"), sometimes called "serpent stars" because of the snakelike shape and movement of the rays. A typical species has five long, brittle rays joined to a flattened central disc, but some species have six to eight arms. Unlike sea stars, brittle stars do not have pedicellariae (pinching structures), and the tube feet, which are used only in feeding, do not have suckers. They are both deposit and suspension feeders, and they move by a writhing or "rowing" motion of the rays. Brittle stars of a single species often cluster together in large numbers in a tangled web. Individuals drop off portions of their rays when disturbed, hence the term "brittle."

Basket stars capture food by extending a forest of arms into the currents.

DAISY BRITTLE STAR

Ophiopholis aculeata (Linnaeus, 1767).
Alternate name: Painted brittle star.
Size: Disc to 7/8" (2.2 cm) diameter, arm radius to 31/2" (9 cm).
Range: Bering Sea to Santa Barbara, California.
Habitat: Under rocks or in kelp holdfasts, intertidal to 5,435' (1,630 m).
Description: Scalloped disc, long, broad rays with blunt spines; lobes between the rays. Variable colours and patterns: spots, lines and bands of pink, red, orange, blue, green, grey and black.
Comments: Variability in colour may confuse gulls and other predators.

LONG ARM BRITTLE STAR

Amphioda urtica (Lyman, 1860).
Size: Disc to 3/4" (2 cm) diameter, arm length to 6" (15 cm) or more.
Range: Alaska to Baja California.
Habitat: In sand–mud, intertidal to 5,330' (1,600 m).
Description: Smooth disc and long rays. Yellow-brown with white markings, occasional red marks.
Comments: One of the largest and most common brittle stars found in sand–mud. Occurs in high densities, to 1,500 per square metre. A similar species, *A. periecta*, is shown here (lower photo) in a spawning position in March.

GREY BRITTLE STAR

Ophiura lütkeni (Lyman, 1860).
Size: Disc to 3/4" (2 cm) diameter; arm radius to 6" (15 cm).
Range: Alaska to Mexico.
Habitat: In sand–mud, intertidal and subtidal.
Description: Grey, green-grey or blue-grey with dark bands on rays.

BASKET STAR

Gorgonocephalus eucnemis (Müller & Troschel, 1842).
Etymology: *Gorgonocephalus* = Gorgon's/head.
Size: To 18" (46 cm) diameter.
Range: Bering Sea to Laguna Beach, California.
Habitat: On rocks in current, subtidal 33–6,600' (10–2,000 m).
Description: 5 arms branching into thousands of branchlets. White to tan, beige, orange-red, pink mottling.
Comments: Young are often associated with soft coral (see p. 37).

Sea Cucumbers Class Holothuroidea

The typical sea cucumber is an elongated animal. It has a mouth at one end, bearing one or two circles of tentacles, and an anus at the other. Five rows of tube feet running along the body are used to hold a position or to move about. In sedentary species, the tube feet may be limited to the bottom or one side of the animal, where it holds to the sea floor. Microscopic calcite plates (ossicles), found in the body wall, are key identifying features for many species.

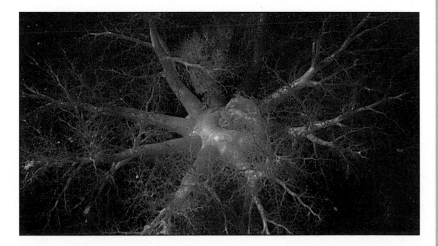

Worldwide there are 700 species of sea cucumbers described (some as long as 6.6'/2 m), 30 to 40 of them between southeast Alaska and southern California. The identification of the many similar white sea cucumbers and others can be aided by Lambert's (1997) handbook. Some can be identified by colour, shape and external features in the field but many require closer examination.

PREY–PREDATORS

Many sea cucumbers are mostly sedentary suspension feeders, gathering food that passes in the currents. Others are free-moving and are surface grazers or deposit feeders.

The major predators of sea cucumbers are sea stars and fishes.

REPRODUCTION

Sea cucumbers typically have separate sexes. A few brood their young, but most are aggregated and reproduce by broadcasting eggs and sperm into the water.

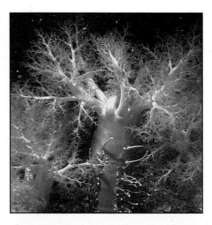

ORANGE SEA CUCUMBER

Cucumaria miniata (Brandt, 1835).
Alternate names: Red, vermilion sea cucumber.
Etymology: *miniata* = bright red.
Size: To 8" (20 cm) long.
Range: Aleutian Islands to southern California.
Habitat: Body in between rocks with tentacles showing, intertidal to 740' (222 m).
Description: 10 tentacles of equal size, bushy and orange-red to brown. Orange body with rows of brown tube feet.
Comments: Common and abundant in current areas.

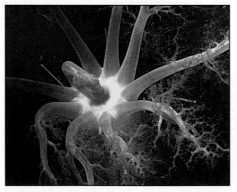

PALE SEA CUCUMBER

Cucumaria pallida Kirkendale and Lambert, 1995.
Etymology: *pallida* = pale.
Size: To 10" (25 cm) long.
Range: Auke Bay, Alaska to Santa Rosa Island, California.
Habitat: Body in between rocks with tentacles showing, intertidal to 300' (90 m).
Description: 10 tentacles of equal size, pale orange to white. Similar to orange sea cucumber (above), but with thinner, wispier tentacles.
Comments: Tends to live in cleaner areas than the similar looking white sea cucumber (see p. 141).

WHITE SEA CUCUMBER

Eupentacta quinquesemita (Selenka, 1867) or *E. pseudoquinquesemita* Deichmann, 1938.
Alternate name: Stiff-footed sea cucumber.
Etymology: *quinquesemita* = five-foot paths.
Size: To 4" (10 cm) long.
Range: Sitka, Alaska to Baja California.
Habitat: In between rocks or exposed, especially in currents, intertidal to 180' (55 m).
Description: 8 large tentacles and 2 smaller ones (close examination is required to distinguish these). White body, sometimes with yellow or pink at bases of tentacles.
Comments: Two very similar species can be distinguished only by examination of ossicles (calcite plates) in the tissues. *E. quinquesemita* is more common in BC, *E. pseudoquinquesemita* in Alaska. Both are toxic to fish.

PEPPERED SEA CUCUMBER

Cucumaria piperata (Stimpson, 1864).
Etymology: *piperata* = peppered.
Size: To 4³/4" (12 cm) long.
Range: Queen Charlotte Islands, BC to Baja California.
Habitat: In between rocks and cobble, shallow subtidal to 450' (137 m).
Description: 10 tentacles of equal size. White-yellow with brown to black spots.

BLACK SEA CUCUMBER

Pseudocnus curatus (Cowles, 1907).
Alternate name: Formerly known as *Cucumaria curata*.
Etymology: *curatus* = to care for: refers to protection of juveniles by adults.
Size: To 1¹/8" (2.7 cm) long.
Range: Northern BC to southern California.
Habitat: On exposed rocky coasts, shallow subtidal.
Description: Black to brown body with light-coloured tube feet, more scattered than in rows.
Comments: Similar species forming mats in mussel beds are *Cucumaria pseudocurata*, with tube feet in rows, or *C. vegae*, found only in Alaska.

CALIFORNIA SEA CUCUMBER

Parastichopus californicus
(Stimpson, 1857).
Alternate name: Giant red sea cucumber.
Size: To 20" (50 cm) long.
Range: Gulf of Alaska to Cedros Island, Baja California.
Habitat: In a variety of habitats, intertidal to 820' (249 m).
Description: Large and small fleshy papillae (nipplelike projections). A circle of 20 bushy feeding tentacles at one end. Mottled brown-red body, rarely white; juveniles red. Light cream underside, often with commensal scale worm (*Arctonoe pulchra*).
Comments: This species, the largest sea cucumber in our waters, is harvested commercially for the 5 internal muscle strips and the body wall, which is processed and dried.

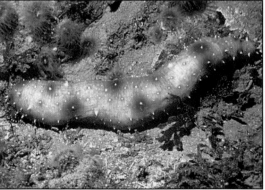

GIANT ORANGE SEA CUCUMBER

Parastichopus leukothele
Lambert, 1986.
Etymology:
leuko/thele = white/nipples (papillae).
Size: To 15" (37.5 cm) long.
Range: Queen Charlotte Islands, BC to Pt. Conception, California.
Habitat: In a variety of habitats, subtidal 65–935' (20–280 m).
Description: Small, white, fleshy papillae. 20 feeding tentacles arranged in two circles. Orange body with rusty patches. Lighter underside; tube feet tipped with orange.
Comments: Not abundant.

CREEPING PEDAL SEA CUCUMBER

Psolus chitonoides H. L. Clark, 1901.
Alternate names: Slipper sea cucumber; armored cucumber.
Etymology: *chitonoides* = resembling a chiton.
Size: To 2³/4" (7 cm) long.
Range: Aleutian Islands to Baja California.
Habitat: On rocks, in currents, intertidal to 810' (243 m).
Description: Dome-shaped body with overlapping plates. Underside has tube feet. Yellow to orange body with 10 brilliant orange tentacles; pale orange to white underside.
Comments: Eaten by a variety of sea stars.

PALE CREEPING PEDAL SEA CUCUMBER

Psolidium bidiscum Lambert, 1996.
Alternate name: Formerly thought to be *Psolidium bullatum* Ohshima, 1915.
Etymology: *bidiscum* = two discs: refers to the two different types of ossicles on the sole.
Size: To 1¹/4" (3 cm) long.
Range: Southeast Alaska to central California.
Habitat: On rocks, intertidal to 720' (216 m).
Description: Pink to pale purple body has fine overlapping plates. 10 translucent white tentacles with red-brown blotches: 8 larger (equal in size) and 2 smaller.
Comments: Species is newly described. *Psolidium bullatum* lives only in deep Alaskan waters.

SEA CUCUMBER

Chiridota sp.
Size: To 12" (30 cm) long.
Range: Southeast Alaska to central California.
Habitat: Partially buried in sand–mud, shallow subtidal to unknown depths.
Description: White, worm-like translucent body with large yellow-white bumps and smaller brown spots in longitudinal rows.
Comments: Poorly described from only a few specimens.

Sea Urchins, Sand Dollars Class Echinoidea

Unlike the other echinoderms, the echinoid has a globular or flattened disc-like body without rays or arms. It also has stalked pincers to keep the test clean, which discourages settling organisms, and in some cases to deter predators.

The Pacific Northwest has few species of echinoids relative to other regions of the world. Approximately 800 species of echinoids have been described.

PHYSICAL FEATURES

A sea urchin has a hard, calcareous skeleton called the test. The test is covered with spines, and a ball and socket joint allows the spines to move, in order to deter predators. Five double rows of tube feet protrude from holes running down the test; the urchin uses these tube feet to move and to attach to kelp and other objects. The standard measurement of sea urchins is their test (shell) diameter.

Sand dollars are flattened irregular sea urchins with reduced spines which typically incline backwards rather than standing erect. Some 150 species are found in the seas of the world, with a variety of common names including cake-urchins, sea-biscuits, keyhole urchins and six-hole urchins.

PREY–PREDATORS

Sea urchins feed primarily on kelps and algae but also eat animal matter. On the underside, the urchin has a ring of five calcareous teeth around the mouth, called "Aristotle's lantern" because its shape resembles that of an ancient lantern. Wastes are discharged from the anus, on the upper side.

The major predators of sea urchins and sand dollars are sea otters, sea stars, fishes and fishers.

REPRODUCTION

Sea urchins and sand dollars typically have separate sexes. Most are aggregated, and broadcast eggs and sperm into the water. Young red sea urchins (see p. 145) live under the protective spine canopies of the adults.

Sea Urchins Order Echinoidea

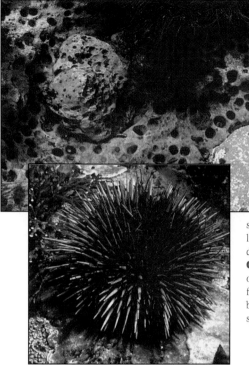

PURPLE SEA URCHIN

Strongylocentrotus purpuratus
(G. O. Sars, 1871).
Etymology:
Strongylocentrotus = ball of spines.
Size: Test (shell) diameter to 3½" (9 cm), to 1¾" (4.5 cm) high.
Range: Southern Alaska to Mexico.
Habitat: On rocks on exposed coasts, intertidal to 525' (160 m).
Description: Short purple spines to 1" (2.5 cm) in the intertidal; longer spines to 2³/8" (5.9 cm) subtidally.
Comments: Purple urchins in surf conditions often erode the rock and fit into the depressions. There has been interest in harvesting this species commercially.

RED SEA URCHIN

Strongylocentrotus franciscanus
(A. Agassiz, 1863).
Etymology:
Strongylocentrotus = ball of spines.
Size: Test (shell) diameter to 6" (15 cm), to 2" (5 cm) high.
Range: Alaska to Mexico.
Habitat: On rocky shores; intertidal to 300' (90 m).
Description: Long, sharp, abundant spines to 3" (7.5 cm). Red to purple-black.
Comments: Juveniles shelter under the spine canopy of adults (see inset photo) to avoid predators. Sea urchins graze extensively on drift and attached algae, creating "barrens." They are eaten by sea stars, fishes and sea otters. Commercial fisheries are located along the Pacific coast. The gonads are processed and shipped to Japan.

GREEN SEA URCHIN
Strongylocentrotus droebachiensis (O.F. Müller, 1776).
Etymology: *Strongylocentrotus* = ball of spines.
Size: Test (shell) diameter to 3¹/₂" (9 cm), to 1¹/₂" (4 cm) high.
Range: Circumpolar, Alaska to Washington.
Habitat: On rocky shores and in kelp beds, intertidal to 3,795' (1138 m).
Description: Short, crowded, pale green spines equal in size; dark tube feet. Sometimes a purple colour.
Comments: Species is a voracious feeder on algae and other organic matter. Harvested and shipped live to Japan, where gonads are processed for sushi.

WHITE SEA URCHIN
Strongylocentrotus pallidus (G. O. Sars, 1871).
Size: Test (shell) diameter to 3¹/₂" (9 cm), to 1¹/₄" (3 cm) high.
Range: Northern Alaska to Oregon.
Habitat: On rocks, subtidal to 65' (20 m) and deeper.
Description: Sparse white spines of different lengths; white tube feet.
Comments: More flattened than the green urchin (above), with sparser spines. Not abundant.

Sand Dollars: Order Clypeasteroida

ECCENTRIC SAND DOLLAR
Dendraster excentricus (Eschscholtz, 1831).
Alternate name: West coast sand dollar.
Etymology: *Dendr/aster* = tree/star; *excentricus* = off centre: refers to five-leaf petal-like pattern.
Size: To 4" (10 cm) diameter, ¹/₄" (6 mm) high.
Range: Alaska to Baja California.
Habitat: In sheltered habitats and open coast, in sand, intertidal to 130' (40 m).
Description: Flattened spines to ¹/₁₆" (2 mm) long on both surfaces. Star area (petaloid) is a series of holes arranged like petals of a flower, where the respiratory tube feet stick out. Lavender-grey, red-brown to purple-black. The white shell ("test") is commonly found washed up on the beach.
Comments: Common and abundant. Burrowing and locomotion are accomplished by spine movement rather than tube feet. Species is typically found oriented to the current patterns, flat or standing vertically in currents, with a third or more of the body buried. May live as long as 13 years. Eaten by starry flounder (see p. 174) and spiny pink star (p. 136).

Feather Stars (Sea Lilies) Class Crinoidea

There are approximately 600 species of crinoids worldwide, but only one feather star is commonly found in the shallow waters of the Pacific Northwest. The animal's feathery arms capture food, and the cilia and tube feet transport it along grooves to the mouth on the upper side of the cupped plate. Crinoids' arms fragment quickly when disturbed by predators, and are regenerated.

Living crinoids are small, relative to some fossil species that had stalks 80' (25 m) long!

FEATHER STAR

Florometra serratissima (A. H. Clark, 1907).
Size: To 10" (25 cm) high.
Range: Southern Alaska to South America.
Habitat: On rock walls in currents, 33–3,300' (10–990 m).
Description: 10 feathery arms, tan to reddish tan from a plate that has a ring of jointed appendages (cirri), which hold on to the rocks. Not stalked.
Comments: Can move using the cirri or swim by using the rays.

CHAPTER 8

Sea Squirts, Ascidians

Tunicates

PHYLUM UROCHORDATA

The urochordates, or tunicates, are colourful jelly-like animals that often carpet the sea floor and floating structures. The encrusting forms are sometimes confused with sponges or bryozoans. The Phylum Urochordata (formerly Tunicata, hence *tunicates*, a broad term) has 3,000 known species and includes the Class Ascidiacea (2,000 species)—common sea squirts or ascidians; the Class Thaliacea, a type of tunicate that lives near the water surface;

pelagic salps—often mistaken for jellyfish—typically found in the open oceans; and the Class Larvacea, small, transparent planktonic forms. The urochordate larval stages are tadpole-like, having a notochord and a rod similar to the backbone; consequently this group of animals is sometimes considered with the chordates (Phylum Chordata).

Ascidians Class Ascidiacea

At least 90 species of Ascidians are found in the waters of the Pacific Northwest. Ascidians, or sea squirts, are colourful, soft-bodied individuals or masses that have obvious openings (siphons) for the intake of waterborne nutrients and oxygen and for the discharge of wastes. Ascidians settle in large numbers and are sometimes regarded as "fouling" organisms. They compete for food and space with other organisms, and have been a problem to mussel farmers.

PHYSICAL FEATURES
The ascidians have attached sac-like forms, the larger solitary sea squirts and social forms topped by a pair of tubular or elevated siphons. The colonial ascidians consist of many tiny individuals called zooids, which have a common skin-like covering (tunic), and sometimes individuals circle and share exhalant siphons. Inside the tunic, some have globular calcareous rods (spicules) but they are unique and different in structure from sponge spicules.

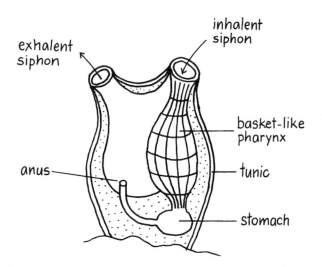

Physical features of tunicates.

PREY–PREDATORS

Water is taken in through the siphons, food is collected by mucous sheets in a basket-like pharynx and wastes are expelled through the exhalant siphon.

Ascidians are often eaten by polyclad flatworms; by sea stars, including the blood star (see pp. 134–35), leather star (p. 133) and mottled star (p. 135); by some snails, including topsnails (p. 103); and by some fishes.

REPRODUCTION

Colonies of compound ascidians divide and are built up by asexual division. Most ascidians are hermaphroditic and reproduce sexually as well.

Solitary Ascidians

STALKED HAIRY SEA SQUIRT

Boltenia villosa (Stimpson, 1864).
Alternate names: Bristly or shaggy tunicate; spiny-headed tunicate.
Etymology: *villosa* = shaggy.
Size: To 1 5/8" (4 cm) high, 1 1/4" (3 cm) wide.
Range: BC to southern California.
Habitat: Low tide to 330' (101 m).
Description: Solitary. May or may not have stalk; red-orange-tan to brown leathery tunic covered with hairs or spines.

MONTEREY STALKED SEA SQUIRT

Styela montereyensis (Dall, 1872).
Etymology: *Styela* = pillar.
Size: To 10" (25 cm) high.
Range: BC to San Geronimo, Baja California.
Habitat: On rocks, pilings in current areas, intertidal to 100' (30 m).
Description: Solitary. Long, thin-stalked, grooved tunic with 2 siphons at the tip, one straight, one curved or bent over. Orange-red or brown.
Comments: Grows rapidly, lives 1–3 years.

PEANUT SEA SQUIRT
Styela gibbsii (Stimpson, 1864).
Size: To 1½" (4 cm) high.
Range: BC to southern California.
Habitat: On rocks, intertidal to 50' (15 m) and more, in protected waters.
Description: Distinct individuals, in groups. Wrinkled, hairy, peanut-shaped with a short stalk. Tan to brown-orange.
Comments: Sometimes hosts pea crabs (*Fabia subquadrata* and *Pinnixa faba*).

GLASSY SEA SQUIRT
Ascidia paratropa (Huntsman, 1912).
Size: To 6" (15 cm) high.
Range: Aleutian Islands to southern Monterey, California.
Habitat: Stands stiffly erect on rocks in current areas, intertidal to 265' (80 m).
Description: Solitary. Clear cylindrical tunic with obvious fleshy spines, prominent siphons.
Comments: Hosts several small animals, hydroids and crustaceans within. The specimen in the photo has a yellow ring in the exhalant siphon, which is a hydroid (*Endocrypta huntsmani*). Sometimes eaten by vermilion star (see p. 130).

FLATTENED SEA SQUIRT
Ascidia callosa Stimpson 1852.
Size: To 1¼" (3 cm) wide.
Range: Alaska to Washington.
Habitat: On and under rocks in current areas, intertidal to 50' (15 m) and deeper.
Description: Solitary. Flattened, smooth, translucent tan oval tunic with small siphons to one side. Has white eggs.
Comments: Species is also found in Japan and the north Atlantic. A similar-looking species, the flattened California sea squirt (*Ascidia ceratodes*), found in Saanich Inlet, has red eggs.

SPINY SEA SQUIRT
Halocynthia igaboja Oka, 1906.
Alternate name: *Halocynthia hilgendorfi igaboja* Oka, 1906.
Size: To 4" (10 cm) diameter.
Range: Prince Rupert, BC to Channel Islands, California.
Habitat: On rocks, intertidal to 540' (165 m).
Description: Solitary. Globular, spiny body, opaque with reddish siphons that close to form a cross shape. When siphons are closed they are covered over by the dense spines. Body spines collect mud and detritus, giving animal a grey-black appearance.
Comments: Also found in Japan.

PACIFIC SEA PEACH

Halocynthia aurantium (Pallas, 1787).
Size: To 6" (15 cm) high.
Range: Chukchi Sea, Arctic to Puget Sound.
Habitat: On rocks, subtidal to 330' (100 m).
Description: Solitary. Smooth, barrel-shaped orange-red tunic with large projecting siphons at the end.
Comments: Similar to Atlantic sea peach (*Halocynthia pyriformis*).

SHINY ORANGE SEA SQUIRT

Cnemidocarpa finmarkiensis (Kiaer, 1893).
Alternate name: Broad-base sea squirt.
Size: To 3" (7.5 cm) high, 2" (5 cm) wide.
Range: Alaska to Point Conception, California.
Habitat: On rocks, intertidal to 165' (50 m).
Description: Solitary. Smooth, flattened pearly orange-red tunic. Short projecting retractable siphons.
Comments: Also found in Asian and Arctic waters.

SEA VASE

Ciona intestinalis (Linnaeus, 1767).
Size: To 6" (15 cm) high, 1" (2.5 cm) wide.
Range: Cosmopolitan; Alaska to southern California.
Habitat: Intertidal to 1,650' (500 m).
Description: Solitary, sometimes in groups. Vase-like, cylindrical. Translucent pale yellow, greenish. Siphon openings ringed with yellow.
Comments: Also found in Atlantic waters, and in many other places worldwide.

WRINKLED SEA SQUIRT

Pyura haustor (Stimpson, 1864).
Alternate name: Warty sea squirt.
Size: To 3" (7.5 cm) high, 3" (7.5 cm) diameter.
Range: Aleutian Islands to San Diego, California.
Habitat: On rocks, intertidal to 660' (200 m) and more.
Description: Solitary. Distinct long, slender red-pink siphons from a brown warty base.
Comments: Species is the most common intertidal sea squirt. Often covered by sediment and debris. Eaten by striped sunstar (see p. 131).

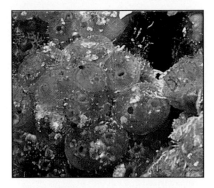

HORSESHOE ASCIDIAN
Chelysoma productum Stimpson, 1864.
Size: To 2¹/₂" (6 cm) high, disk to 1" (2.5 cm).
Range: Prince William Sound, Alaska to San Diego, California.
Habitat: On rocks, intertidal to 165' (50 m).
Description: Individuals, often clumped. Oval body topped with a flattened disk with thin plates and short siphons. Thin, hard, whitish opaque tunic.

TRANSPARENT SEA SQUIRT
Corella willmeriana (Herdman, 1898).
Size: To 2" (5 cm) high.
Range: Sitka, Alaska to Monterey Bay, California.
Habitat: On floats and rocks, intertidal to 165' (50 m).
Description: Often solitary or in groups of compressed, clear, colourless bodies.

TRANSPARENT SEA SQUIRT
Corella inflata Huntsman, 1912.
Size: To 2" (5 cm) high.
Range: BC to Washington.
Habitat: Clumps on floats and rocks, intertidal to 165' (50 m).
Description: Individuals form clumps of compressed, clear, colourless bodies.
Comments: Broods young.

GLOBULAR ASCIDIAN
Molgula pacifica (Huntsman, 1912).
Size: To 3/4" (2 cm) high.
Range: BC and other locations. Abundant in Barkley Sound.
Habitat: On open coast, on rocks, floats, intertidal and shallow subtidal.
Description: Dense clusters of individual globular bodies, bright orange siphons protruding above a layer of adherent sand.
Comments: A similar abundant, cosmopolitan species, *Molgula manhattensis*, was introduced to harbours in California.

Social Ascidians

These ascidians occur in clusters of individuals, clearly separated or sometimes joined at the base.

YELLOW SOCIAL ASCIDIANS

Pycnoclavella stanleyi Berrill & Abbott, 1949.
Size: Less than 1/2" (1 cm) high, large mats to 20" (50 cm) across.
Range: Vancouver Island to Baja California.
Habitat: On rocks where wave action shifts sand, intertidal to 50' (15 m) or more.
Description: Social; individuals clustered but clearly separated. Yellow-orange striped from a background of sandy tubes.

ORANGE SOCIAL ASCIDIANS

Metandrocarpa taylori Huntsman, 1912.
Alternate name: Taylor's colonial tunicate.
Size: Individuals to 1/4" (6 mm) high and in diameter, groups to 8" (20 cm) across.
Range: BC to San Diego, California.
Habitat: On rocks in current areas, intertidal to 65' (20 m) or more.
Description: Social. Contiguous individuals joined by slender stolon, or thin tunic sheet. Bright orange-red.

FUSED ORANGE SOCIAL ASCIDIANS

Metandrocarpa dura (Ritter, 1896).
Size: To 1/4" (6 mm) high and in diameter, groups to 12" (30 cm) and more across.
Range: BC to San Diego, California.
Habitat: On rocks, subtidal.
Description: Similar to orange social ascidians (above) but zooids tightly packed within a common tunic.

SEA GRAPES

Perophora annectens Ritter, 1893.
Size: To 1/4" (6 mm), colonies to 4" (10 cm) across.
Range: BC to San Diego, California.
Habitat: On rocks on open coast or current areas, low tide to 100' (30 m).
Description: Clusters of yellow-green globular bodies, separated or attached together.

Colonial-Compound Ascidians

These ascidians are individuals (zooids) embedded in a common skin-like tunic.

LIGHTBULB ASCIDIAN

Clavelina huntsmani Van Name, 1931.
Etymology: *Clavelina* = little club.
Size: To 1¼" (3 cm) high, clusters to 20" (50 cm) across.
Range: BC to San Diego, California.
Habitat: On rocks in currents; subtidal to 100' (30 m).
Description: Transparent tubes with two orange-pink "filaments."
Comments: Actually a colonial ascidian, with the zooids independent of one another in the adult stage. Annual, abundant in summer.

LOBED ASCIDIAN

Cystodes lobatus (Ritter, 1900).
Size: Patches to 1½" (4 cm) thick, 10" (25 cm) or more across.
Range: Central BC to San Geronimo, Baja California.
Habitat: On rocks on exposed coasts, intertidal to 660' (200 m).
Description: Encrusting colony that folds into irregular ridges and lobes. Grey or purple-pink. Has calcareous disk-shaped spicules that form capsules around each zooid in the tunic.
Comments: Eaten by blue topsnail (see p. 103). May easily be confused with another species, *Eudistoma purpuropuctatum*, which forms huge, thick, lobed colonies but without spicules.

SEA PORK

Aplidium californicum (Ritter & Forsyth, 1917).
Size: To 1¼" (3 cm) thick, 12" (30 cm) across.
Range: Vancouver Island to La Paz, Baja California; possibly Galapagos.
Habitat: On rocks in currents or wave-exposed areas, intertidal to 280' (85 m).
Description: Encrusting sheets. Yellow, grey, opalescent white or transparent colonies.

Comments: Eaten by leather star (see p. 133), cushion star (p. 131) and other stars.

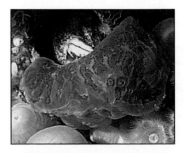

RED ASCIDIAN

Aplidium solidium (Ritter & Forsyth, 1917).
Size: Slabs to 2" (5 cm) thick, 8" (20 cm) across.
Range: Vancouver Island to San Diego, California.
Habitat: Rocks and pilings in current areas, intertidal to 50' (15 m) and more.
Description: Bright red to orange-brown lumps. Zooids arranged in clusters.

MUSHROOM ASCIDIAN

Distaplia occidentalis Bancroft, 1899.
Size: Colonies to 4" (10 cm) across.
Range: Vancouver Island to San Diego, California.
Habitat: On rocks in surge or currents, among roots of surfgrass, intertidal to 50' (15 m).
Description: Mushroom-shaped or flattened colonies. Variable combinations of colours: white, grey, yellow, pink, red, purple-brown.

PADDLE ASCIDIAN

Distaplia smithi Abbott & Trason, 1968.
Size: Stalks to 2" (5 cm) long.
Range: Prince William Sound, Alaska to Monterey, California.
Habitat: Open coast and semi-protected coasts, intertidal to 50' (15 m).
Description: Colony with paddle-like or leaf-like lobes. Cream, grey to orange-brown.

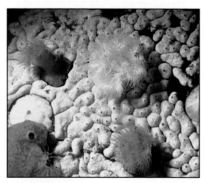

PACIFIC WHITE CRUST

Didemnum carnulentum Ritter & Forsyth, 1917.
Size: Less than 1/4" (6 mm) high, to 5" (12.5 cm) across.
Range: BC to Panama.
Habitat: Rocks and other hard surfaces, intertidal to 100' (30 m).
Description: Thin, flat colonies. Opaque white to grey tunic with pink to orange colours. Many small pores and a few larger holes.

WHITE GLOVE LEATHER

Didemnum albidum (Verrill, 1871) / *Tridemnum* spp.
Size: Crust to 1/2" (2 cm) thick, 6" (15 cm) wide.
Range: Bering Sea to Washington.
Habitat: Rocks and other hard surfaces; intertidal to 50' (15 m) and deeper.
Description: White glove leather appearance.
Comments: The two species of white glove leather cannot be distinguished in the field by examining physical features. Both have globular calcareous spicules. This ascidian is also found in Japan.

HARBOUR STAR ASCIDIAN

Botryllus schlosseri (Pallas, 1776).
Size: To 1/8" (3 mm) thick, colonies to 6" (15 cm) or more across.
Range: Vancouver Island to southern California.
Habitat: On pilings, floats, rocks and kelp fasts, intertidal to shallow subtidal.
Description: Star-shaped to groupings of zooids around a common opening. Striking orange, white, reddish brown to black.
Comments: Also found in Atlantic and Mediterranean waters.

COMPOUND ASCIDIAN

Diplosoma listerianum (Milne Edwards, 1841).
Alternate name: *Diplosoma macdonaldi* Herdman, 1886.
Size: Colonies to 15' (4.5 m) across.
Range: Vancouver Island to San Diego, California.
Habitat: On rocks, pilings, algae or as a sheet over sandy, gravel or mud substrates, intertidal to 165' (50 m).
Description: Encrusting colonies. Thin transparent sheets to 1/8" (3 mm) thick, sometimes in convoluted lumps. Yellow to grey to brown. Exhalant opening raised.
Comments: Also found in Atlantic waters.

LINED COMPOUND ASCIDIAN

Botryllus sp.
Alternate name: *Botrylloides* spp. currently included in genus *Botryllus*.
Size: To 6" (15 cm) across.
Range: Vancouver Island to southern California.
Habitat: On rocks, floats and pilings on mussels and tube worms.
Description: Thin sheet with distinct lines of systems of zooids. Dark orange.

Class Thaliacea

These are species that live near the water surface, swimming and drifting in the currents.

PELAGIC TUNICATE

Salpa fusiformis Cuvier, 1804.
Alternate names: Salp; beach bubble wrap.
Size: Chains to 8" (20 cm) long.
Range: Bering Sea to South America.
Habitat: Drifting near the water surface.
Description: Solitary barrel-shaped individuals (sexual forms) or chains of budding individuals (asexual). Clear to translucent white with internal organs visible.
Comments: Eaten by some rockfishes, particularly the blue rockfish (see p. 167) and the offshore ocean sunfish *Mola mola*. There are likely several species of this tunicate in Pacific Northwest waters. Species is also found in Japan, and in the Atlantic and Indian oceans.

CHAPTER 9

Fishes

PHYLUM CHORDATA

F ishes are animals with backbones (vertebrates), members of the phylum Chordata. More than 325 species of fishes live in Pacific Northwest waters. Included here are 40 of the most common fishes observed by divers and tidepool explorers, and landed in fisheries. The salmonids are not included.

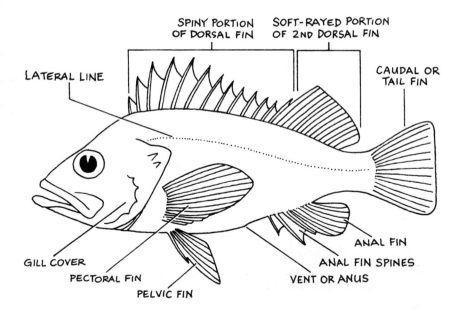

Physical features of fish.

Cartilaginous Fishes Class Elasmobranchii

These sharks, skates and rays have cartilaginous skeletons, well-developed jaws and hard teeth, often with elongated gill openings.

SPINY DOGFISH

Squalus acanthias Linnaeus, 1758.
Etymology: *Squalus* = shark; *acanthias* = referring to the spines.
Size: To 5'3" (1.6 m), to 20 lbs (9 kg).
Range: Cosmopolitan: Bering Sea to Baja California; Chile.
Habitat: In schools, feeding on fishes.
Description: Slate grey to brown with grey-white underside; juveniles are spotted. A single spine is located at the front of each of the 2 dorsal fins.
Comments: Species is taken in commercial fisheries, originally for liver oil, now as a food fish. Spiny dogfish bear young rather than laying eggs. Sometimes schools of these sharks surround divers. Species is also found China to Korea, and in Atlantic, Mediterranean and Black seas. There have been Canadian tag returns from Japan and Mexico.

SIX GILL SHARK

Hexanchus griseus (Bonnaterre, 1788).
Etymology:
Hex/anchus = six/gills; *griseus* = grey.
Size: To 26'5" (8 m).
Range: Gulf of Alaska and along Pacific coast.
Habitat: Usually in deep water, but as shallow as 30' (9 m).
Description: Dark brown to grey with pale underside. Large head, 6 gill slits and a single dorsal fin.
Comments: Species is one of the so-called cow sharks, named for their large size. The six gill shark cruises slowly at 30' (9 m) and deeper, close to bottom. Eats a variety of fishes and crustaceans but does not appear aggressive to divers. Individuals are catalogued by scars, fin shapes and other features.

SKATE EGG CASE (MERMAID'S PURSE)

Each species of skate has a unique egg case shape, many of them flattened and rectangular. The egg case of the big skate *Raja binoculata* may be up to 12" (30 cm) long and contain up to 7 eggs. The cases are often found washed up on the beach.

Ratfish Class Holocephali

RATFISH
Hydrolagus colliei (Lay & Bennett, 1839).
Alternate names: Chimaera; rabbit fish.
Etymology: *Hydro/lagus* = water/hare; *colliei* = after Alexander Collie, ship's surgeon and naturalist on the *Blossom*.
Size: To 39" (1 m).
Range: Southeast Alaska to Baja California.
Habitat: Often in shallow water, 30' (9 m) to 3,085' (925 m).
Description: Grey-brown with white spots and silver underside. Large bulky snout, small mouth with forward-directed teeth, long tapering tail. Swims by flapping large forward fins. Stout spine on forward dorsal fin. Males have claspers on the underside, looking like "fish with legs."
Comments: The female lays several eggs, each enclosed in an elongated leather-like case (inset).

Bony Fishes Class Actinopterygii

These fishes, which some authorities classify as Class Teleostomi, include a great variety of forms. They include the species shown here—frequently seen in tidepools and by snorkellers and divers—and harvested fish such as salmon, blackcod, halibut and other harvested groundfish.

Sculpins

Some 350 types of sculpins (Family Cottidae), common and abundant bottom fishes, can be found worldwide. More than 40 species live in Pacific Northwest waters. They typically have broad, flat heads and slender, tapering bodies, and range in size from small tidepool sculpins to the large cabezon. The sculpins rely on their body colours and patterns for camouflage and often will not move unless threatened.

TIDEPOOL SCULPIN

Oligocottus maculosus Girard, 1856.
Etymology:
Oligo/cottus = few/sculpin;
macula = spot.
Size: To 3¹/₂" (9 cm).
Range: Bering Sea to southern California.
Habitat: Common and abundant in shallow rocky areas, in tidepool and under rocks.
Description: Colours variable, often red-brown, green. Slender. Single, forked spine on gill cover. 5 irregular dark saddles across back.

SCALYHEAD SCULPIN

Artedius harringtoni (Starks, 1896).
Etymology: Artedi was an early scientist studying fish, associated with Linnaeus; Mark W. Harrington was a president of the University of Washington.
Size: To 4" (10 cm).
Range: Kodiak, Alaska to south of Monterey, California.
Habitat: On rocky reefs and pilings; frequently intertidal to 35' (10.5 m).
Description: 2 pairs of prominent bushy appendages (cirri) on head of mature male. Variable colours, including mottled brown, orange and red; white spot at base of caudal fin. Females and males coloured differently; female has prominent red spots near tips of first 2 dorsal spines.
Comments: Species is territorial. Males are aggressive in guarding a space.

LONGFIN SCULPIN

Jordania zonope Starks, 1895.
Alternate name: Band-eye sculpin.
Etymology: David Starr Jordan was a US ichthyologist; *zon/ope* = zone/window.
Size: To 6" (15 cm).
Range: Baranoff Island, SE Alaska to Point Lobos, California.
Habitat: On rocky reefs.
Description: Brightly coloured; olive green with dark red bands along back. Slender body.

Distinctive pale bands on head form 3 dark bars under the eye.
Comments: Species is territorial. Males guard egg masses.

BUFFALO SCULPIN

Enophrys bison (Girard, 1854).
Etymology:
En/ophyrs = on/eyebrow;
bison = buffalo.
Size: To 14 1/2" (37 cm).
Range: Kodiak Island, Alaska to Monterey, California.
Habitat: On rocky reefs, shallow subtidal.
Description: Colours vary from mottled brown to pink and green, with 4 dark saddles across back. Large head with prominent pair of spines on gill cover, top one pointed up and back, lower one flattened and pointed down; raised plates along lateral line.
Comments: Relies on camouflage, stays fixed when disturbed. Female deposits and male guards eggs in shallows in winter–spring.

GREAT SCULPIN

Myoxocephalus polyacantho-cephalus (Pallas, 1811).
Etymology: *Myoxos* = doormouse;
poly/acantho/cephalus = many/spines/on head.
Size: To 30" (75 cm).
Range: Bering Sea to Washington.
Habitat: On rocks and sand–mud; 40' (12 m) and deeper.
Description: Large head, broad body, long snout. Reddish-orange eyes in adults.
Comments: A very large fish, slow to move.

SAILFIN SCULPIN

Nautichthys oculofasciatus (Girard, 1857).
Etymology: *Nautys* = sailor, referring to sail-like shape; *ichthys* = fish; *oculo/fasciatus* = eye/banded.
Size: To 8" (20 cm).
Range: Kodiak Island, Alaska to Point Sal, southern California.
Habitat: In rock crevices, on pilings, on soft bottoms near rubble; shallow subtidal.
Description: Pink-orange to brown with dark bands on the back; dark diagonal band runs down and back through eye. Tall, sail-like first dorsal fin.
Comments: Nocturnal, seen often at night. Long dorsal fin moves in a series of waves.

RED IRISH LORD

Hemilepidotus hemilepidotus
(Tilesius, 1810).
Etymology: *Hemi* = half; *lepidotus* = scaled.
Size: To 20" (50 cm).
Range: Bering Sea to Monterey, California.
Habitat: In rocky areas, on wharves and pilings; intertidal to 162' (49 m).
Description: Red patches and brown, black and white mottling. Large eyes. Conspicuous band of scales, 4–5 scales wide, along sides. Single dorsal fin in 3 steps.
Comments: Female spawns masses of pink to purple eggs in shallows in winter. Eggs are guarded by the male.

CABEZON

Scorpaenichthys marmoratus
(Ayres, 1854).
Alternate name: Marbled sculpin.
Etymology: *marmoratus* = marbled.
Size: To 39" (1 m), to 30 lbs (13.5 kg) or more.
Range: Sitka, Alaska to Point Abreojos, Baja California.
Habitat: On rocky reefs, intertidal to 250' (76 m).
Description: Marbled, olive green to brown or grey with light patches. Flap-like bushy appendage (cirrus) on snout and above each eye. Deeply embedded scales appear to be absent.
Comments: Well-camouflaged males guard eggs in shallows January–March.

GRUNT SCULPIN

Rhamphocottus richardsoni
Günther, 1874.
Etymology:
Rhampho/cottus = snout/sculpin; *richardsoni* = after John Richardson, a naturalist and explorer.
Size: To 3¼" (8 cm).
Range: Bering Sea to Santa Barbara, California.
Habitat: In the cover of rocks or algae, in empty barnacles or sponges.
Description: Tan to orange with dark bands pointed down and forward; orange fins. Unique short, stout body with pointed snout. Very small mouth for a sculpin.
Comments: Species "hops" along the bottom.

Rockfishes

Some 330 species in the Family Scorpaenidae have been identified worldwide, with 68 species described along the Pacific coast of North America. The rockfishes or scorpionfishes are common and popular sport and commercial species. Rockfishes are found from the intertidal zone to depths of 9,200' (2,800 m). To reproduce, the female releases millions of tiny live larvae after the eggs hatch inside her body.

CAUTION: The term *scorpionfishes* refers to the toxicity of species in this family, which includes tropical members such as the well-known stonefishes and lionfishes. Rockfish species in the Pacific Northwest are not as harmful, but fin spines of local species carry venom that can cause throbbing and burning pain, swelling, and in some cases fever.

QUILLBACK ROCKFISH

Sebastes maliger (Jordan and Gilbert, 1880).
Etymology: *Sebasto* = magnificent; *malus/gero* = mast, to bear.
Size: To 24" (60 cm).
Range: Prince William Sound, Alaska to Point Sur, California.
Habitat: On rocky reefs, surface (in kelp beds) to 480' (146 m).
Description: Dark brown to black, mottled with yellow and orange. High, spiny dorsal fin with yellow streak in forward fin region. Brown speckling in lower head region and across breast.
Comments: Common and abundant in many areas, often in shelter of rocks or sponges. Not a schooling species. Has been depleted in some areas by sport and commercial fisheries.

COPPER ROCKFISH

Sebastes caurinus Richardson, 1845
Etymology: *Sebastos* = magnificent; *caurinus* = northwest; John Richardson was a naturalist and explorer.
Size: To 22" (55 cm).
Range: Gulf of Alaska to Baja California.
Habitat: On rocky reefs, 30–600' (9–183 m).
Description: Olive brown to copper with yellow blotches, white on sides and belly and along rear two-thirds of lateral line. Dark bands radiating from eye.
Comments: Common and abundant in many areas. Has been depleted in some areas by sport and commercial fisheries. Loosely aggregated, not usually a schooling species.

CHINA ROCKFISH

Sebastes nebulosus Ayres, 1854.
Alternate name: Yellow-stripe rockfish.
Etymology: *Sebastos* = magnificent; *nebulosus* = clouded.
Size: To 17" (43 cm).
Range: Cook Inlet, Alaska to San Miguel Island, central California.
Habitat: On rocky reefs, along outer coast; 13–422' (4–128 m).
Description: Black body with broad yellow stripe from dorsal fin downward and along lateral line to tail.
Comments: Solitary species. Resident to an area for years, likely for life.

YELLOWEYE ROCKFISH

Sebastes ruberrimus (Cramer, 1895).
Alternate name: Red snapper.
Etymology: *Sebastos* = magnificent; *ruberrimus* = very red.
Size: To 36" (1 m).
Range: Prince William Sound, Alaska to northern Baja California.
Habitat: On rocky reefs, 60–1800' (18–550 m).
Description: Orange-red to red-yellow; fins may be black at tips. Adult has brilliant yellow eye, rough and tuberculate head ridges. Juveniles have dark eyes and 2 light bands along side, one on lateral line and a shorter one below.
Comments: Divers have found individuals are resident to a specific site, likely for life. Juveniles were originally described as a different species. Harvested in Native and commercial fisheries.

CANARY ROCKFISH

Sebastes pinniger (Gill, 1864).
Etymology: *Sebastos* = magnificent; *pinna/gero* = fin/to bear.
Size: To 30" (75 cm).
Range: Southeast Alaska to Cape Colnett, Baja California.
Habitat: In rocky areas, adults at 60–1200' (18–360 m); subadults shallower.
Description: Orange with white to grey stripe along lateral line, 3 bright orange stripes across head. Second anal fin pointed, not round. Juvenile has prominent dark spot at rear of spiny dorsal fin.
Comments: Schooling species, often with black rockfish (see p. 167) or others.

PUGET SOUND ROCKFISH

Sebastes emphaeus Starks, 1911.
Etymology: *Sebastos* = magnificent; *emphaeus* = display.
Size: To 7" (17.5 cm).
Range: Prince William Sound, Alaska to Punta Gorda, California.
Habitat: On rocky reefs, surface to 60' (18 m) and deeper.
Description: Slender orange body, often with dusky stripe along lower side and greenish-brown or coppery blotches.

VERMILION ROCKFISH

Sebastes miniatus (Jordan & Gilbert, 1880).
Etymology: *Sebastos* = magnificent; *miniatus* = vermilion.
Size: To 36" (1 m).
Range: Cape Bartolome, southeast Alaska to San Benito Islands, Baja California.
Habitat: On rocky reefs, adults at 60–900' (18–275 m); juveniles at 10' (3 m) and deeper.
Description: Vermilion red with grey mottling on sides, thin light stripe along lateral line. 3 light, obscure orange stripes radiating from eye. Juveniles tan with brown and yellow mottling.
Comments: Species resembles canary and yelloweye rockfish (see p. 165). Moves in small schools near sea bottom (p. 165).

YELLOWTAIL ROCKFISH

Sebastes flavidus (Ayres, 1862).
Etymology: *Sebastos* = magnificent; *flavidus* = yellow.
Size: To 26" (65 cm).
Range: Kodiak Island, Alaska to San Diego, California.
Habitat: On rocky reefs, surface to 1,800' (550 m).
Description: Olive green to green-brown with pale spots along back, yellow-green on fins. Streaks of yellow on gill cover behind eye.

Comments: Species schools, often with other rockfish.

BLACK ROCKFISH

Sebastes melanops Girard, 1856.
Alternate name: Black bass.
Etymology: *Sebastos* = magnificent; *melan/ops* = black/face.
Size: To 25" (63 cm).
Range: Amchitka Island, Alaska to southern California.
Habitat: On rocky reefs and kelp beds, surface to 1200' (360 m).
Description: Light to dark grey, with dark grey and black mottling along upper back and a pale band below lateral line.
Comments: Species schools, often with other rockfish. Resembles blue rockfish (see below).

BLUE ROCKFISH

Sebastes mystinus (Jordan & Gilbert, 1880).
Etymology: *Sebastos* = magnificent; *mystas* = priest.
Size: To 21" (53 cm).
Range: Bering Sea to northern Baja California.
Habitat: On rocky reefs and kelp beds, surface to 1800' (550 m).
Description: Blue-grey to black, 2–4 dark bands on head.
Comments: Species schools, often with other rockfish. Resembles black rockfish (see above). Differentiation requires close examination of fin shapes. Feeds on a variety of prey including pelagic tunicates (see p. 157).

TIGER ROCKFISH

Sebastes nigrocinctus Ayres, 1859.
Alternate name: Black-banded rockfish.
Etymology: *Sebastos* = magnificent; *niger/cinctus* = black/belt.
Size: To 24" (60 cm).
Range: Prince William Sound, Alaska to Point Buchon, California.
Habitat: In crevices, on rocky reefs; adults at 3–900' (1–275 m), juveniles often shallower.
Description: Pink to red with 5 vertical dark bands. Head has rough ridges.
Comments: Species is solitary and territorial.

Greenlings

This well-known but small family of fishes (Family Hexagrammidae) has only about 13 described species. About half of these live in our region and the rest inhabit Asian Pacific waters. The family includes the lingcod and the greenlings commonly found in shallow waters. The greenling is medium in size and moderately elongated, and has a single long dorsal fin.

LINGCOD
Ophiodon elongatus Girard, 1854.
Etymology:
Ophio/odons = snake/tooth; *elongatus* = elongate.
Size: To 60" (1.5 m), to 105 lbs (47 kg).
Range: Bering Sea to Ensenada, California.
Habitat: Adults on rocky reefs and in kelp beds, to 6,600' (2,000 m); juveniles on sand and mud bottoms, at surface.

Description: Large head, mouth and teeth; dark blotches on a slender, tapering, mottled brown, grey or green body.
Comments: Species is important food fish. Males guard large masses of white eggs in crevices or under rocks. Lingcod eat herring and other fishes, squid and octopus. Some stay in one place while others migrate. All adult lingcod migrate from shallows to deep water seasonally.

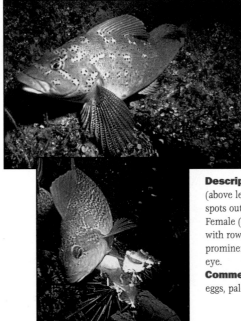

KELP GREENLING
Hexagrammos decagrammus (Pallas, 1810).
Etymology:
Hexa/grammos = six/line; *deca/grammus* = ten/line, referring to 5 lateral line canals on each side.
Size: To 24" (60 cm).
Range: Aleutian Islands to La Jolla, California.
Habitat: In rocky areas and kelp beds, intertidal to 150' (45 m).
Description: Distinctive in colour: male (above left) brownish-olive, with bright blue spots outlined with black on head and back. Female (below left) light brown, golden to blue with rows of orange-brown round spots. Small, prominent bushy appendage (cirrus) above each eye.
Comments: Males actively guard masses of eggs, pale blue to mauve.

FISHES

PAINTED GREENLING
Oxylebius pictus Gill, 1862.
Etymology: *Oxys/lepys* = sharp/fish; *pictus* = picture.
Size: To 10" (25 cm).
Range: Aleutian Islands to Baja California.
Habitat: On rocky reefs in protected waters, to 162' (49 m).
Description: Elongated, pointed head with 2 pairs of bushy appendages (cirri). One lateral line. Dark vertical bars crossing body and dorsal fin.
Comments: Juveniles take protection in tentacles of white-spotted anemone (see p. 44). Adults often sleep at base of anemone. Male guards deposit of orange eggs.

Surfperches

Perches are laterally compressed and elliptical fishes. There are only 23 described species of the Family Embiotocidae, all found in the north Pacific. Surfperches bear relatively small numbers of well-developed young, rather than releasing or depositing eggs.

SHINER PERCH
Cymatogaster aggregata Gibbons, 1854.
Etymology: *Cymato/gaster* = fetus/belly; *aggregata* = crowded together.
Size: To 6" (15 cm).
Range: Wrangell, Alaska to San Quintin Bay, Baja California.
Habitat: On pilings and floats, in bays and kelp beds; surface to 480' (146 m).
Description: Small, silvery body, oval and compressed, with large scales.
Strong dark bars along sides, interrupted by 3 light yellow vertical bars.
Comments: Common in large schools. Fully developed young are born tail first.

STRIPED PERCH
Embiotica lateralis Agassiz, 1854.
Etymology: *Embios/tocos* = living/bring forth; *lateralis* = lateral, referring to blue stripes.
Size: To 15" (37.5 cm).
Range: Port Wrangel, Alaska to Point Cabras, northern Baja California.
Habitat: On rocky reefs and pilings, in kelp beds; surface to 70' (21 m).
Description: Copper colour with about 15 iridescent blue horizontal stripes below lateral line.
Comments: Common species, usually solitary or in small schools. Fully developed young released in late spring–early summer.

PILE PERCH
Rhacochilus vacca (Girard, 1855).
Etymology: *Racos/chelios* = ragged/lip; *vacca* = cow, referring to bearing young.
Size: To 17" (43 cm).
Range: Port Wrangel, Alaska to San Martin Island, northern Baja California.
Habitat: On floats, pilings and reefs; surface to 260' (78 m).
Description: Silvery coloration, usually with dark indistinct vertical bars.

Black spot behind mouth. Dorsal fin much higher in rear section; deeply forked tail fin.
Comments: Solitary or in small schools.

Pricklebacks

This family of slender, elongated fishes includes the pricklebacks, cockscombs, warbonnets, shannies and eelblennies. Many have distinctive ornamentation on the head.

DECORATED WARBONNET
Chirolophis decoratus (Jordan & Snyder, 1903).
Etymology:
Chiro/lophis = hand/crest; *decoratus* = ornamental.
Size: To 16½" (42 cm).
Range: Bering Sea to Humboldt Bay, California.
Habitat: In crevices and sponges, 5–300' (1.5–90 m).

Description: Body orange to brown with dark mottling and bars on fins. Dark bars run down from eyes. Long head with bushy appendages (cirri) centred in front of eyes; cirri on first 4 dorsal spines.
Comments: Species lays and guards eggs in crevices and chimney sponges. Often several warbonnets will occupy a crevice.

MOSSHEAD WARBONNET
Chirolophis nugator (Jordan & Williams, 1895).
Etymology:
Chiro/lophis = hand/crest; *nugator* = fop, elegant appearance.
Size: To 6" (15 cm).
Range: Aleutian Islands to San Miguel Island, California.
Habitat: In holes, crevices and

empty barnacle shells; intertidal to 200' (60 m).
Description: Numerous bushy appendages (cirri) on head to dorsal fin. Black eye-spots on males, dark bars on females, evenly spaced along dorsal fin. Pale, outlined bars along lower side.
Comments: Often only the mossy head appears from a hiding place.

Wolf-Eels

WOLF-EEL

Anarrhichthys ocellatus Ayres, 1855.
Etymology: *Anarhichas* = ancient name for related species; *ichthys* = fish; *ocellatus* = eye-like spots.
Size: To 8' (2.5 m).
Range: Aleutian Islands to Imperial Beach, southern California.
Habitat: In dens and near rocky reefs, intertidal to 700' (210 m).
Description: Large head and mouth. Long, tapering grey body with black eye-spots on body and fins. Female (at left in top photo) has dark rounded head; male (right) has lighter, bulbous head. Juveniles orange with yellow stripe along fin.
Comments: Males and females pair for life. They take turns wrapping around egg mass in the den. Divers can hand-feed opened scallops and urchin roe to these fish. Species was sacred to some coastal Natives; only the medicine man ate the *mukah*, or doctorfish, to enhance his healing powers.

Ronquils

NORTHERN RONQUIL

Ronquilus jordani (Gilbert, 1888).
Etymology: *Ronquilis* = a similar fish (Spanish ronquilis); David Starr Jordan was an eminent American ichthyologist.
Size: To 7" (18 cm).
Range: Bering Sea to Monterey Bay, central California.
Habitat: In rock rubble on sand–mud; 10–540' (3–162 m).
Description: Pale to dark orange-cream to brown, olive-green and grey. Elongated body with orange band or spots below eyes. Single, continuous dorsal fin.
Comments: Species quickly retreats into shelter when approached.

Gobies

BLACK-EYED GOBY

Coryphopterus nicholsi (Bean, 1881).

Etymology:
Coryphos/pterus = summit/fin, referring to dark colour on top of fin; Captain H. E. Nichols, US Navy, discovered this species.
Size: To 6" (15 cm).
Range: Wales Island, northern BC to central Baja California.
Habitat: In rock rubble on sand–mud; intertidal to 340' (102 m).

Description: Black eyes, black patch at top of forward dorsal fin. Pale to dark tan-orange body with large scales. Rounded tail fin. Males have black pelvic fins in breeding season.
Comments: Common species. Territorial and aggressive.

Clingfish

NORTHERN CLINGFISH

Gobiesox maeandricus (Girard, 1858).

Etymology: *Goby/esox* = from names of other fish which actually bear little resemblance; *maeandricus* = meandering colour streaks.
Size: To 6" (15 cm).
Range: Queen Charlotte Islands, BC to Baja California.
Habitat: Attached under rocks, intertidal to 30' (9 m).
Description: Flattened body with large head, large mouth and body tapering to tail; adhesive disc on underside. Single dorsal fin is set back toward tail end. Dark, net-like pattern over head and body, often with pale band between and below eyes.
Comments: Species is common under rocks. Deposits and guards small yellow eggs.

Midshipman

PLAINFIN MIDSHIPMAN

Porichthys notatus Girard, 1854.
Alternate name: Singing fish.
Etymology:
Poros/ichthys = pores/fish; *notatus* = spotted.
Size: To 15" (37.5 cm).
Range: Sitka, Alaska to Gulf of California.

Habitat: On sand and mud bottoms, intertidal to 1,200' (360 m).
Description: Dark grey-brown, iridescent purple with rows of white spots which are luminous organs. Large mouth and head. Single spine on gill cover, mildly venomous.
Comments: Species is often found buried during the day or hiding under rocks. In spring, deposits clusters of yellow eggs under rocks in the intertidal. The common name "midshipman" is from rows of lumininous organs, resembling brass buttons on early naval uniforms; "singing fish" is from loud grunting noises made by males as they use muscles on the swim bladder.

Flounders

There are some 100 described species of flounder in the Family Pleuronectidae, nearly all in the northern waters of the Pacific and Atlantic oceans. Fossils dating back at least 50 million years, to lower Eocene times, have been identified. The flounder has a flattened body with both its eyes on the right side (dextral) of the head. (*Pleuron* means "side.") Occasional individuals have their eyes on the left side (sinistral), including the Pacific halibut and starry flounder. A challenge in identifying this species in the field is that the shape of the lateral line, a key feature, can be difficult to determine underwater and from photographs.

C-O SOLE

Pleuronichthys coenosus Girard, 1854.
Alternate name: Popeye flounder.
Etymology:
Pleuron/ichthys = side/fish; *coenosus* = muddy.
Size: To 14" (35 cm).
Range: Sitka, Alaska to San Quintin Bay, Baja California.
Habitat: On sandy patches near rocks, in eelgrass beds; shallows to 1,200' (360 m).

Description: Oval body with high side (dorsal and anal) fins. Large, dark spot on centre of back resembles the letters *C O*. Large, prominent eyes.
Comments: Species is a common and easily identified flounder due to unique markings.

ROCK SOLE
Pleuronectes bilineatus (Ayres, 1855).
Alternate name:
Lepidopsetta bilineata.
Etymology:
Pleron/ectes = side/fish; *bilineata* = two lines.
Size: To 24" (60 cm).
Range: Bering Sea to San Nicholas Island, California.
Habitat: On sand or mud bottoms, intertidal to 1,500' (450 m).

Description: Black and yellow patches on fins; yellow spots at margins of side. Prominent arch in lateral line. Rough scales. Often rests up on fins, unlike most other flounders.
Comments: Species is commonly encountered by divers.

ENGLISH SOLE
Pleuronectes vetulus (Girard, 1854).
Alternate names:
Parophrys vetulus; lemon sole.
Etymology:
Pleron/ectes = side/fish; *vetulus* = old man, resemblance.
Size: To 22¹/₂" (57 cm).
Range: Aleutian Islands to central Baja California.
Habitat: On sand and mud bottoms, intertidal to 1,800' (550 m).

Description: Pointed head, slender body, lateral line without high arch.
Comments: Species is commonly encountered, but often partially or completely buried.

STARRY FLOUNDER
Platichthys stellatus (Pallas, 1811).
Etymology:
Platy/ichthys = flat/fish; *stellatus* = starry.
Size: To 36" (1 m), to 20 lbs (9 kg).
Range: Bering Sea to Santa Barbara, California.
Habitat: In soft substrates, eelgrass, estuaries; intertidal to 1,200' (360 m).

Description: Large, banded dorsal and anal fins, dark bars on tail. Rough skin with raised plates on body. Can be right-eyed or left-eyed.
Comments: Species is taken incidentally with other commercial flatfish, and sold.

Marine Mammals

CHAPTER 10

PHYLUM CHORDATA

Class Mammalia

More than 30 species of marine mammals have been reported on the Pacific coast between the Bering Sea and Baja California. These animals have several characteristics in common: they breathe air, give birth to live young, and suckle their young. But there is also wide variety. They range greatly in size and feeding patterns; many species are covered with hair, others have little hair; some species avoid contact with humans and others are quite friendly; some species frequent coastal waters and spend time on land, oceanic species of whales and dolphins move inshore and offshore and undertake long seasonal migrations.

Marine mammals have long occupied an important place in aboriginal cultures, and some centuries ago they played a key part in the exploration and settlement of North America by newcomers, who sought the skins of fur-bearing animals and essential whale products such as lamp oil. Populations of some whales and other marine mammals have been depleted by hunting activity, and now several species are protected by law. Whale watching and eco-tourism are rapidly growing businesses in the Pacific Northwest area, replacing the more consumptive activities, although in recent years several aboriginal groups have considered resuming traditional whale hunting in the region. Nowadays entanglement in fishing gear is one of the most serious threats to dolphins, porpoises and other sea mammals.

REPRODUCTION
Marine mammals have mammary glands and nurture their young on milk. Whales and dolphins bear and nurture their young at sea, while seals and sea lions require land to reproduce and to rest. Sea otters live and pup at sea, while river otters have dens on land.

IDENTIFICATION TIPS
Marine mammals can be difficult to observe and identify. They spend much of their time underwater and often live far from shore. Researchers study critical habitats, migration and feeding patterns of groups, and they photograph and study individuals for distinctive sounds, colour patterns, fin or tail shapes, and scars, scratches and nicks. Experienced whale watchers can often identify a whale from the characteristics of the blow and a glimpse of the animal's back. Special tours and viewing sites can help the beginner identify species, and so can the observation of certain behaviour—blowing, leaping from the water, foraging, resting, spyhopping, migrating, and slapping of tail and fins. But you will need to see at least two physical characteristics to make a positive identification.

Seals and Sea Lions Order Carnivora

These animals require land to bear and nurture their young, and to rest.

Earless ("True") Seals

These seals, members of the family Phocidae, lack external ear flaps and have short, fur-covered flippers.

PACIFIC HARBOUR SEAL

Phoca vitulina richardsi Linnaeus 1758.

Alternate names: Common seal; spotted seal.

Etymology: *Phoca* = seal, from root word meaning "to swell up," referring to the animal's plumpness; *richardsi* = Capt. G. H. Richards, of HMS *Hecate*, collected some of the first scientific specimens from this region in 1860–62.

Size: To 6' (1.8 m) and 250 lbs (113 kg). Males and females similar in size.

Range/habitat: Temperate coastal areas of north Pacific; seal also travels up rivers and into lakes.

Description: Markings variable, from nearly black with white spots to white with black spots. Large, round, smooth head, large eyes. Short flippers covered with hair.

Behaviour: Found in groups of several individuals to 500 or more. Most seals haul out on land

at low tides, on calm days, often in the morning. They also "sleep" on the ocean bottom adjacent to haulout sites. Seals often swim on the surface, sticking their heads out of the water, and swimming at speeds of 4.3 knots (5 km/h) to pursuit speeds of 12.5 knots (14.5 km/h). They also swim submerged, usually for 5–8 minutes at a time, but they can dive to 1,380' (420 m) and remain submerged for as long as 28 minutes.

Comments: The north Pacific coast population is estimated to be in excess of 350,000 (1988), with northern populations on the decline and southern populations, southeast Alaska to California, increasing (1998). The life span of males is 20 years; of females 30 years. Harbour seals are relatively territorial and do not migrate long distances. They are considered a nuisance by many sport and recreational fishers, and there is great controversy over the impact of seals on fish stocks such as salmon, lingcod and herring. Bounties (1913–64) and a fishery for pelts (1962–69) reduced the BC populations to about 10 percent of historic levels.

NORTHERN ELEPHANT SEAL

Mirounga angustirostris (Gill, 1866).

Etymology: *Mirounga* = from *miouroung,* Australian native name for species; *augusti/rostris* = great/snout.

Size: Females to 10' (3 m) and 2,200 lbs (1 tonne); males to 20' (6 m) and 4,400 lbs (2 tonnes). Largest species of the seals and sea lions (pinnipeds) in northern hemisphere.

Range/habitat: Southern Alaska to Mexico. Seals congregate off Mexico and California to mate and pup, December–March. Pups and adult males range north.

Description: Adults uniform light brown. Males have pendulous snouts, large earless heads and creased necks.

Behaviour: Species hauls out on sandy beaches in California. Some reach BC, feeding on mid-water fish; they rarely haul out but rest vertically in the water, with massive head and neck protruding from water like a large log. They spend much of their time diving and can dive to 3,940' (1182 m) and stay submerged for 45 minutes. They dive continuously for weeks at a time when at sea, surfacing for no more than a few minutes between dives.

Comments: Species was hunted in the 1800s for blubber, reducing the population to about 100 animals. Population has since been restored to near historic levels, estimated at 120,000 in 1997.

Eared Seals

Members of this family of seals, sea lions and walrus (family Otariidae) have short, stiff external ear flaps and large hairless flippers. They are gregarious animals. They tend to be shallow divers, and they breed in large rookeries on offshore islands.

STELLER SEA LION

Eumetopias jubatus (Schreber, 1776).

Etymology: *Eu/metopias* = well/broad forehead or brow; *jubatus* = mane; Georg Wilhelm Steller was a German naturalist on Bering's expedition to Alaska in 1741. **Size:** Females to 8' (2.5 m) and 600 lbs (270 kg); males to 10' (3 m) and 2,200 lbs (1 tonne). Largest member of this family. **Range/habitat:** Coastal rim of north Pacific, Bering Sea and Kurile Islands to California, typically close to shore. Adults are largely nonmigratory.

Description: Low forehead. Males (bulls) tan above and reddish-brown below; females slimmer and uniformly brown.

Behaviour: Species roars and growls deeply rather than barking; sometimes swims by to inspect divers. Swims and makes shallow dives; usually dives for less than 2 minutes but can stay submerged for 16 minutes or more.

Comments: Species has been protected since 1970; population is 100,000–140,000 worldwide (1997). Rookeries are located at Forrester Island, southeast Alaska, and at Cape St. James, North Danger Rocks and the Scott Islands, BC. Life span of males is 20 years; of females 30 years. Most feeding takes place shallower than 600' (180 m) and usually not more than 15 miles (24 km) from shore. These sea lions are considered a nuisance by commercial fishers.

CALIFORNIA SEA LION

Zalophus californianus (Lesson, 1828).

Etymology: *Za/lophus* = prominent/crest.

Size: Females to 5'6" (1.7 m) and 250 lbs (113 kg); males to 8' (2.5 m) and 900 lbs (405 kg).

Range/habitat: Sea lions congregate in rookeries off California and Mexico, Gulf of Mexico, Galapagos Islands May–August. Estimated population of 67,000 or more from Washington to California. Females and juveniles remain in California and Mexico; males (below) range up the coast to southern BC..

Description: Smaller and darker than Steller sea lion (see previous page); mature males have bump on forehead and light-coloured fur.

Behaviour: Species has a honking bark. Hauls out on log booms and wharves; often rests in rafts, with flippers held out of the water to minimize heat loss. Rolls and dives, often leaping out of the water ("porpoising"). Can stay submerged for 20 minutes.

Comments: Species feeds mainly on schooling fish, herring, hake, pollock and dogfish, with a small amount of salmon. Sea lions get caught in nets during the herring fishery, tearing gillnets and posing problems of releasing them from seine nets.

NORTHERN FUR SEAL

Callorhinus ursinus (Linnaeus, 1758).

Alternate names: *Ursus marinus*; sea bear.

Etymology: *Callo/rhinus* = beautiful/skin or hide; *ursinus* = bear.

Size: Females to 4' (1.2 m) and 110 lbs (50 kg); males to 6' (1.8 m) and 600 lbs (270 kg); pups 12 lbs (5.4 kg) at birth.

Range/habitat: Bering Sea and Sea of Okhost to southern California, in offshore waters throughout north Pacific.

Description: Small head with sharp, pointed nose; very large flippers. Males have much larger, thicker necks than females. Males dark above, reddish below, with massive grey shoulders. Females are slimmer, grey above and reddish below.

Behaviour: Individuals live solitary at sea. Often leaps out of the water ("porpoising"); may dive for up to 7 minutes and to depths of 600' (180 m). During May–October, fur seals of the Pacific Northwest gather on the Pribilof Islands, Bering Sea, to mate and give birth.

Comments: Species was hunted for its fur from the late 1700s to the 1980s. Northwest coast population is approximately 1 million. Life span of males is about 15 years; of females 25 years.

Whales, Dolphins, Porpoises Order Cetacea

In all, 79 species of whales, dolphins and porpoises (cetaceans, from the Latin *cetus*—"large sea animal," and the Greek *ketos*—"sea monster") have been described, and there are likely others that have not been identified. Their offshore distribution and elusive behavior make them difficult to study.

Whale watching has gained such popularity in the Pacific Northwest that regulations and guidelines are necessary to ensure minimal disturbance for marine mammals. These vary from site to site, so consult Fisheries and Oceans Canada or the National Marine Fisheries Service in the United States for specific information.

TIPS FOR WHALE WATCHERS:

- If a whale or whales are sighted near your vessel, avoid sudden speed or course changes.

- Approach whales from the side rather than heading directly toward them. Always be on the lookout to ensure you are not breaking up pods or separating females from their young. Avoid disturbing resting whales.

- Stay at least 300' (100 m) away from any whale, dolphin or porpoise. The animal may choose to come much closer to you; if it does, do not chase it. Be wary of individuals that appear to be tame, and keep clear of the flukes.

- If you are in a power boat, shift your motor into neutral or idle when you are within 300' (100 m) of the animal. If you must use your motor to hold position, keep your speed down. If you are in a sailboat, idle your auxiliary motor to signal your presence or turn on your echo sounder.

- Minimize the time spent with any one group of whales, and the number of vessels in the area. When you leave the location, start out slowly and wait until you are more than 1,000' (300 m) from the animal before accelerating.

- Travel parallel to whales.

Orcas, Dolphins, Porpoises Suborder Odontoceti

This suborder includes dolphins, porpoises and the toothed whales. The terms *dolphin* and *porpoise* are often used interchangeably. *Porpoise* is a name often used for any small dolphin, but it is scientifically used for the Family Phocoenidae, six species of small coastal marine mammals having small, rounded heads without beaks and spade-shaped teeth. Porpoises often travel up rivers and some live out in the open sea. The "true" dolphins, Family Delphinidae, are small cetaceans, including orcas, false killer whales, and a variety of dolphins with prominent to indistinct beaks, cone-shaped teeth and generally prominent dorsal fins.

Toothed whales, including several sperm whales and beaked whales, are sometimes sighted offshore in Pacific Northwest waters. They feed on fish, squid and, in a few cases, other marine mammals.

Orcas and Dolphins
Family Delphinidae

KILLER WHALE (ORCA)
Orcinus orca (Linnaeus, 1758).
Alternate name: Formerly *Grampus rectipinna* (Cope, 1869).
Etymology: *Orcinus* and *orca* = demon from hell (the Latin *orcus* means "the lower world"). Linnaeus originally called the species *Delphinus orca*, "the demon dolphin."
Size: Females to 23' (7 m) and 8 tons (7.2 tonnes); males to 30' (9 m) and 11 tons (10 tonnes); newborns to 8'6" (2.5 m) and 400 lbs (180 kg).
Range/habitat: Range is one of the greatest among all mammals: all oceans, tropics to polar ice packs. Largest populations in cooler coastal waters of northern Pacific coasts, with more than 725 killer whales inhabiting the coastal waters of Alaska, BC and Washington. Of these, 305 are fish-eating "residents," which live in stable family groups or pods in northern and southern resident communities. The rest are "transient" and "offshore" whales, which travel in more loosely associated groups.

Description: Largest member of dolphin family. Black (rarely white) with white chin, elliptical white patch behind each eye, white patches on the sides, white underside of tail fluke, grey saddle patch behind dorsal fin. Individuals can be identified by fin shape, nicks and marks, and grey saddle markings. Male has tall dorsal fin to 6' (1.8 m) and longer and broader paddle-shaped pectoral fins than the females. Female has shorter, curved dorsal fin, to 3' (1m) (see photo at bottom of page).

Behaviour: Species shows a number of exciting behaviours, including blowing, breaching, tail-slapping, pectoral fin-slapping and spyhopping. They often rest in a tight group or line, and travel in groups, quite close to one another. They cruise at 2–4 knots (4–7 km/h), but can reach speeds of 17 knots (30 km/h) or more. When two pods meet after a separation of a day or more, they may engage in a "greeting ceremony." Northern residents sometimes rub their bodies on stones in shallow water.

The basic social group of "resident" killer whales is a mother and her offspring, up to 9 whales. A subpod is one or more mothers and offspring, closely related, that travel together and rarely split up. A pod of 10 to 20 whales consists of several subpods that often travel together but may separate for weeks or months. Each pod can be distinguished by its vocalizations. The northern and southern communities of whales may overlap in their distribution, but have never been seen to travel together.

When a hydrophone is used, whales' vocalizations can be heard from several miles away, and from their unique "dialects" individual resident pods and clans can be identified. "Transient" killer whales are much quieter. Resident populations feed primarily on fishes; transients feed on marine mammals, including seals and sea lions. This is the only "whale" that regularly feeds on other whales.

Comments: Several thousand orcas live worldwide (1998). Life span is 50 years for males, 80 years for females. Orcas have been captured for display in aquaria. Until 1980 they were harvested, often as a bycatch, when hunting other whales for meat and oil. Until the late 1970s, orcas were killed in Norway to reduce predation on herring.

PACIFIC WHITE-SIDED DOLPHIN

Lagenorhynchus obliquidens Gill, 1865.

Alternate name: Lag's.

Etymology:
Lageno/rhynchus = bottle/nose;
obliqui/dens = slanting/teeth.

Size: Adults to 8' (2.5 m) and 300 lbs (135 kg); newborns to 4' (1.2 m).

Range/habitat: Usually offshore in temperate north Pacific. Occasionally inshore; usually in groups of up to 50, but also in large groups of several hundred to more than 1,000.

Description: Dark upper body with pale grey streak along sides, widening at tail end. White underside. Small, hooked dorsal fin, usually dark at front and grey in rear two-thirds. Short, indistinct black beak. Individuals can be identified by markings and coloration of dorsal fin.

Behaviour: Lots of splashing is often seen before dolphins are actually sighted. Active groups swim fast at 15 knots (28 km/h), leaving the water and creating a "rooster tail" of water similar to Dall's porpoise (see p. 187). Dolphin breaches frequently and is curious, often bowriding and approaching stationary boats; swimmers can snorkel and dive with travelling schools. Dives for 3–7 minutes.

Comments: Species lives about 45 years. It feeds on schooling fishes such as herring, anchovy, sardines (pilchards) and squid.

Porpoises
Family Phocoenidae

HARBOR PORPOISE

Phocoena phocoena (Linnaeus, 1758).
Alternate name: Common porpoise.
Etymology: Original name was *Delphinus phocoena*: *Phocaen* = porpoise (from Greek *phoke*, referring to seal-like appearance).
Size: To 6'3" (1.9 m) and 145 lbs (65 kg); newborns 34" (1 m).
Range/habitat: In coastal waters Beaufort Sea to California, usually within 6 miles (10 km) of land. Also swims up rivers. Both resident and migrating populations live in this area.
Description: Small, rounded head. Dark back, white to grey zone on lower sides and white to speckled belly. Low, triangular dorsal fin. 1 to 3 dark stripes run from jawline to flippers.
Behaviour: Species is typically seen alone or in small groups of 2 to 5. It avoids vessels and does not bowride. Swims at 12 knots (22 km/h); rolls about 4 times, emitting short puffing blows, then dives quietly at surface, rarely raising the flukes, and stays submerged for 2–6 minutes. When travelling, this porpoise surfaces repeatedly, up to 8 times at 1-minute intervals.
Comments: Species is smallest cetacean found in Canadian waters. It feeds on a variety of small fishes and lives about 13 years. Size of Pacific population is unknown.

DALL'S PORPOISE

Phocoenoides dalli (True, 1885).

Alternate name: Spray porpoise.

Etymology: *Phocaen* = porpoise (from Greek *phoke*, referring to seal-like appearance); *dalli* = William H. Dall, US Geological Survey, US National Museum, collected specimens in Alaska in 1873, on board the *Humboldt*.

Size: To 7'3" (2.2 m) and 485 lbs (218 kg); newborns to 39" (1 m).

Range/habitat: In northern reaches of north Pacific, close to shore and in open ocean. Inshore–offshore and north–south migrations.

Description: Dark grey to black with distinctive white patch, well behind flippers, on sides and belly. Dorsal fin has hooked tip, grey-white above and black below.

Behaviour: Small groups of 2 to 20 often rush to approach boats and bowride, but soon lose interest in anything travelling slower than 11 knots (20 km/h). Species rarely leaves the water but produces a "rooster tail," similar to Pacific white-sided dolphin (see p. 185). Swims to speeds of 20 knots (55 km/h) and makes short dives of 2–4 minutes.

Comments: Hundreds of thousands of individuals live in the north Pacific and Bering Sea (1998). Life span to 15 years.

Baleen Whales Suborder Mysticeti

Gray, minke and humpback whales are mysticete (*mystax* = moustache; *cetus* = large sea animal) or baleen whales. They have paired blowholes and, instead of teeth, plates of baleen (fingernail-like material) that hang down from the upper jaw.

GRAY WHALE

Eschrichtius robustus (Lilljeborg, 1861).

Alternate names: *E. glaucus* (Cope, 1868); Pacific gray; California gray; musseldigger.

Etymology: *Eschrichtius* = Daniel Frederciht Eschricht was a Danish zoologist at Copenhagen (1798–1863); *robustus* = strong.

Size: Adults to 50' (15 m) and 33 tons (30 tonnes); newborns to 16'6" (5 m) long.

Range: In shallow coastal waters of the north Pacific and Arctic oceans. Some whales stop to feed along Washington and BC coasts but most migrate annually between the lagoons of Baja California and the Arctic seas.

Habitat: Migrating along coast; feeding in shallow mud-sand bottoms.

Description: Grey patches and white mottling on dark grey skin; scattered patches of white barnacles and orange whale lice. Low hump instead of dorsal fin, followed by 6 to 12 "knuckles" on rear third of back. Paired nostrils on long, slender head, small in relation to overall size. Upper jaw has coarse, yellowish baleen with long, thick bristles. Flukes 10–12' (3–3.6 m) across, pointed at tips and deeply notched in centre. Newborns are jet black.

Behaviour: Species produces occasional sounds—low groans, grunts, clicks and bongs—but these are rare and barely audible on a hydrophone. They spyhop (left) and breach. Gray is often approachable; "friendlies"

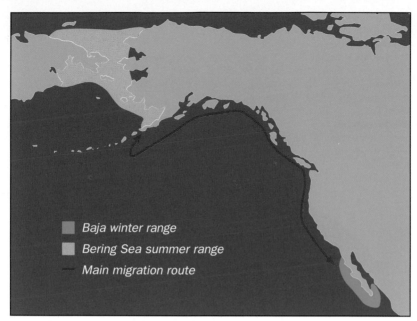

■ Baja winter range
■ Bering Sea summer range
— Main migration route

Grey whale migration

approach small boats and allow themselves to be touched by humans. When migrating, grays travel at 2–5 knots (4–8 km/h), occasionally to 10 knots (18 km/h). The whale produces 4 to 6 blows with quick, shallow dives at 15- to 30-second intervals, then raises its flukes and dives for 3–5 minutes, or as long as 18–20 minutes. The blows are often heart- or V-shaped due to the two blowholes.

Comments: Species was harvested commercially until 1947, and the north Atlantic population is extinct as a result. Approximately 22,000 now inhabit Pacific Northwest waters (1998), and there may be small population in the Pacific off northeast Asia, and near Korea.

Grays make one of the longest mammal migrations, 10,000–14,000 miles (16,000–22,400 km) round trip (see above). From December to April they breed, calve and rear their young in lagoons in Baja California; from February to July they migrate north along the coast; from April to November they feed in the Arctic; from October to February they return south. An estimated 35–50 "resident" gray whales spend the summer off Vancouver Island.

The whale feeds on a variety of planktonic animals in the water column, and by opening its mouth and running it along the bed of shallow sand and mud bays, scooping up worms, crustaceans and other organisms. The life span is about 70 years.

MINKE WHALE

Balaeanoptera acutorostrata acutorostrata Lacépède, 1804.

Alternate name: Piked whale.

Etymology: *Balaeano/ptera* = whale/wing or fin; *acuto/rostrata* = sharp/snout. The common name originates from a Norwegian whaler, Captain Meinke, known for overestimating the length of whales taken by his crew. Whalers came to call all small or undersize whales "Minke's whales," and the name was eventually adopted.

Size: To 33' (10 m) in total length and 10 tons (9 tonnes); newborns to 9'3" (2.8 m).

Range/habitat: Found worldwide but more common in polar and temperate seas, including north Pacific. Some individuals are resident to an area, others migrate seasonally.

Description: Sharp, pointed snout; longitudinal ridge on head. Small dorsal fin curves toward rear. Dark grey to black above, white underside; often a broad white band on upper surface of pectoral flippers. Flukes have pointed tips, slight notch in the middle. Individuals can be identified by subtle natural marks and scars on dorsal fin and pigmentation on flanks.

Behaviour: Species may leap out of the water. Swims at 6–8 knots (11–15 km/h), but can reach 30 knots (55 km/h). When diving, head surfaces first and small dorsal fin is exposed, then whale typically produces 5 to 8 low, indistinct blows at intervals of less than a minute, followed by a long dive to 8 minutes, but as long as 20 minutes. The flukes do not show when whale surfaces or dives.

Comments: Species is one of the smallest baleen whales. Approximately 900,000 live worldwide (1998), about 9,000 of them in the north Pacific (north Atlantic and Pacific stocks have been considered different subspecies). They are seen alone or in small groups, often detected when a flock of seabirds feeding on small fish and krill is disrupted by the feeding whale. Life span is about 50 years.

HUMPBACK WHALE

Megaptera novaeangliae (Borowski, 1781).
Alternate name: The singing whale.
Etymology: *Mega/ptera* = large/wing or fin; *novae/angliae* = of New England, where species was first scientifically described.
Size: To 49'3" (14.8 m); newborns to 16'6" (5 m).
Range/habitat: All oceans, from poles to tropics. North Pacific humpbacks feed in colder regions of BC, Alaska and Bering and Chukchi seas in summer, and migrate to Hawaii, Mexico and even Japan for breeding. In winter, humpbacks of Washington, Oregon and California migrate south to warmer waters of Mexico for calving.

Description: Dark grey to black, underside often white or partially white; white on underside of long pectoral flipper, some white patches on underside of tail flukes. Flippers are proportionally longer than those of any other whale. Knobs on top of head and along lower jaw. 12–26 grooves in throat region. Low, stubby dorsal fin with broad base.
Behaviour: Species is seen single, or in groups to 15 whales. Produces sounds during feeding that may scare prey or coordinate feeding activities. A group of whales produce bubbles, forming a "bubble-net" that forces prey to the surface for easier capture by lunge feeding (see photo below). Males only "sing" some of the longest and most complex songs of any animal, especially on breeding grounds. All males on a breeding ground sing the same song. Humpbacks swim slowly, 4–5 knots (7–9 km/h). They breach, spyhop, tail-slap and often roll on the surface and flap the flipper. They feed by charging through schools of small fish and crustaceans, trapping food in the baleen plates that line the upper jaw.
The humpback produces 5 to 10 tall bush blows at the surface, then arches the back and dives, raising the tail flukes, and stays submerged for 10–20 minutes.
Comments: This is a threatened species, with several geographically distinct populations. Approximately 7,000 humpbacks live in the northern hemisphere (1998). Catalogues have been prepared of individual whales, identified by shape, colour pattern and marks on underside of the tail flukes. Over 5,700 were harvested in BC waters.

Otters Order Carnivora

Otters are part of a family (family Mustelidae) of sea otters, river otters, weasels and their allies. Those seen in protected, inshore waters on the beach are likely river otters; those in more exposed, offshore waters are likely sea otters.

SEA OTTER

Enhydra lutris (Linnaeus, 1758).
Etymology: *Enhydra* = living in water; *lutris* = otter.
Size: Over 5' (1.5 m) long and to 80 lbs (36 kg). Smallest marine mammal.
Range: Isolated populations in Alaska, BC, Washington and California.

Habitat: In offshore kelp beds, rocky islets and reefs. Species lives almost entirely at sea.
Description: Short, flattened tail, one-third of body length. Broad, flat, light-coloured head and short, thick neck with loose skin folds on neck and chest. Rusty red to dark brown to black fur, lighter on head, throat and chest.
Behaviour: Sea otters always eat while floating on their backs in the water. They do not go ashore to eat, as river otters often do. They tend to stay in open, exposed waters, gathering and "rafting" together in large groups of various ages and sexes. They squeal, hiss, snarl and grunt but do not whistle like river otters.
Comments: Early records show sea otters occurred from northern Japan along the Pacific rim to Baja California. When they were protected in 1911, there were fewer than 2,000 animals in populations from Russia to Prince William Sound, Alaska, and a population in California. Sea otters from Alaska were introduced to the west coast of Vancouver Island in 1969–72. A population has also become established along BC's central coast, off the Goose Islands.

Sea otters have a high metabolic rate and eat as much as 25–30 percent of their body weight each day! They feed primarily on sea urchins, mussels, abalone and a variety of invertebrates from the intertidal zone to 65' (20 m), and occasionally to 330' (100 m). Sea otters use rocks as tools to dislodge prey and break open food items. They live about 15 years.

RIVER OTTER

Lutra canadensis (Schreber, 1776).
Etymology: *Lutra (lytra)* = otter.
Size: To 4'6" (1.3 m) and 30 lbs (13.5 kg).
Range: Pacific coast, coastal marshes, lakes and streams throughout North America.
Habitat: Most abundant on the coast, in bays and inland marine waters. Also found in lakes, rivers and marshes.

Description: Long, streamlined body and long, tapered tail, 16-20" (40-50 cm). Broad, flat head; neck longer than that of sea otter. Short, very dense fur, dark brown above, lighter below.
Behaviour: Species is seen in groups, each group usually a single family with up to four young. A shrill whistle is used to communicate, as well as chuckles and grunts to sound alarm. River otters tread water with neck and head out of water, peering about. They are at home on land. They construct "beds" in hollow logs, stumps or roots, or they take over the burrow of a beaver or muskrat. They do not excavate their own burrows. The young are tended in the nest for 10-12 weeks before they venture out to learn to swim and hunt.
Comments: There are 8 or more subspecies of river otters recognized across North America. The subspecies *L.c. mira* is found in SE Alaska, the mainland coast of BC and Vancouver Island. A subspecies is recognized for the the Queen Charlotte Islands, *L.c. periclyzomae*.

Less Common Whales and Dolphins

A number of marine mammals are encountered only occasionally or seasonally in deep and offshore waters at the continental shelf and beyond. They are recognized by their "blows" and dive sequences and by their visible body features. Many of these whales were hunted in the past and were landed at coastal whaling stations. Today they sometimes stray into coastal waters or become stranded on Pacific Northwest shores. The figure below shows the shape and relative sizes of many of the whales, dolphins and porpoises of the north Pacific.

Humpback Whale

Gray Whale

Stejneger's Beaked Whale

Sei Whale

Northern Right Whale

Pacific White-Sided Dolphin

Harbor Porpoise

DOLPHINS, KILLER WHALES, FALSE KILLER WHALES, PILOT WHALES

In addition to the commonly encountered killer whale (see p. 183) and Pacific white-sided dolphin (p. 185), five other members of the dolphin–killer whale family inhabit the North Pacific. These species have been seen in offshore waters but rarely move inshore.

The **false killer whale**, *Pseudorca crassidens*, is common (but not abundant) in deep offshore waters. They range from the Aleutian Islands to central America, but sightings north of California are unusual. Adults reach 20' (6 m) in length. They travel in groups of 10 to 50, and sometimes hundreds. When encountered, they approach boats readily and bow-ride or wake-ride. The false killer whale has a uniformly dark body colour, a prominent dorsal fin and a long, slender body.

Blue Whale

Beluga Whale

Fin Whale

Dall's Porpoise

Minke Whale

Sperm Whale

Killer Whale

Baird's Beaked Whale

Cuvier's Beaked Whale

195

The **short-finned pilot whale**, *Globicephala macrorhynchus*, is found offshore, from the Aleutian Islands to Guatemala. The adult reaches 21 1/2' (6.5 m) in length. It is jet black or dark grey, with a rounded bulbous forehead and a low dorsal fin set forward on the body. These mammals travel in groups of 10 to 30, or occasionally several hundred. Entire pods rest at the surface, a behaviour called "logging," which allows vessels to approach.

Both the **common dolphin** (or **saddle-backed dolphin**), *Delphinus delphis*, and the **striped dolphin**, *Stenella coeruleoalba*, travel in active groups of 10 to 500, to larger herds—sometimes more than 1,000. Both have been sighted following warm water currents from the equator to Victoria, BC. They are usually found well offshore over the continental shelf.

Risso's dolphin, *Grampus griseus*, has often been sighted in groups of 3 to 50, well out at sea at the continental shelf, and very occasionally a carcass has washed ashore. This species is also known as the **grey dolphin**. It has a tall, crescent-shaped dorsal fin and can be identified by extensive scars on the body, caused by the teeth of other Risso's dolphins, either mates or rivals. Adults reach 12 1/2' (3.8 m) in length.

Less common Toothed Whales

Beluga, Sperm, Beaked Whales

The uniformly white **beluga (belukha) whale**, *Delphinapterus leucas*, is found in Alaska, in shallow coastal waters, rivers and estuaries of the Arctic and in the Bering Sea. It is also seen off the north and central coasts of Alaska. Adults are 9 1/4–16 1/2' (3–5 m) long. This whale has a rounded, bulbous head and no dorsal fin. Belugas are called the "sea canaries" because they are very vocal and emit a variety of clicks, squeaks and moos. In fact they are often heard rather than seen. Belugas pay little attention to passing boats. They frequently spyhop, and are known to dive down to 1,805' (550 m) and beyond in search of fish.

The **sperm whale**, *Physeter macrocephalus*, is found offshore at the edge of the continental shelf, in waters deeper than 655' (200 m). The best-known sperm whale is Herman Melville's *Moby Dick*. Adults are 36–59' (11–18 m) long and weigh 20–50 tons (18–45 tonnes). Sperm whales are deep divers, spending up to 90 minutes diving to depths of at least 9,845' (3,000 m). They have a distinctive blow, off-centre and directed forward. Sperm whales are listed as endangered, having been one of the world's most heavily exploited whales. Almost 6,000 individuals were harvested commercially off British Columbia, mostly during summer months.

On rare occasions, **dwarf sperm whales**, *Kogia simus*, which grow to only 9' (3 m) in length, have been stranded on Pacific Northwest shores.

The **beaked whales** are the least known, and some species have never been seen alive. The largest of the Pacific beaked whales is the **North Pacific bottlenose whale** (**Baird's beaked whale**), *Berardius bairdi*. Adults reach 42' (12.8 m) in length. More than 50 of these whales were hunted and landed at BC's coastal whaling stations. They occur near shore, but are usually seen offshore at the continental shelf and beyond.

Only the skulls and carcasses of the **Cuvier's beaked whale**, *Ziphius cavirostris*, that washed ashore have been studied. The living whales, to 23' (7 m) long, are rarely encountered and have not been studied. **Stejneger's beaked whale**, *Mesoplodon stejnegeri*, known mostly from strandings, has also been sighted in small groups off our coast. These whales reach 17¹/2' (5.3 m) in length. They are most frequently seen in the Aleutian Islands.

Less common Baleen Whales

Blue, Sei, Fin, Right whales

In addition to the commonly encountered baleen whales, the gray (see p. 188), minke (p. 190) and humpback (p. 191) whales, a few other large whales are occasionally seen offshore. These include the blue, sei, fin and northern right whale. The rorqual whales—blue, sei, fin, humpback and minke—have throat grooves, while gray and right whales do not.

The rare **blue whale**, *Balaenoptera musculus* (below), is seen in summer off the Aleutian Islands and offshore from the Gulf of Alaska to central California. It is the largest animal known to have lived on earth, larger than dinosaurs, reaching a length of 110' (33 m) and a weight of about 196 tons (176 tonnes). Blue whales travel in small groups of 1 to 5, sometimes up to 60. The blue-grey and

mottled body has only a tiny, stubby dorsal fin set far back. Yellowish coloured algae often grow on the underside, giving rise to another common name, "sulphur-bottom whale." Whalers hunted the blue whale close to extinction. The population was estimated at only 6–14,000 worldwide by the 1990s. Between 1905 and 1967, 1,400 blue whales were taken off the BC coast.

The **sei whale** (or **pollock whale**), *Balaenoptera borealis*, is found offshore or occasionally near islands, from the Gulf of Alaska to Baja California. They occur far off the BC coast each summer. Adults reach 62' (18.9 m) in length. They travel in small groups of 2 to 5, occasionally up to 30 at good feeding grounds. The sei whale has a long, slender, bluish-grey to black body, a longitudinal ridge on the head, throat grooves and a small sickle-shaped dorsal fin. These whales were hunted commercially, but are elusive and fast, capable of burst speeds of 25 knots (46 km/h). The common names, sei and pollock whale, come from the name of a fish that it follows as it feeds in the Norwegian fjords.

The **fin whale**, *Balaenoptera physalus*, prefers deep, offshore waters from the Bering Sea to Baja California. This is the second largest animal on earth (after the blue whale), about the size of the large dinosaurs, reaching 72 1/4' (22 m) and 80 tons. It has a grey to brown-black back, a longitudinal ridge on the back, throat grooves and a small dorsal fin set well back. This whale is unusual in having white markings on the lip and head on the right side only. Unlike that of the blue whale, its body is free of mottling. Fin whales travel in small groups of 3 to 7, sometimes 100 or more on feeding grounds, and are indifferent to boats. More than 7,600 fin whales were landed at BC whaling stations.

As well, very small numbers (estimated at 220) of the **northern right whale**, *Eubalaena glacialis*, occur in the offshore waters of the north Pacific, usually near the ice edge at high latitudes. This whale is close to extinction; only a few hundred remain in the world from a population of tens of thousands. The common name originates from whaling—these were the "right" whales to kill. They were slow, easy to approach and kill, and they floated when they were dead. The carcasses provided large quantities of oil, meat and whalebone. Fewer than 10 were landed at whaling stations on the Queen Charlotte Islands and on the west coast of Vancouver Island. The northern right whale reaches a length of 60' (18 m) and a weight of 100 tons (90 tonnes). It has a brown to black body, a large head with distinctive white bumps or patches (callosities), and a broad back with no dorsal fin.

Seaweeds & Seagrasses

An estimated 7,000 seaweeds (large attached algae), 4,000 microalgae (individuals not visible to the naked eye) and 50 seagrasses live in marine environments worldwide, and according to recent estimates the Pacific coast between Alaska and California is home to nearly 700 species of them. Included here are some of the large, visible seaweeds of the region, which occur from the intertidal zone to depths of 100' (30 m) or more. Within this zone, seaweeds generally inhabit distinct subzones, depending on their tolerance of conditions, competition from other species and activity of predators such as sea urchins.

Archibald Menzies, a botanist on Captain George Vancouver's voyage in 1791–95, was the first naturalist to collect marine algae in this area. He collected a few specimens on an earlier voyage, 1786–89, with Colnett.

STRUCTURE

Algae and seagrasses are non-vascular plants: they do not have true roots, stems and leaves. They do not need a conducting system, because all parts of the plant are in constant contact with water, from which it takes the nutrients and dissolved gases it needs to grow and reproduce.

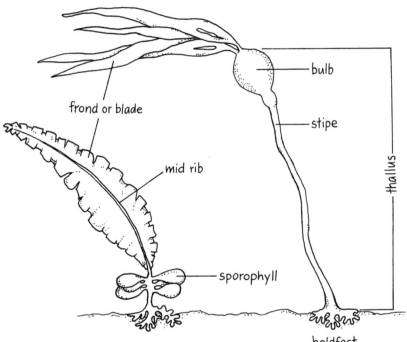

Physical features of seaweeds.

Seaweeds are attached to the sea floor by a holdfast, which often looks like a root but is primarily for attachment. The main portion of the plant, the thallus, may be encrusting, leafy, filamentous or branched. The thallus is made up of a supporting stem-like structure called a stipe, and leaf-like fronds or blades.

REPRODUCTION AND LIFE CYCLES

Marine algae often have complicated life cycles. Many are seasonal, sometimes microscopic and other times large and visible.

Seaweeds are non-flowering plants. They reproduce by sexual means, producing swimming gametes, and also by asexual means, including budding and division. Sexual stages often develop at the tips of the blades. Winter storms can break plants down to the holdfasts, and in the spring new blades begin to grow. Some species, such as the coralline algae, are truly perennial and live many years.

HARVESTING AND ECOLOGICAL IMPORTANCE

The marine algae make up much of the basis of life in the sea. Some, like the bull kelp and giant kelps, form extensive underwater forests that support communities of organisms.

Many species of algae are edible. Seaweeds have long been harvested by Native peoples for a variety of foods, and today they are cultivated commercially. Giant kelp (see p. 206) is still used to collect herring roe. Other seaweeds are dried and used for extracts, a source of iodine, vitamins, minerals and trace elements. Alginate, an extract of kelp, is an emulsifier and stabilizer used in many foods, such as ice cream, and other products.

RED TIDES—HARMFUL ALGAL BLOOMS (HABS)

The Pacific Northwest is unfortunately an area where toxic marine algae flourish. Most people are aware of "red tides" of microscopic algae (several dinoflagellates of the *Alexandrium*, *Pyrodinium* and *Gymnodinium* genera; not included in this guide). Algae are concentrated by filter-feeding bivalve (two-shelled) shellfish and can cause paralytic shellfish poisoning (PSP). Over time, many people have become sick and some have died from eating clams (especially butter clams), mussels, oysters, scallops and other bivalve shellfish.

Recently other harmful algal blooms (HABs) have received attention. The microscopic algae of the *Pseudo-nitzschia* genus produce demoic acid, which killed fish and caused illnesses in people. Demoic acid from algae causes "amnesic shellfish poisoning" in humans and has resulted in fishery closures of Dungeness crab (see p. 78) and razor clams (p. 94) on our coast and mussel closures on the Atlantic coast. Demoic acid has also been a contributing factor in the death of birds (pelicans and cormorants) and marine mammals along the California coast. Sea lions eat anchovies and sardines, which can accumulate demoic acid.

HABs also pose significant threats to shellfish and finfish aquaculture industries. Blooms of the alga *Heterosigma*, which are not toxic to humans, have caused gill damage and respiratory paralysis leading to fish kills in Washington and British Columbia since the late 1980s.

PHYLUM (DIVISION) CHLOROPHYTA

Green Seaweeds Class Ulvophyceae

About 13 percent of green algae species live in salt water. To utilize light most efficiently, they usually live in shallow water and in the intertidal zone: blue and red wavelengths, which these plants require, are filtered by seawater and do not penetrate much more than a metre. Marine green algae of the Pacific Northwest occur in diverse shapes and are usually less than 12" (30 cm) long.

SEA STAGHORN

Codium fragile (Suringar) Hariot, 1889.
Alternate names: Felty fingers; dead man's fingers.
Size: To 12" (30 cm) tall.
Range: Prince William Sound, Alaska to Baja California.
Habitat: On rocks on open coast, in current-swept transition areas, low intertidal and subtidal.
Description: Dark green-black, felt-like appearance and spongy texture. Cylindrical branches 1/4" (6 mm) in diameter; each fork divides into 2 equal branches.
Comments: Has an unpleasant pungent odour. Species is also found in Japan and has been introduced to the north Atlantic.

SPONGY CUSHION

Codium setchellii Setchell & Gardner, 1903.
Etymology: *setchellii* = from William A. Setchell, University of California, who studied algae and published from the late 1890s–1940s. He was the west coast's first resident phycologist.
Size: To 10" (25 cm) diameter and 5/8" (1.6 cm) thick.
Range: Sitka, Alaska to Baja California.
Habitat: On rocks, low intertidal.
Description: Smooth, irregular, dark green cushions.
Comments: Eaten by nudibranchs in some locations.

GREEN ROPE

Acrosiphonia coalita (Ruprecht) Scagel, Garberry, Golden & Hawkes, 1986.
Alternate name: *Spongomorpha coalita.*
Size: To 18" (46 cm) long, but more commonly to 12" (30 cm).
Range: Alaska to San Luis Obispo County, California.
Habitat: On rocks, low intertidal.
Description: Spongy texture, resembles branched, much-frayed rope. Bright grass-green to dark green, frequently with yellow tips.

SEA HAIR

Enteromorpha intestinalis (Linnaeus) Link, 1820.
Alternate name: Link confetti.
Size: To 8" (20 cm) long, to 1/4" (6 mm) diameter.
Range: Cosmopolitan on temperate coasts; Aleutian Islands to Mexico; Chile.
Habitat: Free-floating in tidepools, in fresh water seepage or growing on other algae on rocks. High to mid-intertidal.
Description: Bright green, yellowish at reproduction and bleached white. Hollow tubes of a single layer of cells.

Comments: Favourite food of the isopod sea slater (*Ligia pallasii*), high in the intertidal zone. One of several species of *Enteromorpha*. Also found in Chukchi Sea, Russia, and in Mediterranean and Atlantic waters.

SEA LETTUCE

Ulva spp.
Size: To 7" (18 cm) long; sometimes broader than long.
Range: Alaska to southern California.
Habitat: On rocks in protected areas, mid- to low intertidal.
Description: Light to medium grass-green blades, often with ruffled or deeply incised edges; 2 cells thick with a small, distinct stipe (stem).
Comments: 9 or more species of *Ulva*, and many similar bladed greens, occur between Alaska and California. All species are edible, but some are tastier than others. Positive identification often requires microscopic examination of cell layers.

PHYLUM (DIVISION) PHAEOPHYTA

This classification (which has also been called Heterokontophyta) includes the brown, golden and yellow-green algae under a common phylum, or division.

Brown Seaweeds Class Phaeophyceae

These algae, the largest and most visible on our coast, are often thick and tough, and range in colour from light olive-green to dark brown and almost black. Included among them are the kelps, whose name is derived from an English term for the ash made by burning brown algae. This ash was used in making soap and other products. Today the giant kelp (*Macrocystis*) is harvested by underwater mowing machines mounted on self-propelled vessels. They are used in making vitamins and alginate, an extract used as an emulsifier and stabilizer in foods, paint and other items.

ROCKWEED
Fucus gardneri (Linnaeus) Silva, 1953.
Alternate names: Bladderwrack; popweed; often listed as *Fucus distichus.*
Size: To 20" (50 cm) long.
Range: Bering Sea and Aleutian Islands to central California.
Habitat: On rocks, mid- to low intertidal.
Description: Olive-green to yellow-brown. Flattened thallus with a midrib and branches which keep dividing into 2 parts. Blades to 1/2" (1 cm) wide. Some terminal branches are swollen and warty: these are sites where eggs and sperm are produced.
Comments: Common and abundant; the most conspicuous plant on rocky intertidal shores. Eaten by periwinkle snails, falselimpets and isopods. Avoid walking on this plant. Rockweed is also found in Russia.

LITTLE ROCKWEED
Pelvetiopsis limitata Gardener, 1910.
Size: To 3¹/4" (8 cm) tall.
Range: Vancouver Island to Cambria, northern California.
Habitat: Usually atop rocks, upper intertidal on open coast.
Description: Light tan-olive. Erect, compact growths with flattened stems that branch several times.
Comments: Swollen terminal ends contain reproductive structures. Species is similar in appearance to rockweed (above), but no midrib, and blades are not as flattened.

WIREWEED
Sargassum muticum (Yendo) Fensholt, 1955.
Alternate name: Japweed.
Size: To 6½' (2 m) tall.
Range: Southeast Alaska to Baja California.
Habitat: Attaches to rocks or shells, low intertidal to 16' (5 m).
Description: Typically a yellowish-brown short stalk that branches repeatedly; flat leaf-like growth and reproductive structures in spherical floats.
Comments: Introduced from Japan on shells with oyster spat. Species is also found in Japan, southern England, Netherlands, France, Spain and the north Atlantic.

SEA CAULIFLOWER
Leathesia difformis (Linnaeus) Areschoug, 1847.
Alternate names: Golden spongy cushions; sea potato.
Size: To 1" (2.5 cm) tsll, to 5" (12 cm) diameter.
Range: Bering Sea to Baja California; Mexico; Chile.
Habitat: On rocks or on other algae, in tidepools and exposed in the mid-intertidal.
Description: Convoluted, globular, brain-like spongy growths. Yellowish-brown to golden.
Comments: May form a bumpy carpet in the mid-intertidal. Species is also found in north Atlantic and in the North Sea.

BULL KELP
Nereocystis luetkeana (Mertens) Postels & Ruprecht, 1840.
Alternate names: Bullwhip kelp; ribbon kelp.
Size: Stalk to 65' (20 m) long, float to 5" (12 cm) diameter, blades to 10' (3 m) long.
Range: Aleutian Islands to San Luis Opisbo County, California.
Habitat: On rocks from protected shores to open coast, lowest intertidal zone and subtidal to 65' (20 m).
Description: Forms large kelp forests. Branching holdfast; long tubular stalk ending in a bulbous gas-filled float with four groups of broad, flat, elongated blades.
Comments: An annual plant that dies off in winter and is washed ashore during storms. The resulting kelp drift is important food for urchins, and food and shelter for a variety of organisms. Has been harvested commercially for fresh and dried products for human consumption and for manufacturing fertilizer.

GIANT KELP

Macrocystis integrifolia Bory, 1826.

Alternate name: Giant perennial kelp.

Size: To 33' (10 m) long, blades to 16" (40 cm) long and 3" (7.5 cm) wide.

Range: Kodiak Island, Alaska to Monterey Peninsula, California.; Peru; Chile.

Habitat: Attached to rocks in somewhat sheltered areas of the open coast, lowest intertidal zone and subtidal to 33' (10 m).

Description: Thick canopy of kelp blades, olive to dark brown. Branched stipes (stems) with split blades; hollow, gas-filled, pear-shaped floats where blades join stipe. Flattened holdfast creeps over the rocks.

Comments: Giant kelp is harvested and ponded with spawning herring, which deposit eggs on it, producing for edible and valuable "roe on kelp." The giant perennial kelp *Macrocystis pyrifera* is harvested by machine for alginate extracts, which are added to food products to make them smooth and creamy. *Macrocystis* is also used in making kelp tablets, a source of vitamins and minerals.

FEATHER BOA KELP

Egregia menziesii (Turner) Areschoug, 1876.

Etymology: Named in honor of Archibald Menzies, the botanist on Captain George Vancouver's voyages, 1791–95, who collected many marine algae specimens from Nootka Sound on the west coast of Vancouver Island.

Size: To 65' (20 m) long.

Range: Alaska to Punta Eugenio, Baja California.

Habitat: On rocks along moderately exposed open coasts, intertidal to 65' (20 m).

Description: Long, strap-like stem (stipe) densely covered with numerous broad to linear blades to 2" (5 cm) long, some forming ellipsoid to rounded floats. Olive to dark brown.

Comments: One of the largest intertidal brown kelps. *Notoacmaea incessa*, a species of limpet, is often found rasping depressions on the rib of the kelp.

SEA PALM
Postelsia palmaeformis Ruprecht, 1852.
Etymology: *palmae/formis* = resembling a small palm tree.
Size: To 2' (60 cm) tall.
Range: Vancouver Island to Morro Bay, California.
Habitat: On surf-beaten rocks along the open coast, mid- to low intertidal.
Description: Stubby holdfast; long, flexible, rubbery stalk topped with numerous (to 100) drooping blades to 10" (25 cm) long. Greenish to olive brown. Blades have grooves in which spores form and release.
Comments: Grows at same high to mid-intertidal range as goose barnacles (see p. 85) and California mussels (p. 89). Sea palms are beaten down by the surf and spring back as each wave recedes.

SPLIT KELP
Laminaria setchellii (Kjellm, 1889) Silva, 1957.
Alternate name: *Laminaria dentigera.*
Etymology: *denti/ger* = toothlike projections/bear.
Size: To 5' (1.5 m) long.
Range: Eastern Gulf of Alaska to Ensenada, Baja California.
Habitat: On moderately exposed rocky shores.
Description: Branched holdfast; long, stiff stipe (stem) to 1¼" (3 cm) diameter. Long, smooth divided blades to 4½" (11 cm), which droop from upright stipe at low tide on a calm day.
Comments: Common in groups at lowest tide levels.

RIBBON KELP
Alaria marginata Postels & Ruprecht, 1840.
Alternate names: Wing kelp; edible kelp.
Size: To 10' (3 m) long, 8" (20 cm) wide.
Range: Kodiak Island, Alaska to Point Conception, California.
Habitat: On rocks in open and protected waters, often in currents, mid- to low intertidal and shallow subtidal.
Description: Well-branched holdfast; short stipe (stem) to a dark tan blade, with a distinctive single golden midrib ½" (1 cm) wide. Blade to 10' (3 m) long and 8" (20 cm) wide.
Comments: One of the largest and most abundant algae.

PHYLUM RHODOPHYTA

Red Seaweeds Class Rhodophyceae

The common name "red seaweeds" hardly does justice to the many species in this group, whose hues range from reds to browns to purples to black, and whose forms range from encrusting patches to large, conspicuous blades. The red seaweeds have pigments that absorb red, blue and green light, which penetrate deeply into the water and allow red algae to live at greater depths than other kinds of seaweeds.

PURPLE LAVER
Porphyra perforata J. G. Agardh, 1882.
Alternate names: Red laver; Nori.
Size: To 12" (30 cm) wide and long.
Range: Bering Sea; Aleutian Islands to Baja California.
Habitat: On rocks, mussels or other algae along protected and exposed shores, upper and mid-intertidal.
Description: Tiny disk-shaped holdfast; broad, delicate, often lobed or ruffled blades, 1 cell layer thick. Iridescent purple, purple-green.
Comments: Species is also found in Russia. It is one of the least tasty species of *Porphyra*.

SEA SACS
Halosaccion glandiforme (S. G. Gmelin) Ruprecht, 1851.
Size: To 6" (15 cm) tall, 3/4" (2 cm) wide.
Range: Bering Sea; Aleutian Islands to Point Conception, California.
Habitat: On rocks along exposed and transition shores, mid-intertidal.
Description: Groups of finger-like individuals, often inflated with water. Bright purple-red (younger plants) to pale yellow.
Comments: Sea sacs often form a distinct band of growth in the intertidal zone. They are eaten by limpets. Amphipods often shelter inside the sac.

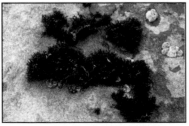

SEA MOSS
Endocladia muricata (Postels & Ruprecht) J. Agardh, 1847.
Alternate name: Nail brush seaweed.
Size: To 3" (8 cm) tall.
Range: Aleutian Islands to Baja California.
Habitat: On rocks and mussels along exposed shores, upper and mid-intertidal.
Description: Dense, stiff, bushy clumps of cylindrical spiny branches. Pinkish, dark red to black-brown.
Comments: Common and abundant. Sometimes grazed by limpets.

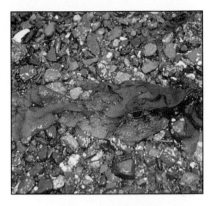

TURKISH TOWEL
Chondracanthus exasperatus (Harvey & Bailey)
Hughey, 1996
Alternate name: *Gigartina exasperata.*
Etymology: *exasperatus* = rasp-like blades.
Size: To 3.3' (1 m) long, 12" (30 cm) wide.
Range: Vancouver Island to Punta Maria,
Baja California.
Habitat: On rocks, subtidal to 65' (20 m).
Description: One or more broad, thick
blades with edges and flat surfaces bearing
tall, stiff projections. Brick red to purple, iri-
descent when wet.
Comments: Often washed up on the beach.

TURKISH WASHCLOTH AND TARSPOT SEAWEED
Mastocarpus papillatus (C.A. Agardh)
Kützing, 1843.
Alternate names: *Gigartina*
papillata = *Petrocelis middendorfii*
(encrusting phase).
Size: To 6" (15 cm) tall.
Range: Alaska to Punta Baja, Baja
California.
Habitat: On rocks, high to mid-
intertidal.
Description: Blades to 6" (15 cm)
long, with broad and various-shaped
branches. Dark reproductive
encrusting stage, formerly described as the genus *Petrocelis*, often found adjacent to blade form.
Comments: One of the more common red algae on the Pacific coast. Botanists first believed
the tarspot was a different alga, but it is now known to be a phase in the life cycle of this species.

BLACK PINE
Neorhodomela larix (Turner)
Masuda, 1982.
Alternate name: Formerly
known as *Rhodomela larix.*
Etymology: *larix* = larch, referring
to larch-like branches.
Size: To 8" (20 cm) long.
Range: Bering Sea to Government
Point, California.
Habitat: On sand-swept rocky
reefs; usually low but sometimes
upper intertidal.
Description: Wiry branches with
clusters of small branchlets to 3/8"
(1 cm) long. Dark black-brown.
Comments: Dense growth of black pine provides shelter for a variety of organisms.

Coralline Red Algae

In 1901–02, Professor K. Yendo from the University of Tokyo spent time at the Minnesota Seaside Station, operated by the University of Minnesota at Botanical Beach near Port Renfrew, BC. He described 21 species of coralline algae from that one location alone.

These abundant algae are difficult to identify in the field to the species level. As a group they are very distinctive, containing large amounts of calcium carbonate and ranging in colour from reddish-pink to purplish-pink. (They do not, however, retain their colour when they die.) Some are strictly encrusting, while others are jointed and branched.

Chitons and limpets graze on these algae. Sea urchins graze on them extensively to maintain their own shell-skeletons.

PINK ROCK CRUST

Lithothamnion spp. and others.
Alternate name: Encrusting coralline algae.
Size: To 1/8" (3 mm) thick. Often round, to 4" (10 cm) diameter.
Range: Alaska to California.
Habitat: On rocks and some shells, intertidal and subtidal.
Description: Thin, pink perennial growths, smooth or covered with bumps. May grow over worm tubes or shells of some mollusks.
Comments: Often found on the shell of the whitecap limpet (see p. 104). This limpet, abalone and several chitons graze on coralline algae. Several species of pink rock crust, *Lithothamnium* and others, occur in the Pacific Northwest and can be distinguished only by microscopic examination of reproductive structures.

GRACEFUL CORALLINE ALGAE

Corallina vancouverensis Yendo, 1902.
Alternate names: *Corallina gracilis* forms.
Etymology: Originally described from Botanical Beach, Vancouver Island, hence *vancouverensis*.
Size: To 4" (10 cm) tall.
Range: Alaska to Mexico.
Habitat: In tidepools, lower intertidal and shallow subtidal, mostly on outer coasts.
Description: Feather-like growths, segments longer than wide. Pink to light purple, bleached white.

BEAD CORALLINE ALGAE

Calliarthron sp.

Size: To 8" (20 cm) tall.
Range: Alaska to Baja California.
Habitat: Low tidepools and shallow subtidal, on rocks of kelp beds.
Description: Branching, both cylindrical and flattened segments, widely spaced. Pinkish to reddish-purple. Species is very brittle and breaks when handled.
Comments: Resembles beads stuck on a wire. Often has another disc-like coralline algae (*Mesophyllum*) encrusting on the branches.

TIDEPOOL CORALLINE ALGAE

Corallina officinalis var. *chilensis* (Decainse in Harvey) Kützing, 1858.
Alternate names: Common coralline algae; *Corallina chilensis*.
Size: To 6" (15 cm) tall.
Range: Prince William Sound, Alaska to Baja California; Chile.
Habitat: On moderately exposed shores; tidepools, low intertidal and shallow subtidal.
Description: Cylindrical but somewhat flattened branches, feather-like side branches. Pale pink to purplish.
Comments: Often covered with bryozoans, other algae and small calcareous worms. Species is also found in Russia and Japan.

CORAL LEAF ALGAE

Bossiella spp.
Etymology: Named in honour of Anna Weber van Bosse, a Dutch phycologist.
Size: Stems 1/2–11/2" (1–4 cm) tall.
Range: Alaska to California.
Habitat: On rocks, mid- to low intertidal.
Description: Segments are regularly flattened, sometimes leaf-like. Pink to deep purple.
Comments: May be confused with bead coralline algae (above), which sometimes has flattened segments as well as cylindrical segments. Coral leaf algae is also found in Russia and Japan.

PHYLUM ANTHOPHYTA

Flowering Plants

Seagrasses Class Monocotyledoneae

These are not true grasses but flowering plants related to lilies. Seagrasses evolved on land and "returned" to the sea.

EELGRASS

Zostera marina Linnaeus, 1753.
Size: Blades to 4' (1.2 m) long, 1/4" (6 mm) wide.
Range: Alaska to Mexico.
Habitat: Rooted in mud and sand in protected waters, low intertidal and subtidal to 3' (1 m) or more.
Description: Blades have 3–7 longitudinal veins, sometimes only a midvein. Dull green.
Comments: Eelgrass is a common surface for deposit of herring spawn. Numerous other plants and animals thrive on or under the canopy of the blades. The tangled mat of rhizomes and roots stabilizes the bottom and provides habitat for numerous organisms. Perennial; overwinters as leafy shoots. The word *Tanu* (the name of a village in the Queen Charlotte Islands), comes from the Haida word for eelgrass.

DWARF EELGRASS

Zostera japonica Ascherson and Graebner, 1907
Alternate names: Formerly *Zostera nana*; *Z. nolti.*
Size: Leaves to 8" (20 cm) long, less than 1/8" (3 mm) wide.
Range: BC to Coos Bay, Oregon.
Habitat: Sand–mud bays; mid-intertidal.
Description: Thinner and shorter than the native eelgrass. Leaf shield is a complete tube encircling inner leaves.
Comments: Introduced from Japan. Annual or short-lived perennial; overwinters as buried seed which germinates in the spring.

SCOULER'S SURFGRASS

Phyllospadix scouleri Hooker, 1838.
Alternate name: Basket grass.
Size: Blades to 3' (1 m) long; narrow, flat blades to 1/8" (3 mm) wide.
Range: Sitka, Alaska to Mexico.
Habitat: Attached to rocks on shores exposed to surf, at lowest tide levels.
Description: Bright emerald green leaves; small flowers in summer.

Comments: Two other surfgrasses are likely to be found, *Phyllospadix torreyi*, on rocks in the subtidal zone, having narrow, wiry leaves. The serrulated surfgrass (*P. serrulatus*), found in rocky habitats from Alaska to Oregon, has truncated leaf tips, flat, broad leaves with microscopic spines (hence *serrulatus*).

Semi-Marine Plants of Saltwater Marshes
Class Dicotyledoneae

SEA ASPARAGUS

Salicornia virginica Linnaeus, 1753.
Alternate names: Glasswort; pickleweed.
Size: To 10" (25 cm) tall.
Range: Alaska to California.
Habitat: High intertidal, along protected shores, tideflats and saltwater marshes.
Description: Spreading mats of green-grey jointed stems, with leaves reduced to little scales. Flowers at tips of branches.

Comments: Perennial, but dies back in winter. Is harvested commercially just before summer flowering and served fresh as a salty salad item.

Glossary

A

Aboral: side opposite to the mouth (oral).

Alga (pl. algae): Large group of plants, including microscopic plants (microalgae) or phytoplankton and larger attached seaweeds.

Algin, alginate: Extract from seaweeds, used commercially as emulsifier and stabilizer.

Ambulacral groove: sea star, groove on the underside that contains tube feet.

Amnesic Shellfish Poisoning (ASP): Poisoning from demoic acid produced by blooms of algae; see also *HABs, Paralytic Shellfish Poisoning (PSP)* and *red tide*.

Aperture: In snails, opening from which the soft body, foot and head extend from the shell.

Ascidians: Colourful jelly-like animals, attached individuals or colonies with siphons.

B

Baleen: Fibrous plates on the upper jaws of some whales, instead of teeth, used to strain food from the water.

Benthic: Referring to the sea floor.

Blade: Flattened leaf-like part of a seaweed.

Bladelet: Small blade.

Blow: Release, often audible, of moisture-laden air by whales, dolphins and porpoises; also called *spout*.

Breach: In whales and other marine mammals, the action of leaping out of the water, exposing two-thirds or more of the body, and landing with a splash.

Bryozoan: Moss-like animal; a type of small, filter-feeding colonial animal.

Budding: Process of asexual reproduction by which an outgrowth of an organism develops and forms a new individual.

Byssal threads (byssus): Tough, silken threads of mussels and certain other bivalves, used to attach to rocks or other objects.

C

Calcareous, calcified: Made of calcium carbonate; hard and crusty.

Carapace: Shell on the back of a crab or shrimp, covering the head and thorax.

Cilia: Microscopic hair-like processes used in locomotion, food gathering and other functions.

Cirrus (pl. cirri): Soft hair-like or fleshy, finger-like projection resembling a tentacle.

Clan: Group of killer whale pods that have a similar dialect, thus considered to be closely related to one another.

Cnidarians: Members of the Phylum Cnidaria, including the hydroids, corals, anemones and jellyfish; characterized by their stinging capsules, especially in the tentacles surrounding the mouth.

Commensal: Referring to a relationship between one animal or plant living with another, sometimes sharing its food. One benefits while the other neither benefits nor is harmed.

Coralline algae: Group of red algae having a hard, crusty texture.

Cosmopolitan: Found in many seas of the world.

Crustose algae: See *coralline algae.*

Cryptic: Camouflaged.

D

Detritus: Debris containing organic particles for food.

Disc: Central body of a sea star from which the arms (rays) extend.

Dorsal: Back or upper surface of the body.

E

Echinoderms: Spiny-skinned animals, including sea stars, brittle stars, sea cucumbers, sea urchins, sand dollars and feather stars; having tube feet, radial and five-part symmetry.

Etymology: Study of the origin of words; in plants and animals often the Greek, Latin and other combining forms used in the names of plants and animals.

Exoskeleton: The rigid outer covering of a crab, shrimp or other arthropod.

F

Filter feeding: Feeding by straining food particles out of the water.

Flipper-slapping: Raising a flipper out of the water and then slapping it on the surface.

Fouling organism: Organism occurring in large numbers and competing with other organisms for food and space.

Frond: See *blade.*

G

Girdle: A band of muscular tissue that surrounds and binds the shell plates of a chiton.

H

HABs: "Harmful algal blooms," toxins produced by algae resulting in fish kills and illness and death in humans; see also *Amnesic Shellfish Poisoning (ASP), Paralytic Shellfish Poisoning (PSP)* and *red tide.*

Holdfast: Root-like point-of-attachment structure with which seaweeds attach to objects.

I

Intertidal: Area of shore exposed when the tide recedes.

Invertebrates: Animals without backbones.

Iridescent: Having a rainbow-like shine.

L

Logging: In marine mammals, resting at or near the surface of the water.

M

Madreporite: Sieve plate of a sea star, sea urchin or other echinoderm through which water is taken in or expelled.

Mantle: Interior sheet of tissue that encloses the soft body of a mollusk. The mantle has sensory perception and sometimes small tentacles or eyes, as in scallops. The shell is secreted from the edge of the mantle.

Midrib: Thickened axis of a seaweed blade.

N

Nematocysyt: Stinging capsule, unique to animals in the phylum Cnidaria, which when stimulated shoots out a stinging or entangling thread.

O

Operculum: In snails, the trap door attached to the foot that covers the shell opening, to seal and protect the soft body parts within the shell. May be horny or calcareous material.

Osculum (pl. oscula): In sponges, excurrent pore from which water exits the sponge.

Ossicles: Microscopic crystals (rods, crosses, plates) of calcium carbonate embedded in the skin of echinoderms.

Ostium (pl. ostia): In sponges, one of the incurrent pores where water enters the sponge.

P

Papillae: In nudibranchs, finger-like projections that do not contain digestive gland; may be used in respiration and for camouflage.

Paralytic Shellfish Poisoning (PSP): Poisoning caused by eating bivalves affected by toxic algal blooms; see also *Amnesic Shellfish Poisoning (ASP)*, *HABs* and *red tide*.

Pedicellariae: Simple pincer-like or scissor-like appendages on sea stars and sea urchins that help keep the upper surface free of small settling organisms.

Pelagic: Living in the upper waters of the sea, drifting or free-swimming.

Petaloid: Petal-like in shape; in sand dollars, referring to the flower-like pattern.

Planktonic: Referring to microscopic plants (phytoplankton) and animals (zooplankton) that are capable of only minor swimming and are carried by water currents.

Pod: A group of resident killer whales (orcas), comprising one or more subpods (closely related family groups) that travel together. Subpods may break off for weeks or months.

Polyp: In cnidarians, an individual (usually of a colony), typically cylindrical, one end having a mouth surrounded by tentacles, the other end attached.

Porpoising: Leaping out of the water, a behaviour exhibited by many seals, sea lions, whales, dolphins and porpoises.

R

Radula: The flexible, rasp-like "tongue" of a mollusk used to scrape food.

Rays: Arms of a sea star or brittle star.

Red tide: Algal bloom concentrated enough to turn the water a reddish colour, sometimes toxic, resulting in closures of bivalve fisheries; see also *Amnesic Shellfish Poisoning (ASP)*, *HABs* and *Paralytic Shellfish Poisoning (PSP)*.

Regeneration: Process of growing and replacing lost body parts, exhibited by sea stars, crabs, worms and other organisms.

Rooster-tail: Spray of water caused by a cone of water flying from the head of a dolphin or porpoise travelling along the surface at high speed.

S

Seagrasses: Common and abundant marine flowering plants including eelgrass and surfgrass, often called seaweeds.

Sea squirts: See *ascidians*.

Seaweeds: Large attached marine plants or algae (not planktonic).

Segmented: Divided into many sections; referring to the body in worms and shrimp, the legs in crabs, etc.

Sessile: Fixed, permanently attached to the sea bottom or other objects.

Spicules: In sponges, tunicates, sea cucumbers and other species, the limy or glass rods that form support.

Sporophyll: A specialized blade where spores are formed on seaweeds.

Spout: Blow.

Spyhopping: In whales and other marine mammals, raising the head vertically above the water for a view, then slipping back into the water with little or no splashing.

Stipe: Erect stem-like portion of a seaweed.

Subpod: In killer whales (orcas), a subgroup of a pod of mainly resident killer whales; a group that stays together almost all the time but may separate from other groups in a pod.

Substrate: The surface on or in which an organism lives.

Subtidal: Area below the zone or part of the shore that is exposed when tides recede.

Symbiosis: A close relationship between different species of organisms, including parasitism, where one organism lives off the other and may harm it, commensalism, where one benefits and the other is not affected, and mutualism, where both gain from the relationship.

Sympatric: Species that occur together.

T

Tail-slapping: In whales and other marine mammals, raising the tail and slapping it on the surface of the water.

Tentacles: Long, finger-like, fleshy or flexible projections used as a sensory organ or, when located around the mouth or head, for feeding.

Thallus (pl. thalli): Main body of a seaweed, including stipe and blades but excluding holdfast.

Tube feet: Numerous fleshy appendages of sea star and other echinoderms, often having a disk at the end, operated by water pressure and used in locomotion, feeding and/or defence.

Tubercles: Small, rounded bumps that increase the surface area of the skin.

Tunic: Sheet or skin-like covering.

Tunicates: Members of the phylum Urochordata, formerly Tunicata; see *Ascidians*.

Type specimens: Specimens used by authors to describe a species or subspecies.

V

Valve: Shell; referring to a gastropod shell, one of the 2 shells of a bivalve or one of the 8 shell plates of a chiton.

Vertebrates: Animals with backbones.

Vocalizations: Social sounds of communication between whales, important in killer whale groups, each of which has a unique dialect, or set of calls. Male humpback whales have long and complex songs during mating season.

Z

Zooids: In bryozoans, ascidians and hydroids, individual members of a colony, structurally continuous with others in box-like, tube-like or other types of units.

Further Reading

INVERTEBRATES—GENERAL

Austin, W. C. 1985. *An Annotated Checklist of Marine Invertebrates in the Cold Temperate Northeast Pacific*, Vols. 1–3. Cowichan Bay, BC: Khoyatan Marine Laboratory.

Kozloff, E. N. 1983. *Seashore Life of the Northern Pacific Coast: An Illustrated Guide to Northern California, Oregon, Washington and British Columbia*. Vancouver: Douglas & McIntyre.

_____. 1996. *Marine Invertebrates of the Pacific Northwest*. Seattle: University of Washington Press.

Morris, R. H., D. P. Abbott and E. C. Haderlie. 1980. *Intertidal Invertebrates of California*. Stanford CA: Stanford University Press.

Snively, G. 1978. *Exploring the Seashore in British Columbia, Washington and Oregon: A Guide to Shorebirds and Intertidal Plants and Animals*. Vancouver: Gordon Soules Book Publishers.

HYDROIDS, CORALS, SEA ANEMONES, JELLYFISH, COMB JELLIES

Wrobel, D. and C. Mills. 1998. *Pacific Coast Pelagic Invertebrates: A Guide to the Common Gelatinous Animals*. Monterey CA: Sea Challengers.

MOLLUSKS

Harbo, R. M. 1997. *Shells and Shellfish of the Pacific Northwest: A Field Guide*. Madeira Park BC: Harbour Publishing.

Behrens, D. W. 1991. *Pacific Coast Nudibranchs*, 2nd ed. Monterey CA: Sea Challengers.

CRABS, SHRIMP, BARNACLES

Butler, T. H. 1980. "Shrimps of the Pacific Coast of Canada," *Can. Bull. Fish. Aquat. Sci.* 202.

Cornwall, I. E. 1970. *Barnacles of British Columbia* (Handbook No. 7). Victoria: British Columbia Provincial Museum.

Hart, J. F. L. 1982. *Crabs and their relatives of British Columbia* (Handbook No. 40). Victoria: Britsh Columbia Provincial Museum.

Jensen, G. C. 1995. *Pacific Coast Crabs and Shrimp*. Monterey CA: Sea Challengers.

SEA STARS, SEA CUCUMBERS

Lambert, P. 1997. *Sea cucumbers of British Columbia, Southeast Alaska and Puget Sound* (Royal British Columbia Museum Handbook). Vancouver: UBC Press.

Lambert, P. 1981. *The Sea Stars of British Columbia* (Handbook No. 39). Victoria: British Columbia Provincial Museum Handbook.

FISHES

Gillespie, G. E. 1993. "An Updated List of the Fishes of British Columbia, and Those of Interest in Adjacent Waters, with Numeric Code Designations." *Can. Tech. Rep. Fish. Aquat. Sci.* 1918.

Hart, J. L. 1973. *Pacific Fishes of Canada* (Bulletin 180). Ottawa: Fisheries Research Board of Canada.

Humann, P. 1996. *Coastal Fish Identification. California to Alaska.* Jacksonville FL: New World Publications Inc.

Kramer, D. E. and V. M. O'Connell. 1988. *Guide to Northeast Pacific Rockfishes: Genera Sebastes and Sebastolobus* (Marine Advisory Bulletin #25). Juneau: University of Alaska.

Lamb, A. and Edgell, P. 1986. *Coastal Fishes of the Pacific Northwest.* Madeira Park BC: Harbour Publishing.

MARINE MAMMALS

Banfield, A. W. F. 1977. *The Mammals of Canada.* Toronto: University of Toronto Press, National Museum of Natural Sciences.

Carwardine, M. 1995. *Whales, Dolphins and Porpoises: The Visual Guide to the World's Cetaceans.* (Eyewitness handbook), Toronto: Stoddart Publishing Co. Ltd.

Ford, J. K., G. M. Ellis and K. C. Balcomb. 1994. *Killer Whales: The Natural History and Genealogy of* Orcinus orca *in British Columbia and Washington State.* Vancouver: UBC Press.

King, J.E. 1983. *Seals of the World,* 2nd ed. Oxford: Oxford University Press, British Museum.

Leatherwood, S., R. Reeves and L. Foster. 1983. *The Sierra Club Handbook of Whales and Dolphins.* San Francisco: Sierra Club Books.

Nickerson, R. 1989. *Sea Otters: A Natural History and Guide.* San Francisco: Chronicle Books.

Rice, D.W. 1998. *Marine Mammals of the World: Systematics and Distribution.* Special Publication 4. The Society for Marine Mammalogy, Lawrence, KS.

Sugarman, P. 1984. *Field Guide to the Orca Whales of Greater Puget Sound and Southern British Columbia.* Friday Harbor WA: The Whale Museum.

SEAWEEDS

Abbott, I. A. and G. J. Hollenberg. 1976. *Marine Algae of California.* Stanford CA: Stanford University Press.

O'Clair, R. M., S. C. Lindstrom and I. R. Brodo. 1996. *Southeast Alaska's Rock Shores: Seaweeds and Lichens.* Auke Bay AK: Plant Press.

Scagel, R. F., P. W. Gabrielson, D. J. Garbary, L. Golden, M. W. Hawkes, S. C. Lindstrom, J. C. Oliveira and T. B. Widdowson. 1993. *A Synopsis of the Benthic Marine Algae of British Columbia, Southeast Alaska, Washington and Oregon* (Phycological Contribution No. 3). Vancouver: University of British Columbia, Department of Botany.

Acknowledgements

Scientific editing and advice were generously provided by numerous experts. My thanks to Ronald L. Shimek, William C. Austin, Claudia Mills, Daphne Fautin, Dale Calder, Paul Scott, Eugene V. Coan, James McLean, Roger N. Clark, Sandra Millen, William Merilees, Neil McDaniel, Philip Lambert, Gretchen Lambert, Charles Lambert, Andy Lamb, Graham Gillespie, Graeme Ellis, John Ford, Jane Watson, Edward Gregr, Michael Hawkes and Sandra Lindstrom. Many others provided advice, specimens or assistance in collecting specimens.

Special thanks to Mary Schendlinger who edited many drafts of the text, Patricia Wolfe for proofreading and Ann Macklem for preparing the index. Peter Robson and Howard White provided valuable direction in the development of the book. Mary White scanned photographs and Martin Nichols of Lionheart Graphics contributed his skill in the design and layout of the book.

Photo credits (25): Exceptional photographic images were contributed by Ronald L. Shimek: cemented tube worm (page 52), globular ascidian (153), compound ascidian (157); Neil McDaniel: spiny dogfish and six gill shark (159), blue rockfish (167), starry flounder (174); Greg Jensen: humpback shrimp and sidestripe shrimp (81); Philip Lambert, Royal British Columbia Museum: giant orange sea cucumber (142); Susan Bower: bivalve flatworm (57); Roland Anderson, Seattle Aquarium: red octopus (2 photos, 122); Finn Larsen, Ursus Photography, northern elephant seal (178); Andrew Trites, northern fur seal (175, 181); Jim Borrowman, killer whales (184 top), Dall's porpoise (187), gray whale (188); Alexandra Morton, killer whale (front cover), Pacific white-sided dolphin (185); Robin Baird, harbor porpoise (186), gray whale (189), humpback whales (191); Graeme Ellis / Ursus Photography, minke whale (190); Kevin Oke: river otter (193). All other photographs (486) by Rick Harbo.

Illustrations were prepared by Pieter Folkens: Pacific harbour seal (page 177), northern elephant seal (178), Steller sea lion (179), California sea lion (180), northern fur seal (181), killer whale (183), Pacific white-sided dolphin (185), harbor porpoise (186), Dall's porpoise (187), gray whale (188), minke whale (190), humpback whale (191), whales and dolphins (194–95), blue whale (197); Nola Johnston Graphic Design and Illustration: sponges (18), crab (65), clams (88), snail (102), nudibranchs (111), chitons (123), sea stars (127), fish (158); Amy Harbo: sea squirt (149); Jennifer Harbo: seaweed (200); Martin Nichols, Lionheart Graphics, map (7) and chart (189).

Index

Page numbers set in bold-face type indicate black and white figure drawings.

Other Outdoor, Science & Nature books from
HARBOUR PUBLISHING

WHALES OF THE WEST COAST
David A.E. Spalding

Here is a book that will answer every question you ever had about whales of the west coast. Includes information on whale watching, a west coast whale chronology, a calendar of whale events throughout the Pacific Northwest, and listings of museums, parks, hotlines, archives, research agencies and readings.
ISBN 1-55017-199-2 • 216 pages • 6 x 9 • 80 photos • $18.95 paper

THE BEACHCOMBER'S GUIDE TO
SEASHORE LIFE IN THE PACIFIC NORTHWEST
Duane Sept

The 275 most common animals and plants to be seen along the saltwater shores of the Pacific Northwest are described here. Packed with expert information but wonderfully accessible to any interested layperson, this book is perfect for a family or a school group, a Saturday beachwalker or a naturalists' club.
ISBN 1-55017-204-2 • 240 pages • 5 ½ x 8 ½ • 200 colour photos • $21.95 paper

FIELD IDENTIFICATION OF COASTAL JUVENILE SALMONIDS
W.R. Pollard, G.F. Hartman, C. Groot and Phil Edgell
Illustrations by C. Groot, photos by Phil Edgell

This important field guide is a must for biologists, resource assessment workers, forestry workers, salmon enhancement groups, naturalists, fisheries students and members of the public interested in fisheries projects.
ISBN 1-55017-167-4 • 32 pages • 5 ½ x 8 ½ • 15 colour photos & over 60 b&w and colour illustrations • Inside pocket with waterproof viewing bag • $12.95 paper

LAKE, RIVER AND SEA-RUN FISHES OF CANADA
Frederick H. Wooding

The only popular guide to freshwater fishes in all parts of Canada, this book is a must for naturalists, anglers and anyone who loves fine nature writing. This revised edition includes a foreword by Professor Joseph Nelson of the University of Alberta and an updated essay on endangered species by Dr R.R. Campbell.
ISBN 1-55017-175-5 • 304 pages • 6 x 9 • 36 colour illustrations, 14 line drawings, index • $18.95 paper

SHELLS & SHELLFISH OF THE PACIFIC NORTHWEST
Rick M. Harbo

This comprehensive, easy-to-follow, full-colour guide introduces more than 250 species of mollusks—the clams, oysters, scallops, mussels, abalone, snails, limpets, tuskshells and chitons found along the beaches and intertidal and shallow waters of the Pacific Northwest.
ISBN 1-55017-146-1 • 272 pages • 5 ½ x 8 ½ • 350 colour photos, index • $24.95 paper

COASTAL FISHES OF THE PACIFIC NORTHWEST
Andy Lamb & Phil Edgell

Written by a marine biologist and illustrated in colour by a prize-winning under-water photographer, this is the only comprehensive field guide to marine fishes of BC, Washington and southern Alaska.
ISBN 0-920080-75-8 • 224 pages • 5 ½ x 8 ½ • index • $21.95 paper

WHERE TO SEE WILDLIFE ON VANCOUVER ISLAND
Kim Goldberg

Colourful, info-packed and user-friendly, this guide introduces the 50 best wildlife viewing hot spots on Vancouver Island, from the busy Victoria waterfront to Nanaimo's Buttertubs marsh to "Gator Gardens" in Alert Bay.
ISBN 1-55017-160-7 • 174 pages • 5 ½ x 8 ½ • 100 colour photos, index • $20.95 paper

These titles available at your local bookstore or from:

HARBOUR PUBLISHING
P.O. Box 219, Madeira Park, BC, Canada V0N 2H0
Toll-Free Order Line: 1-800-667-2988
Fax: 604-883-9451
E-mail: harbour@sunshine.net